William
CONGREVE

a reference guide

*A
Reference
Publication
in
Literature*

Arthur Weitzman
Editor

William
CONGREVE,

a reference guide .

LAURENCE BARTLETT

G.K.HALL&CO.

70 LINCOLN STREET, BOSTON, MASS.

Copyright © 1979 by Laurence Bartlett

Library of Congress Cataloging in Publication Data

Bartlett, Laurence.
   William Congreve, a reference guide.

   (A Reference publication in literature)
   Includes index.
   1. Congreve, William, 1670-1729—Bibliography.
I. Title. II. Series: Reference publication in
literature.
Z8189.6.B37   [PR3366]   016.822′4   79-19661
ISBN 0-8161-8142-X

Contents

Congreve's Major Works
and
Dates of First Publication

Introduction

The 250th anniversary of the death of William Congreve affords a timely opportunity to consolidate some facts regarding publications of the author's works and to discern various trends and patterns in the criticism that has accumulated since 1729. For the sake of clarity and brevity, the Introduction focuses upon the major works: Incognita and the five plays. It deals with statistics pertaining to publications of primary material, considers biographical and bibliographical studies, and surveys the criticism, with reference first to Congreve in general and then to specific works. The Introduction concludes with an explanation of (along with a cautionary comment upon) the methods employed in correlating both the primary and the secondary material.

(1) TEXTS

Editions of Congreve's works appear frequently and in different groupings: combined prose, drama, and poetry; the dramatic works, sometimes including The Judgment of Paris and Semele; the complete plays; and the comedies. There is yet to appear, however, a definitive edition of the complete works.

(a) Collected Works

The first publication of The Works, a three-volume edition, appeared in 1710, the two-volume seventh edition in 1774, and the three-volume Baskerville edition in 1761. The first attempt to include extensive annotations and critical notes was made by Montague Summers in the four-volume Nonesuch edition of The Complete Works (1923.A1; reprinted 1964.A1), considered the most complete to date. The twin-volume Oxford World's Classics edition, by Bonamy Dobrée, of the Comedies (1925.A1; with ten reprints up to 1966) and The Mourning Bride, Poems and Miscellanies (1928.A1) follows with minor revisions the 1710 text. F. W. Bateson's The Works (1930.A1) includes only the four comedies, Incognita, and selected poems.

(b) Dramatic Works

Five different editions of Congreve's dramatic works appeared between 1733 and 1773; there were seven reprintings of Leigh Hunt's <u>The Dramatic Works of Wycherley, Congreve, Vanbrugh, and Farquhar</u> (1840.A1) between 1840 and 1880. Alexander Charles Ewald's popular Mermaid edition of the complete plays, <u>William Congreve</u> (1887.A1), was reprinted seven times until 1949, and the New Mermaid edition was reprinted four times between 1956 and 1966. William Archer's <u>William Congreve</u> (1912.A1) does not include <u>The Old Bachelor</u>, an omission that reflects the little critical interest shown in and the decreasing publication of the play at this time. A period of over fifty years elapsed before Herbert Davis' <u>The Complete Plays</u> (1967.A1), based on the Harvard copies of the first quartos. David Mann's <u>A Concordance to the Plays of William Congreve</u> (1973.A7) is based on Davis' edition.

(c) Comedies

Four editions of the comedies have been published since the last decade of the nineteenth century, by G. S. Street (1895.A1), Bonamy Dobrée (1925.A1), Joseph Wood Krutch (1927.A1), and Norman Marshall (1948.A2).

(d) Individual Works

The number of publications of specific works indicates quite clearly the growing popularity of <u>Love for Love</u> and <u>The Way of the World</u> and parallels critical interest in the two comedies. It should be added that the numbers given below (which include reprintings) should be used only as guidelines because of possible duplications in the entries (see p. xxix) and because subsequent research may unearth other editions. However, these should not alter drastically, if at all, the impressions gained from the statistics given in the following sections.

(i) Incognita

As may be expected, separate editions of Congreve's novella appear infrequently. The Dublin edition (1743.A1) was not followed until H. F. B. Brett-Smith's critical edition (1922.A1). <u>Incognita</u> was, however, included in Philip Henderson's collection <u>Shorter Novels: Seventeenth Century</u> (1930.A3; reprinted 1962.A1). The Folio Society's edition contains an introduction by Alan Pryce-Jones and engravings by Van Rossem (1951.A4). <u>Incognita</u> was later published, with <u>The Way of the World</u>, in an edition by A. Norman Jeffares (1966.A3; reprinted 1970.A2).

(ii) The Old Bachelor

Congreve's first comedy appears to be the least popular with critics and publishers alike. With the exception of the facsimile reprint of the 1693 first edition (1972.A2), publication of the play came to an abrupt halt in the 1820s: all twenty-two single editions appeared before 1830, while the play's inclusion in collections, eighteen times, ended in 1811.

(iii) The Double Dealer

A similar pattern to that observed for The Old Bachelor manifests itself for Congreve's second play, although statistics and dates vary slightly. Of the twenty-four separate printings of the play, twenty-two were issued before 1883. There is, in addition, one adaptation of the play by Lord Lebanon for the Jacobite Club (1938.A1) and one facsimile reprint of the 1694 first edition (1973.A1). The play appears in twenty-one collections, all before 1864.

(iv) Love for Love

Of the total of forty-three individual printings of Love for Love, thirty-three were issued before 1894, three between 1920 and 1949, and seven since 1950. Its inclusion in collections totals fifty times: thirty-four until 1894, six between 1920 and 1949, and ten between 1950 and 1977. Three of the most popular and recent separate editions of the play are those by Emmett L. Avery (1966.A4; modern spelling), A. Norman Jeffares (1967.A4; old spelling), and Malcolm M. Kelsall (1969.A3; modern spelling). All include useful and lengthy critical introductions.

(v) The Mourning Bride

Up to the end of the nineteenth century, Congreve's tragedy was the most frequently published of all his works. The Mourning Bride was published separately fifty-four times before 1897, and in collections, fifty-two times before 1866. Along with The Old Bachelor and The Double Dealer, The Mourning Bride lost ground as it gave way to Love for Love and The Way of the World. These figures confirm the findings of several scholars who point to the popularity of the play, especially in the eighteenth century (1941.B1; 1951.A1; 1971.B6).

(vi) The Way of the World

Congreve's last play was printed separately on twenty-four occasions before 1895, ten between 1920 and 1949, and twelve since 1950. Inclusions of the play in anthologies attest to its increasing popularity: twenty-two before 1894, four between 1895 and 1919, thirty-nine between 1920 and 1949, and sixty-eight between 1950 and 1977. Some recent editions are those by Kathleen M. Lynch (1965.A2; modern spelling), A. Norman Jeffares (1966.A3; old spelling), Brian Gibbons (1971.A3; modern spelling), and John Barnard (1972.A3; old spelling).

Not surprisingly, Congreve's two most successful comedies have been published with some regularity since 1729. However, what may be mildly unexpected is that until 1900, Love for Love was printed more frequently, both singly and in collections, than The Way of the World, and that between 1896 and 1919 only the latter was printed, four times in anthologies. No doubt their increasing appearance in anthologies may be partly explained by the fact that both plays are now part of the regular college syllabus.

(2) BIOGRAPHY

Early accounts of Congreve's life are highly unreliable, gossip invariably blurring the distinction between fact and fiction. The authenticity of the Memoirs by "Charles Wilson" (1730.A5) remains extremely questionable; the author has been variously identified as John Oldmixon and, more recently, as Edmund Curll (1970.B19). Forty-three of Congreve's letters to his friend Joseph Keally were printed in Literary Relics (1789.A1), a collection now superseded by the more extensive one found in John C. Hodges's Letters & Documents (1964.A3). The first comprehensive biography, by Edmund Gosse (1888.A3; reprinted 1972.A6), dispelled some of the mystery surrounding the subject, but Gosse bewailed the fact, confirmed in his revised edition (1924.A4), that "unless fresh material should most unexpectedly turn up, the opportunity for preparing a full and picturesque life of this poet has wholly passed away."

Two foreign critical biographies, one in German by D. Schmid (1897.A2) and the other in French by Dragosh Protopopesco (1924.A6), made no significant contributions. D. Crane Taylor's William Congreve (1931.A4; reprinted 1963.A7) has been shown to be far from reliable or complete by Congreve's most successful biographer, John C. Hodges, in his William Congreve the Man: A Biography from New Sources (1941.A2), now regarded as the standard biographical work on the dramatist. Bonamy Dobrée's exceedingly brief account of Congreve's life (1963.A6) depends heavily on Hodges's work. Also recent are Kathleen M. Lynch's A Congreve Gallery (1951.A11) and her "References to Congreve in the Evelyn MSS" (1953.B2), both of which shed new light on some of Congreve's friendships. The nature of Congreve's relationships with the actress Anne Bracegirdle and later with Henrietta, Duchess of Marlborough, has been traced by (among others) Charles W. Collins (1906.B1) and argued about by R. G. Howarth (1961.B1), who questions the accepted view that both women were probably Congreve's mistresses.

Several works on Congreve's library serve, in varying degrees, to fill out the relatively little that is known about the writer. Before John C. Hodges's detailed work on this subject, The Library of William Congreve (1955.A7), articles by Alfred Robbins (1922.B4), J. Isaacs (1939.B2), and M. M. (1942.B4) discussed copies of texts in Congreve's possession.

(3) BIBLIOGRAPHY

Bibliographical information has been, to date, far from exhaustive. The bibliographies in the biographies by Gosse (1888.A3),
Protopopesco (1924.A6), and Taylor (1931.A4) cite some lesser-known
criticism of the eighteenth and nineteenth centuries. Other useful
sources are The British Museum General Catalogue of Printed Books
(1966.B2; 1968.B4; 1971.B5) and the National Union Catalog (1970.B14,
B15; 1973.B14); Montague Summers' A Bibliography of the Restoration
Drama (1934.B4); Clarence S. Paine's brief reference guide to the
comedy of manners (1940.B6; 1941.B3); and three bibliographies edited
by Carl J. Stratman: Bibliography of English Printed Tragedy 1565-1900
(1966.B29), Restoration and 18th Century Theatre Research Bibliography 1961-1968 (1969.B14), and Restoration and Eighteenth-Century
Theatre Research: A Bibliographical Guide 1900-1968 (1971.B16),
with a supplement to the last by Laurence Bartlett (1971.B3). There
are, in addition, two short critical surveys, one by John Barnard
(1975.B1) and the other by Frederick M. Link (1976.B7). Extremely
valuable for its detailed listings of many early editions of
Congreve's works and of Congreveana is The John C. Hodges Collection
in the University of Tennessee Library: A Bibliographical Catalog,
edited by Albert M. Lyles and John Dobson (1970.A6).

(4) CRITICISM

Any attempt to impose a rationale on a quarter of a millennium's
diffuse critical material inexorably involves many problems, the most
significant of which is the tendency either to distort or to over-
simplify subtleties and specifics. However, several general observations may be tentatively made and some broadly outlined patterns may
be recognized.

(a) General

Congreve has on the whole fared very favorably with his
critics, on occasions for what many may consider the "wrong"
reasons. At first, the voices of dissenting critics were heard
quite distinctly, but later they became less audible. Up to the
end of the nineteenth century, critics disagreed about the moral
value of the plays and the function and effect of the language
and wit. They explored Congreve's affinity with other Restoration
dramatists and the relationship between life and the worlds depicted in his comedies. The present century has continued the
debate, but has also shown an increasing interest in Congreve's
plays as important contributions to "the comedy of manners" and
in his characters as embodiments of various social and literary
types. Stimulated by L. C. Knights's diatribe against Restoration
comedy in 1937, critics since then, especially after the 1960s,
have shown how the comedies not only reflect and explore different social, political, and philosophical principles, but also
contain much that is of moral and aesthetic value.

Such a strictly chronological survey, however, fails to distinguish clearly other emerging and equally significant trends
and patterns and to take into account the more detailed attention
given to interpreting and exploring individual works. Consequently, the following survey emphasizes subject matter--with
reference first to Congreve's comedies in general and then to
specific titles--with less regard for chronology, so that
Congreve's critical reputation may be more clearly outlined.
Critical hostility to Congreve's comedies may be traced back
to the unfavorable reception extended toward the first performances of The Double Dealer and The Way of the World, and to
Jeremy Collier's notorious attack on Restoration comedy.
While praising Congreve the man, David Mallet disapproves of the
plays' moral content (1729.B1); Thackerary likens the world of
the comedies to a "temple of Pagan delights" (1853.B2); the memory of reading the plays is compared to a "horrible nightmare"
(1871.B2), and their atmosphere is felt to be "asphyxiating"
(1887.B1). Another critic complains that Congreve laughs with
the vicious characters and makes a joke of vice, with no attempt
to correct it (1888.B1). L. C. Knights has other reasons for
disliking Restoration comedy. Those who would defend it, he
advises, should not address themselves to the question of its
immorality but to the fact that it is "trivial, gross and dull"
(1937.B2), a sentiment echoed later in a work that first set out
to rebut Knights's conclusions (1964.B15). Two more recent critics believe that Congreve is overrated. One finds The Way of the
World an "insufferably dull play," adding that Congreve neither
judges nor tests but only exemplifies the values of the period
(1970.B10); the other asserts that Congreve's limitation as a
poet is that "his own vision is neither large enough nor sufficiently clear to be really satisfying" (1972.B22).
It was a generally accepted conviction that comedy should
teach and delight; but if Congreve's comedies do, or appear to
do, very little to fulfill Horace's first principle, how can they
be defended, if at all, or evaluated? Unable to solve the problem, several critics in the nineteenth century evade the issue
by divorcing content from form. Thus Congreve may be taken to
task for his "immorality" while being lauded for his stylistic
excellencies (1781.B1; 1838.B1; 1883.A6; 1890.B1). This separa-
tion of the aesthetic aspects from the didactic, begs the problem-
atical task of evaluating the plays in toto, as does the parallel
tendency to excuse, if not overlook, the moral value of the comedies by seeing Congreve, ethically indifferent to life (1912.A1)
and perverse in his moral detachment (1914.B4), in one of two
ways: either as part and parcel of that vicious period in
English history (1833.B1) whose code of morals was not ours
(1897.A2), or in the role of historian, as one whose interest
lies not in reforming but merely in reflecting the triviality of
an artificial society (1937.B4)--an amused and detached observer
(1927.A1), a "laughing recording angel" (1940.B3), even a superficial one (1957.B2).

Yet Congreve's ability as an accurate and perceptive historian of his age meets with approval from another group, including
Hazlitt (1819.B1), Clarke (1871.B1), Ewald (1887.A1), Whibley
(1912.B2), and Morse (1922.B3). John Wain assesses the plays
as being better documents than good plays (1956.B6).

A countermovement to the one mentioned above questions
the relationship between "real" life and the worlds illustrated
in the plays, but it also tends to dispense with the moral
issue--this time by relegating the plays to an amoral world of
art, a "Utopia of gallantry," remote from the "world that is"
(1823.B1), and by regarding the dramatist as a romanticist who
transforms the real world into such a Utopia (1916.B1). In the
1920s, a brief debate, including references to Restoration comedy
and to Congreve, centers on the relationship between life and art.
Elmer Edgar Stoll consistently argues that the plays reflect the
taste rather than the life of the time (1924.B5; 1928.B6;
1934.B3; 1943.B6), and Basil Williams points to "implausible"
features in The Way of the World (1928.B9). Both of these views
are challenged, ironically enough, by the historian G. M.
Trevelyan, who, not without some display of wit, affirms that
a recent production of the play suggests that Restoration comedy
is as "artificial" as real men and women (1928.B7).

An emphasis upon the formal elements of the comedies, as
mentioned earlier, greatly assists those who wish to offer a
balanced (if not unified) view of the plays. Congreve's wit,
however, does not always receive unqualified praise. Regarded
by many to be the most attractive and forceful feature of the
comedies, the wit can, paradoxically, be thought of as a weak-
ness, preventing the engagement of the passions and the moral
reformation of the audience (1798.B1), distracting the attention
toward the author (1804.B1), and blurring the distinction between
the characters and obscuring the plot (1940.A5). An extreme view
proposes that The Way of the World is not only too witty for real
life but probably too witty for the stage (1953.A2).

Invariably, the language evokes extremely positive reactions
(for example, 1784.B1; 1913.B1; 1925.B8; 1948.A2; 1972.B7).
Dobrée believes that Congreve is to be appreciated more for
aesthetic than for moral or philosophical reasons (1925.A1).
Yet others show that the wit reflects the "traditional belief
that love and faithfulness accompany marriage" (1916.B2), that
the raillery clarifies the tenets and refines the values of
"conversational man" (1966.B5), and that the style exists not
only for the sake of wit but to define the plays' comic values
(1968.A5). Congreve's style, moreover, serves not to obscure
but to differentiate characters: their idiosyncrasies "seem to
control and inform the manner of their speech" (1930.A1); the
ways in which they speak "individuate their personalities quite
clearly, create dramatic conflict, and establish a moral perspective" (1973.B8). Studies of more specific aspects of the style
include those that deal with puns (1966.B3), raillery (1966.B5),
"idealized speech" (1966.B4), and conjunctions (1962.B4).

The structural features of the comedies are the subject of
several essays. William Archer argues that the early success of
The Old Bachelor and Love for Love and the relative failure of
The Double Dealer and The Way of the World may have arisen from
the structural strengths and weaknesses of the respective plays
(1910.B1). In the last twenty years, several dissertations have
continued to explore the subject: the parallel between Congreve's
growing technical skill and the meaningful structure of his action
(1962.A11); the figurative structure of The Way of the World
(1962.B5); the metaphoric structure and texture in the comedies
(1965.A5); their satiric structure (1972.B4); and the substance,
construction, and disposition of scenes (1966.A10).

Defenses on behalf of Congreve against L. C. Knights were
not immediately forthcoming, but eventually many studies revealed
the serious social, moral, and philosophical ideas implicit in
the themes of the comedies. Prior to Knights's article, Dobrée
had proposed that Restoration comedy attempts to rationalize
sexual relationships (1924.B1). Later writers demonstrate that
the plays also illustrate in a realistic manner the difficulty
involved when the sexes live with each other (1968.B14); that
the only hope for happiness in a fallen world is "the private
love between men and women of sensibility and genuine wit"
(1971.B13); that the comedies deal with the "kind of understanding associated with love, friendship, and the intermediate ground
of family relationships" (1974.B6); and that relationships among
the characters reflect the "ambiguities, indeterminacies and
conflicting perspectives" of real life (1974.A7).

The twin themes of marriage and money are the topic of other
studies that deal with the social and moral ideas of the comedies.
Congreve's satire, it is thought, implies that an ideal marriage
must be based on reason and respect (1965.B5). The libertine in
Congreve's plays is neither the hero nor the heroine, but the
villain, who must be banished from society before the marriage
of the first two can take place (1975.B2). Also explored are
the influence on the comedies of a society that reveres money
as both god and king (1971.B4) and the relationships between
paternity and property (1974.B8).

One critical offshoot of these discussions may be discerned
in the trend that examines various facets of themes not unexpected in comedies that were produced in a society as much concerned with manners as with morals: the conflict and discrepancy
between social conventions and antisocial desires (1959.B5), the
pleasures and perils of deception (1964.B7), the comic valuations
of innocence and experience (1975.B16); and the relationship
between beauty and power (1972.B15), the individual and society
(1976.B9), and time and art (1964.A6). The movement toward
rehabilitating Congreve as a serious and moral dramatist finds
a staunch supporter in Aubrey Williams, who in a series of articles argues, some would say unconvincingly, that the themes and
patterns of Congreve's works illustrate the operation of a Divine
Providence in human affairs (1968.B18, B19; 1971.B20).

Congreve's poetic vision and its effect upon his art evoke different and sometimes ambivalent responses. Congreve, a romanticist, transforms real life into an imaginary world of gallantry (1916.B1). Although he gives Congreve credit for being "too much of a poet to accept the surface of life," Dobrée states that he is "too little a poet to find beauty in the bare facts of existence" (1924.B1). A similar view is developed by one who says that Congreve, seeing beneath the "surface of reality with extraordinary penetration" but unable "to uncover the truth in its nakedness," clothes his "observations upon life in the ribald and fantastic garments of another world" (1938.A1). Congreve's limited and indistinct vision is the subject of a more recent critic (1972.B22). On the other hand, views are advanced that Congreve sees "strange beauties" hidden beneath affectations but that he pulls "his hat over his brows" and keeps "his vision and thoughts to himself" (1948.B2), and that the plays record Congreve's struggle "to reconcile the contradictions in his literary and ideological inheritance" (1972.B19).

Other patterns in criticism revolve around Congreve's literary heritage, the relationship between his comedies and those of other comic dramatists, and the influences of the social, literary, and intellectual milieu of the late seventeenth century. Two works trace Congreve's literary roots back to the satiric tradition of Horace and Jonson (1958.A5; 1963.B10); another, to the influences of Beaumont and Fletcher (1928.B8). The inevitable comparison between Congreve and Molière is made: Congreve's style is seen to be equal to Molière's (1897.B1), as are his wit and treatment of comic situations (1929.B10), but in the range and depth of his humor (1929.B10) Congreve is the French playwright's inferior (1897.B1). His debt to Molière, first thought significant (1890.A2; 1910.B2), may be canceled because there is no demonstrable borrowing from Molière in any of the comedies; Congreve exploits English prototypes (1938.B4).

According to Genest, Congreve is regarded as the best (with the exception of Shakespeare) of English comic writers (1832.B1), and to another writer he is more "decorous" than his predecessors (1833.B1). Considered by one critic to be not as gross as Wycherley (1840.B2), Congreve is, according to another, far less moral than Wycherley (1871.B1). The structural and linguistic elements of Congreve's style are analyzed, being first contrasted (1969.B7) and then compared (1974.B9) with Etherege's and Wycherley's. His comedies, because of their "psychological observation," distinguish themselves from those by these contemporaries (1926.B5). Congreve's achievements as a dramatist are frequently contrasted also with those of his more famous contemporaries and successors. Thus, he is considered superior to Vanbrugh, Farquhar, and Sheridan (1877.B1) and to Cibber (1973.B15), or not as witty as Sheridan (1923.B2). Comparisons are also made between Congreve and Meredith (1971.B19), Sheridan, Wilde, and Coward (1937.B4), and Wilde alone (1974.B12). Congreve's influence on Fielding's comedies (1971.B17) and on The Rape of the Lock (1975.B6) is also examined.

To regard Congreve's comedies as anything but supreme exam-
ples of the Restoration comedy of manners would have been considered perverse until recently. For many the comedies,
capturing the atmosphere of the school of manners in its most
perfect form (1923.B6) and expressing a very special and con-
spicuous phase of the Restoration comic spirit (1925.B9), crys-
tallize the quintessence of the genre. Generally considered
superior to both his immediate predecessors and his successors,
yet inseparable from an apparently continuing but relatively
unchanging comic tradition, Congreve occupied a place at an apex,
as it were, formed by a line rising from the "insouciant"
Etherege and "mordant" Wycherley and descending from Congreve
to the more overtly moral and sentimental Vanbrugh and Farquhar.
Differences between Congreve and the other "big four" have been
frequently noted--differences that can be, and have been, explained by recalling that Congreve wrote his first play long
after the spirit of the Restoration had all but expired.

Some recent works explore in detail the concept of Congreve
as either a transitional dramatist--his development as a playwright is examined with reference to the plays' changing relationships to the older Restoration tradition and the newly
emerging sentimental comedy of the eighteenth century (1970.A1;
1971.A6)--or a writer of the postrevolutionary period (1971.A7).
Robert D. Hume's essays do much to show the fallacy of looking
at the drama of the period en bloc, an approach long overdue,
by pointing out the diversity in aims and methods of Restoration
comedy (1973.B7) and the changes and interactions that occurred
on an "almost season-by-season basis" (1976.B5). But just as
Congreve is about to be rescued from the pitfalls of being
categorized, he may be thought by some to be once again in danger
of being pigeonholed, this time as a writer of a newly coined
and distinct mode--"humane" comedy (1977.B4), a term that does
serve to identify many characteristics in Congreve's comedies
but that carries with it the potential to restrict Congreve's
achievements as a unique dramatist.

Another important trend emerges during the present century,
beginning slowly in the 1920s and gradually gaining momentum:
the concentration upon particular literary, social, political,
and philosophical influences. Studies that include specific
references to Congreve examine the influences of the <u>précieuse</u>
tradition (1926.B3; 1955.B2; 1959.B1) and courtesy literature
(1964.B15); the concept of humours upon comic characterization
(1947.B1), the evolution of the humours character (1966.B25),
and humour characterization as a literary technique (1973.B11);
the application of Restoration comic theories to Congreve's
plays (1939.B5) and the interplay between Congreve's use of the
"neo-classical theory of dramatic structure, his appeal to classical precedent, and his attempt to achieve a seriousness differing in kind from that of other Restoration comedies" (1972.B1);
and themes and conventions of Restoration comedy as evident in
Congreve's comedies (1965.B7). Related to these are writings

that point to such various character types as the learned lady
(1920.B2), crabbed age and youth (1947.B4), the gay couple
(1948.B6), servants (1958.B6; 1961.B4), friends and families
(1960.B2), the cuckold (1962.B9), the fop and related figures
(1965.B6), the social climber (1965.B10), medical men (1967.B11),
and the coquette-prude (1968.B12). Other studies explore friends
and families (1960.B2), and the town's attitudes toward the
country (1961.B7).

Naturally, quite a lot of attention centers on the antag-
onists of the comedies. Essays relevant to Congreve include
discussions of the libertine gentleman (1965.B4), the rake's
progress from court to comedy (1966.B30), the rake hero (1970.B2),
and the myth of the rake (1977.B3). Cazamian points out early in
the century that Congreve's art successfully analyzes the "feminine soul" (1927.B2), an observation that seems to be confirmed
by several recent studies on the women in Congreve's comedies
(1972.A8; 1973.B12), and on the "new woman" (1954.B3) and "independent woman" (1975.B8) in Restoration comedy. Still two other
studies document and describe the moral characteristics of
Congreve's figures (1971.B15) and look at the characters in
terms of their varying degrees and kinds of ignorance (1975.B11).
Attention is also given to such nonliterary influences as matrimonial law (1942.B2); the social results of economic changes
(1959.B6); post-1688 influences (1971.A7); the values of the
Whig aristocracy (1958.B7); Epicureanism, libertinism, and
naturalism (1952.B1); the psychological, ethical, and critical
principles related to Hobbesian doctrine (1953.B4); and the
split consciousness of modern man (1959.B5). Lately, a series
of articles has proposed that Congreve's works conform to a
Christian vision of human experience (1968.B19), that they are
therefore neither Epicurean nor naturalistic (1971.B20), but,
in the case of Love for Love, a witty dramatization of Christian
truths and paradoxes (1972.B29).

This section of the Introduction must include two other subjects, one encompassing Congreve's plays on the stage and the
other, the Collier-Congreve debate. The first includes discussions of the reception given to Congreve's plays in the eighteenth
century (1931.B2; 1971.B7), to his plays on the eighteenth-
century stage (1951.A1) and in the nineteenth-century theater
(1974.B14), and to revivals of Love for Love in Great Britain
and America in the nineteenth century (1966.B10). There are a
detailed study of the popularity of The Mourning Bride in the
English theaters in the eighteenth century (1941.B1), a brief
stage history of The Way of the World (1939.B3), and studies of
Congreve's reputation in the eighteenth-century novel (1960.B6)
and on the stage and in bookstalls (1976.B6). The multivolume
The London Stage 1660-1800 serves as an extremely useful guide to
various interesting facets of the theater in the period, including actors, cast lists, and performances.

The second subject includes a history of the Collier controversy and the subsequent debate between the opposing factions
(1937.B3), an explanation as to why Restoration comedy has been

attacked (1972.B3), and a discussion of the dramatists' awareness
that there were abuses in the theater (1974.B15). Congreve is
defended by, among others, Lytton Strachey against Collier and
Macaulay (1923.B9), Muir against Collier (1949.B7), and Bateson
against Knights and Wain (1957.B1). Further explanations as to
why the Priest and the Poet, the Platonist and the Aristotelian,
disagreed are advanced respectively by Maximillian Novak (1969.B8)
and Aubrey Williams (1975.B17).

(b)   Individual Works

In many respects, criticism of Incognita and the plays follows broadly the patterns traced in the preceding section, but
the focus on specific works results in more detailed analyses of
various topics. Many of these are included in the following
survey.

(i)   Incognita

Samuel Johnson's witty but negative verdict on Incognita,
that he would "rather praise it than read it" (1781.B1), antic-
ipates the dearth of comments on the novella. One writer
points to a possible source for its setting (1932.B1), and an
article in German, which cites Congreve's work, briefly documents the use of sylphs in literature (1952.B2). H. F. B.
Brett-Smith's edition acknowledges the merits of Congreve's
youthful excursion into nondramatic fiction (1922.A1). More
substantial essays discuss Incognita's structure and language
(1967.A10), the narrator's ironic detachment from the romantic
attitude (1930.A3), and the role of the narrator (1976.B11).
Various relationships examined are those among Congreve's
early theory of prose fiction (expressed in the preface to
the work), his use of masks, and Fielding's (1968.B16),
between the situations in Incognita and the stage (1966.A3),
and among Incognita, Restoration comedy, and the novella form
(1969.B9, B13; 1972.B27). The work's design and theme, so it
is believed, foreshadow those of the plays and reveal the
shaping hand of Providence (1968.B18). From Scandinavia comes
the most detailed analysis of Incognita, demonstrating it to
be a significant prologue to the plays (1976.A5).

(ii)   The Old Bachelor

Three articles discuss the date, place, and composition
of The Old Bachelor (1936.B4; 1943.B2; 1946.B2); a theater
ticket for a 1717 performance of the play is reproduced, with
notes (1963.B1); and a possible allusion in the play to the
alleged murderers of the actor-playwright William Mountford
is suggested (1972.B14). Two studies focus upon the character
of Vainlove: they explore his fastidious attitude toward
women, which implies sexual abnormality (1967.B13), and his
similarity to Swift's Gulliver (1968.B3). The play's originality receives attention (1970.B16), as do its observance of

Jonsonian precepts (1972.B10) and its use of Restoration material for the purpose of Augustan satire (1977.B5).

(iii) The Double Dealer

The amount of criticism of The Double Dealer is almost as sparse as that of Congreve's first comedy. A brief bibliographical note deals with the cancel leaf in the first edition (1949.B1), and it is proposed that The Double Dealer must have influenced Gresset's Méchant (1912.B1). An examination of the tradition of the hypocrite in eighteenth-century English literature includes references to the play (1972.B28). Another study deals with the interplay among Congreve's use of the "neoclassical theory of dramatic structure, his appeal to classical precedent, and his attempt to achieve a seriousness differing in kind from other Restoration comedies" (1972.B1). The ambiguous nature of the play, arising chiefly from a combination of comic and vicious characters, has been explained by an exploration and definition of the work as an "ironic dark-comedy" (1968.B6) and as a comedy that fulfills Dryden's specification for "the mixed way of comedy" (1974.B3).

A London revival of The Double Dealer was given in 1978 by the National Company in the Olivier Theatre; directed by Peter Wood, it presented John Harding as Mellefont, Judi Bowker as Cynthia, Robert Stephens as Maskwell, and Sir Ralph Richardson as Lord Touchwood.

(iv) Love for Love

The relative popularity of Love for Love may be seen in the amount and range of the criticism of the play. A textual comparison of the first printed edition and the acting version reveals many interesting variants (1975.B5); it is suggested that the eleventh scene of Act III may have been omitted in the initial production (1963.B4), while revisions of the play in the early nineteenth century indicate changes in taste, manners, and morals (1970.B17). A close look at Ben's song suggests that the author was Congreve himself (1933.B3; 1935.B5), a possible source for Ben being Ravencroft's Durzo (1934.B2). It is believed that two episodes in the play closely resemble similar incidents in Dryden's Wild Gallant (1954.B1).

In the 1940s, John Gielgud's production of Love for Love, a revival that did much to bring Congreve's plays back to the stage and to renew interest in the dramatist, became the topic of several reviews and the stimulus for several critical articles. Revealing are Gielgud's own discussion of his "naturalistic" adaptation of the play (1943.B1) and his further description of the production (1945.B5). Gielgud is praised for his interpretation of Valentine (1947.B2), while the disconcerting discovery is made that the play is as "much of a bore as a delight" (1948.B1). It is observed that the play makes a notable contribution to the "gallery of humorous

character" (1948.B4); that the peculiar quality of the play
rests upon the fact that it is not a comedy in the classic
sense,--that is, it is a parody not of man's work but of
God's (1956.B5); and that it "subsumes the best of Restoration
comedy" and looks forward to the later comedy of Vanbrugh and
Farquhar and to the fictional comedies of Fielding (1973.B17).

Although one early critic complains that for all its
bright and sparkling characters, Love for Love lacks one "pure
and perfect model of simple nature" (1817.A1), the play is
praised for its diversity of characters and their close
approximation to life (1791.A10), as well as for its fusion
of character and dialogue (1936.A1).

Thematic interpretations vary. Neither "insouciant" nor
"morally ambiguous," the play celebrates the "rationality of
an appropriate and real exchange of love" and "affirms the
value of an honest and faithful union in marriage" (1964.B10).
The action explores the various forms of "love (in exchange)
for money" (1968.A2) and the opposing values of love and money
(1972.B30). Seen to be influenced by Locke, Love for Love is
viewed as a "sophisticated and somewhat skeptical statement
of the limitations of human reason" (1972.B12). It is also
regarded as a play that embodies a vision of "secular reality"
(1972.B11) and as a "very witty dramatization of some basic
Christian truths and paradoxes" (1972.B29).

Comparisons of the play with Congreve's other comedies
lead to different evaluations. The characters are more varied
and closer to life than those in any other comedy by Congreve
(1791.A10); yet, inferior in wit and elegance to The Way of
the World, Love for Love remains unquestionably the "best-
acting of all his plays" (1818.B1; 1887.A1), its dramatic
effectiveness being explained in terms of the greater clarity
of plot (1967.A4).

(v) The Mourning Bride

Textual studies of The Mourning Bride and influences upon
it include a comparison of the first quarto edition and the
text in the 1710 collected Works (1975.B9) and acknowledgements
of Congreve's debt to Racine (1904.B1) and Dryden (1956.B1).
The play's première is examined (1942.B3), as are an Italian
adaptation of the play for an opera (1962.B2) and a Hebrew
translation (1967.B9).

Critical hostility to the tragedy emerges quite early and
continues well into the present century. The Mourning Bride
is seen not only as one of the "worst living tragedies"
(1770.B1), but as a defective tragedy (1817.A4), a play demonstrating Congreve's poverty of invention (1925.B6) and destitute prosody (1972.B20). Acknowledged, however, is the
popularity of the play on the stage between 1702 and 1776
(1941.B1). The paradox between the critical failure and the
stage success is discussed in some detail (1943.B5).

Congreve's verse, considered the "best instrument for the drama" of the age (1929.B5), his use of language (1967.B8), and the interplay of visual, verbal, and musical elements in the play (1972.B23) are examined, as are the presence and function of poetic justice (1971.B20; 1973.B5). One critic concludes that the play should be regarded as a "thriller" rather than a tragedy (1929.B5), but other studies point to the play's relationship to Restoration tragedy (1908.B1) and to heroic drama (1966.B14).

(vi) The Way of the World

Congreve's most popular play—if not always with audiences, at least with critics—brings forth a relatively large body of critical material. Attempts to pinpoint sources for the play result in some unconvincing arguments, partly because of the difficulty in identifying such sources in plays that belong to a specific but pervasive dramatic convention. Consequently, sources or influences have been variously traced to Nolant de Fatouville (1938.B3), to Corneille and Betterton (1946.B6), and to Corneille alone (1959.B8).

Other studies include a short stage history of the play (1939.B3), an explanation that the play failed because of the popularity of farce, song, and dance (1940.B5), and an assertion of its affinity with the Horation and Jonsonian satiric tradition (1958.A5). An examination of the structural aspects of the play is included in a detailed analysis (1967.B7), and it is also demonstrated that the structural development parallels a thematic movement from confusion and concealment to clarity and openness (1971.B10). One writer views The Way of the World as a play that illustrates some of the technical problems that every writer of comedy must face (1970.B6), and another questions whether the comic structure can withstand the kind of suffering caused in the play by Fainall and Marwood (1971.B21). The innovative qualities of the play are also discussed (1972.B16).

The Way of the World is thought of not only as the most brilliant example of the Restoration comedy of manners, but sometimes as the finest English comedy of the kind; yet attitudes to the more formal aspects of the play vary. A minority of critics complain, for example, that the plot, characters, and dialogue are not unified (1817.A5) and that the wit blurs distinctions between characters and obscures the plot (1940.A5). Others have sought to demonstrate that the wit both successfully differentiates the characters (1894.A1) and creates dramatic conflict and establishes a moral perspective (1973.B8). The wit, seen by several critics as the most important element in the play (for example, 1950.A3; 1953.A4), invariably raises admiration. The play, it is argued, explores wit in its widest sense (1952.B1; 1965.A4), yet the skeptical wit always remains in control (1968.A4). It is suggested that Dryden's formulation of wit offers a standard indispensable for proper responses to the play (1977.B1).

The proviso scene attracts specific attention, and three
views of it may be cited. One critic states that Millamant's
fanciful provisos result from her desire to prolong and in-
crease the prenuptial glamour and that Mirabell's more judi-
cious ones result from his desire to separate permanent
values from transitory ones (1958.A5). Another feels that
the proposal scene comes as close to romantic drama as is
possible in this "brilliantly cold comedy of manners"
(1964.B2); and a third argues that the scene indicates "a
serious attempt to form a union which would last, and...allow
liberty to both parties without leading to a corruption of
their relationship" (1970.B20).
    Studies also include comments on the characters of the
play. The Way of the World explores how "felicitously they
exemplify the principles which they profess" (1950.A2), how
they attempt to express their "true natures amid the intrica-
cies of civilized social intercourse" (1951.A6), and how the
central characters are distinguished by their flexibility
(1964.B13). More specific treatments of the characters deal
with Mirabell as an "ideal gentleman" (1964.B4), a view with
particular relevance to the interpretations given by Fujimara
(1952.B1), the Mueschkes (1958.A5), and Holland (1959.B5);
with Mirabell as a protagonist in a play that perfects the
"natural form of the comedy of the rake" (1966.B30); with
Mirabell's relationship to the rake-hero (1970.B2) and to the
"extravagant rake" (1972.B13); and with Congreve's use of
Mirabell to criticize the priorities of earlier Restoration
comedy and to explode "the artificies of...'the comic dance'"
(1972.B25). One critic affirms that Mirabell deserves to be
rewarded for his "sincere remorse" and "hearty contrition"
(1977.B7).
    The play's imagery has become a favorite topic in the
last two decades. It is shown that Congreve's use of the
"gambling analogy" establishes both social judgment and
situation (1968.B17); that the "rhetoric of law" involves
the audience in the action and suggests that "true comedy is
entirely compatible with serious art" (1971.B9); that its
"game-structure" molds the material of the play into its
peculiar form (1971.B12), and that Congreve's use of the
traditional comic image of disguise "explores the problem of
value in a world dedicated to appearance" (1971.B10).
    Thematic interpretations focus upon many interrelated
subjects: conflicts between personal desires and social
pressures, among three different ways of life--"presocial,
social and supra-social" (1959.B5), between art and nature
or "passional nature" and "civilized nature" (1963.B8), and
between appearance and reality (1964.A8); sexual aggression
(1966.B20) and sexual morality and monetary marriages
(1972.B24); the "way in which the world behaves about money
and love" (1958.A1); and the "decorum and artifices through
which individual feeling must fulfill itself within a society

where love easily founders on cold financial calculation"
(1972.A3). The Way of the World is also seen as a romantic
comedy because of its "central affirmation of the power of
love" (1971.A3) and as a play that probes the "possibilities
of deeper, more lasting and more complementary relationships
between men and women" (1966.A3), with its conclusion a
"testament to the hopeful and fearful human need to establish
a fostering and enduring love" (1974.A3).   Explored also are
the relationships among men and women and marriage (1894.A1)
and the theme of "marriage fraud" (1975.B13).   Some readings
reveal the play as examining the vagaries of a limited world
of an artificial society (1965.A2) and as reflecting social
experience (1972.B11) and the "best ethical and political
thought of the violent and fascinating" Whig aristocracy
(1958.B7).   One edition of the play, prepared for the university syllabus, includes a discussion of the complexity of the
plot, the system of values, the variation of the theme of
love, the use of irony, and the relationship between the
intrigue plot and the comedy as a whole (1945.A2).

The moral and aesthetic values of the play receive
attention in many of the critical studies just considered,
but particular attention should be given to the following
views, which deal with Congreve's achievement as a poet and
moralist.

The Way of the World, it is believed, mirrors a world in
which "nothing is good or bad, in which there is neither
morality nor feeling, but in which men and women are pretending to be civilized, in which sex is a battle of wits rather
than of emotions, and manners are the prime consideration"
(1928.A5).   The play, despite its wit and brilliance, does
not "provide an object lesson in moral conduct" (1942.A1);
or, it is an "insufferably dull play" that neither judges
nor tests but only exemplifies the values of the period
(1970.B10).   Furthermore, the "ironic gloss" is not "quite
dazzling enough to conceal the moral turbulence beneath"
(1955.B6); the play unexpectedly suggests "the lees beneath
the froth and the tarnish that diminishes the glitter"
(1969.B6).   Yet we are also reminded that the comedy reflects
and criticizes the fashionable world of the Restoration
(1950.A5), seriously examines sexual morality (1962.A7) and
society (1969.A6), possesses a "moral seriousness" that
depends upon a realistic presentation of alternatives to the
happiness of Mirabell and Millamant (1975.B3), and provides
an "exemplary movement by which characters may reach and use
virtue within their flawed society" (1975.B4).

The problem of the play's morality is defined variously
by critics.   One affirms that the play deals with a particular
kind of artistic morality (1959.B7), and the same critic
asserts that Congreve's is "the morality of an ethical, but
worldly, statesman, not of a saintly martyr" (1962.B8).
Others feel that Congreve judiciously contemplates the ways

of the world and metes out rewards and punishments according to the deserts of his characters (1965.B13), or that the play, while it may disregard conventional moral standards, possesses its own intrinsic "social and moral code to which everything is referred, and according to which certain things should be done and others should not" (1971.B18).

As a play, The Way of the World may be praised for its "vivid sense of reality" (1907.B2) and its "stark reality" (1925.B10), or may be considered "artificial rather than realistic comedy" (1958.A3)--even as too witty not only for "real life," but probably also for the stage (1953.A2). One critic feels the play's "brilliance and the cruelty" to be "overwhelming and somewhat wearisome" (1953.A3); yet it is also argued that there is "nothing brutal or repulsive in the ethics" of the play (1916.A1), that Congreve is a "good-mannered satirist" (1966.A5), that Congreve's intellectual brilliance never becomes divorced from compassion (1959.A6), and that he sees all the "follies and imperfections clearly but tolerates what he knows cannot be changed, albeit with an underlying sense of sadness" (1977.B2). To master the way of the world, it is further proposed, requires a "vigilance that Congreve never underestimates, even as he refuses to allow that it need cost us our hearts" (1973.A4).

(c) Conclusion

In retrospect, one may readily assert that Congreve is, as it were, very much alive and well. The increasing material written on him (articles, books, and dissertations) and the inclusion of three of his comedies in the modern repertoire attest not only to Congreve's popularity as a dramatist of some historical interest, but to his significance as a brilliant comic writer and perceptive observer of human nature.

What is striking, however, about much of the critical material is its heavy-handedness. One of the reasons that several reviews of Congreve's plays are included in this Reference Guide is that the reviewer, as opposed to the literary critic (a distinction that unfortunately has to be made), succeeds in capturing on the printed page the sheer delight of viewing the plays in the theaters--an element significantly lacking in the work of the serious scholar. One brief review of a production frequently does more to illuminate the play than do several critical analyses of the same play. Of course, the reviewer has the enviable advantage of basing his responses on a live presentation of the play. Nevertheless, in the attempt to rescue Congreve from his detractors--and there are still several--much of the recent criticism is motivated, implicitly if not explicitly, by the desire to defend Congreve against such a critic as L. C. Knights.

Furthermore, it is to be hoped that the effort to remove Congreve from one slot, that of Restoration dramatist, will

neither result in our placing him, to his detriment, in yet
another nor blind us to the more traditional aspects of the
plays.

Needed, and to some extent already accomplished, is a sane
balance that includes the exhilaration evoked by seeing the plays
on the stage and the more profound sense of what they have to say
about man and society, a balance that acknowledges Congreve's
debt to his literary heritage and his own unique achievements as
a dramatist worthy of attention.

(5) AIMS AND METHODS

The purpose of the Reference Guide is to present chronologically
the posthumous editions and criticism of Congreve's work, which total
approximately 1,315 entries, up to 1977, including as much material
for that year as was available at the time the bibliographical section was being prepared. Category A contains editions of Congreve's
works as well as books and dissertations that deal exclusively or
substantially with Congreve. Category B includes secondary material
that is concerned primarily with Congreve or that touches significantly upon him and that appears in articles, essays, reviews,
dissertations, or chapters or passages in these or in books.

Neither a descriptive nor a critical bibliography, the Reference
Guide attempts at all times to be objective in its annotations of the
criticism. Consequently whenever possible, the critic's own words
serve to summarize the argument. Annotations also include references
to those editions of Congreve's works that are prefaced with a critical introduction. Asterisks indicate all secondary material not
personally examined; and in such cases, reference sources are cited.

Materials not included are as follows:
(a) Works published before Congreve's death in 1729.
    Consequently, early references to the Jeremy Collier con-
    troversy are excluded. These, however, may be found in the
    history of the debate outlined by Sister Rose Anthony
    (1937.B3), in the biographies by Protopopesco (1924.A6) and
    Taylor (1931.A4), and in the brief bibliography by
    Clarence S. Paine (1940.B6).
(b) Annual bibliographies such as appear in Philological Quarterly,
    Restoration and 18th Century Theatre Research, The Scriblerian,
    and Studies in English Literature.
(c) Brief references to Congreve in journals, magazines, news-
    papers, and other obiter dicta that may be found in
    eighteenth- and nineteenth-century records. References to
    these may be found in the biographies by Gosse (1888.A3),
    Protopopesco (1924.A6), and Taylor (1931.A4). Of particular
    value is the eleven-volume work The London Stage 1660-1800,
    published by the Southern Illinois University Press, 1960-68.

Several criticisms from this period are included in the Reference Guide to give a sense of continuity and because they frequently represent one particular trend in Congreve's critical reputation.
(d) Reprints of
    (i) criticism that would reflect the historical reputation of the critic rather than the subject.
    (ii) literary histories that contain surveys of Congreve's career, for example, The Cambridge History of English Literature and A History of Restoration Drama.
    (iii) libretti by Congreve. Information for these may be obtained from the appropriate bibliographies under the name of the composer.
    (iv) English translations of Homer, Ovid, and Juvenal that may contain, but the bibliographical sources of which do not specifically indicate, Congreve's translations.

CATEGORY A

The following order is followed when listing Congreve's works in a given year:
(a) Complete works
(b) Selected works--combined editions of drama and poetry
(c) Selected works--drama
(d) Selected works--poetry
(e) Individual titles, with translations of Homer, Ovid, and Juvenal listed according to author.
Although no attempt was made to exhaust the area of foreign translations of Congreve's works, those editions readily found in bibliographical sources are included for the sake of completeness and interest.

Entry Lines

(a) Titles: Variant spellings are standardized, as in the case of The Old Bachelor, and titles of anthologies and collections reduced as far as is consistent with the claims of brevity and clarity.
(b) Dates: These may vary between that found on the imprint of of the individual work and that of the collection in which the play appears. The latter has been used to determine the appropriate year of entry.
(c) Volume numbers: The volume number of early collections containing Congreve's plays is cited whenever possible. The numbers in brackets following the volume number refer to the location of the play in the collection's sequence.
(d) Pagination: Only the arabic-numbered pages are cited in entries for earlier editions of Congreve's works, because pages with roman numerals can vary in otherwise identical editions. Furthermore, unnumbered pages that contain the play's epilogue and/or other printed matter about the play are frequently to be found.

A cautionary comment: Entries in the period between approximately 1776 and 1883 include references to many editions of Congreve's plays, printed singly and in collections, that may be considered duplications. The scattered location of these editions makes it impractical, if not impossible, to examine and collate each and every one. Different bibliographical sources do not follow one consistent method of measuring the format of the work and either use centimeters or designate the size as quarto, octavo and so on. Consequently, it is not always possible to determine whether different sizes indicate different editions, especially for those entries bearing similar imprints. The problem of distinguishing between the different editions is compounded by the fact that imprint dates may vary, although size and printer remain identical. Furthermore, the volume numbers, especially in the case of Bell's collections, can vary despite the fact that other information suggests that the work may be the same edition. The following list of groupings of the more questionable entries will, it is hoped, alert the researcher to these possible duplications and assist in identifying them:

    1776.A2/3, A8/9, A13/14, A18/19/20, A23/24;
    1778.A5/6;
    1791.A2/3, A4/5, A6/7, A8/9, A11/12, A13/14/15, A16/17/18,
       A20/21, A23/24;
    1795.A2/3, A4/5, A6/7;
    1796.A4/5;
    1797.A3/4, A7/8, A10/12, A11/13, A15/16, A14/17;
    1815.A2/3, A4/5, A6/7, A11/12;
    1817.A3/4;
    1824.A4/5, A7/8, A9/10;
    1864.A4/5;
    1866.A2/3;
    1883.A4/5

CATEGORY B

Those Ph.D. dissertations listed in <u>Comprehensive Dissertation Index</u> and <u>Dissertation Abstracts</u> that do not specifically mention Congreve's work in the abstract but whose titles suggest that Congreve may be referred to in the study are included and the appropriate sources are cited.

ACKNOWLEDGEMENTS

I am indebted to Ohio University for a Summer Research Grant and to the staff of the Inter-Library Loan Department at Ohio University for their invaluable help in obtaining crucial material for the completion of this project. I owe especial thanks to Professor John Dobson, librarian of the special collections at the University of Tennessee at Knoxville, for making available to me John C. Hodges's collection of Congreve's works, and to his staff for their kind assistance.

Annotated Bibliography

<u>1729</u>

<u>A BOOKS</u>

1 CONGREVE, WILLIAM. <u>The Dramatic Works</u>. 5 pts. in 1 vol.
  Dublin: by S. Powell for Thomas Moore; for Phil. Crampton
  and Stearne Brock, 1729-30-31.
  Contains the five plays.

2 _____. "An Hymn to Harmony." London.
  Cited in <u>NUC</u> (1970.B14), p. 586.

3 _____. <u>Last Will and Testament</u>. London: for E. Curll, 38 pp.
  Includes comments on Congreve's writings by Dryden,
  Blackmore, Addison, and Pack, as well as "Of Rightly Improving
  the Present Time. An Epistle [in verse] to Cobham" and "The
  Game of Quadrille. An Allegory."

4 _____. "A Letter...to Viscount Cobham" [in verse]. London:
  for A. Dodd and E. Nutt, 6 pp.

5 _____. <u>Love for Love</u>. Dublin: for P. Crampton, [etc.],
  108 pp.

6 _____. <u>The Mourning Bride</u>. Dublin: by and for George Grierson,
  67 pp.

<u>B SHORTER WRITINGS</u>

1 [MALLET, DAVID]. "A Poem to the Memory of Mr. Congreve."
  London: for J. Millan, 20 pp.
  Praises Congreve the man but disapproves of the morality
  of the comedies. Poem first attributed to James Thomson.
  <u>See</u> 1930.B3; 1939.B4; 1973.B1.

1729

2 MONTAGU, LADY MARY WORTLEY. "To the Memory of Mr. Congreve."
   In Essays and Poems and Simplicity, a Comedy. Edited by
   Robert Halsband and Isobel Grundy. Oxford: Clarendon Press,
   1977, pp. 246-47.
      Pays tribute to Congreve both as man and as writer.

                              1730

A BOOKS

1 CONGREVE, WILLIAM. The Works. 3 vols. The fifth edition.
   London: for J. Tonson.
      Includes the five plays, The Judgment of Paris, Semele,
   and Poems upon Several Occasions.

2 _____. Poems upon Several Occasions. London: n.p.,
   [205]-382 pp.

3 _____. The Old Bachelor. [London], 127 pp.
      Cited in NUC (1970.B14), p. 593.

4 _____. The Way of the World. [London], 149 pp.
      Cited in NUC (1970.B14), p. 595.

5 WILSON, CHARLES. Memoirs of the Life, Writings, and Amours of
   William Congreve Esq. Interspersed with Miscellaneous
   Essays, Letters, and Characters, Written by Him. Also some
   very Curious Memoirs of Mr. Dryden and his Family, with a
   Character of Him and his Writings, by Mr. Congreve. Compiled
   from their respective Originals. London: n.p., xvi + 156 +
   [iv] + 38 pp.
      Bound with Last Will and Testament (1729.A3) and extract
   from Incognita. See 1970.B19.

B SHORTER WRITINGS

1 COLLIER, JEREMY. A Short View of the Profaneness and Immorality
   of the English Stage, &c, with the several defences of the
   same. In answer to Mr. Congreve, Mr. Drake, &c. London:
   G. Strahan, [etc.], 437 pp.
      The fifth edition, corrected. Reissued 1738.B1.

*2 TEMPLE, RICHARD. "Cobham and Congreve. An epistle to Lord
   Viscount Cobham, in memory of his friend the late Mr. Congreve."
   London.
      Cited in BM (1966.B2), col. 990.

                               2

1731

A BOOKS

1 CONGREVE, WILLIAM. The Judgment of Paris; or, The Triumph of Beauty. London: by J. Roberts, 15 pp.
Without the music by Thomas Augustine Arne.

2 _____. The Mourning Bride. In The English Theatre. Part 4, vol. 2. London: for W. Feales, 1731-34.

B SHORTER WRITINGS--NONE

1732

A BOOKS

1 CONGREVE, WILLIAM. "An Epistle on Retirement and Taste....to Lord Cobham" [in verse]. In A Miscellany on Taste by Alexander Pope. London: G. Lawton, T. Osborn, J. Hughes.

2 _____, trans. [Juvenal's Eleventh Satire]. In The Satyrs of Decimus Junius Juvenalis; and of Aulus Persius Flaccus. Translated by Dryden and several other eminent hands. Dublin: by and for S. Fuller, 1732-33.

B SHORTER WRITINGS--NONE

1733

A BOOKS

1 CONGREVE, WILLIAM. The Dramatic Works. 5 pts. in 1 vol. London: for W. Feales.

2 _____. The Double Dealer. London: for J. Tonson and sold by W. Feales, 94 pp.

3 _____. The Judgment of Paris. London: for J. Tonson, 12 pp. Without the music.

4 _____. Love for Love. Dublin: by G. Grierson. Cited in NUC (1970.B14), p. 588.

3

1733

5 _____ . <u>Love for Love</u>. London: for J. Tonson and sold by
W. Feales, 106 pp.

6 _____ . <u>The Mourning Bride</u>. London: for J. Tonson and sold by
W. Feales, 82 pp.

7 _____ . <u>The Old Bachelor</u>. London: for J. Tonson and sold by
W. Feales, 84 pp.

8 _____ . <u>The Way of the World</u>. London: for J. Tonson and sold
by W. Feales, 82 pp.

B SHORTER WRITINGS

1 VOLTAIRE [FRANÇOIS-MARIE AROUET]. <u>Letters Concerning the English
Nation</u>. No. 19. London: for C. Davies and A. Lyon.
Recounts his visit to Congreve: "Il me parlait de ses
ouvrages comme de bagatelles au-dessous de lui, et me dit...
de ne le voir que sur le pied d'un gentilhomme qui vivait
très uniment."

<u>1735</u>

A BOOKS

1 CONGREVE, WILLIAM. <u>Plays</u>. 2 vols. in 1. London: for
J. Tonson.

2 _____ . <u>The Double Dealer</u>. [Dublin]: by Theo. Jones for George
Risk, [etc.], 95 pp.

3 _____ . <u>The Double Dealer</u>. London: for Jacob Tonson, 107 pp.

4 _____ , ed. <u>The Dramatic Works of John Dryden</u>. 6 vols. London:
J. Tonson.
Contains the dedication "To His Grace the Duke of
Newcastle."

5 _____ , trans. "The Impossible Thing," and "The Lout Looking for
His Heifer." In <u>Tales and Novels in Verse</u>. Translated by
several hands. London: Samuel Humphreys.
Translations of two tales by La Fontaine.

6 _____ , trans. [Juvenal's Eleventh Satire]. In <u>The Satyrs of
Decimus Junius Juvenalis: and of Aulus Persius Flaccus</u>.
London: for J. Tonson.

7 _____. <u>Love for Love</u>. Dublin: by Theo. Jones for George Risk, [etc.], 106 pp.

8 _____. <u>Love for Love</u>. London: for Jacob Tonson, 130 pp., 12mo.

9 _____. <u>Love for Love</u>. London: J. Tonson, 130 pp., 16mo.

10 _____. <u>The Mourning Bride</u>. Dublin: by Theo. Jones for George Risk, [etc.], 70 pp.

11 _____. <u>The Mourning Bride</u>. Dublin: by S. Powell for P. Crampton, 60 pp.

12 _____. <u>The Mourning Bride</u>. London: for Jacob Tonson, 80 pp., 12mo.

13 _____. <u>The Mourning Bride</u>. London: for J. Tonson, 82 pp., 16mo.

14 _____. <u>The Old Bachelor</u>. London: for Jacob Tonson, 106 pp.

15 _____, trans. [Book III of the <u>Art of Love</u>]. In <u>Ovid's Art of Love...Together with his Remedy of love</u>. London: for J. Tonson.
   Includes Congreve's notes on Book III.

16 _____. <u>The Way of the World</u>. London: for Jacob Tonson, 116 pp., 12mo.

17 _____. <u>The Way of the World</u>. London: J. Tonson, 116 pp., 16mo.

B SHORTER WRITINGS--NONE

<u>1736</u>

A BOOKS

1 CONGREVE, WILLIAM. <u>The Works</u>. 2 vols. Dublin: by Theo. Jones for George Risk, [etc.].
   Includes the five plays, <u>The Judgment of Paris</u>, <u>Semele</u>, and <u>Poems upon Several Occasions</u>.

2 _____. <u>The Mourning Bride</u>. London: for W. Feales, 70 pp.

1736

3 _____. The Mourning Bride. London: for W. Feales, 82 pp.

4 _____. The Mourning Bride. In The British Theatre. Vol. 2.
     London: for W. Feales, 82 pp.

5 _____, trans. Ovid's Metamorphoses [Part of Book 10]. Trans-
     lated by Mr. Dryden...and other eminent hands. 2 vols. The
     fourth edition. London: J. & R. Tonson.

B SHORTER WRITINGS--NONE

1737

A BOOKS

1 CONGREVE, WILLIAM. The Old Bachelor. Dublin: for P. Crampton,
     71 pp.

B SHORTER WRITINGS--NONE

1738

A BOOKS

1 CONGREVE, WILLIAM. The Way of the World. Dublin: for Philip
     Crampton, 84 pp.
          "No. 4 in a volume of plays with binder's title: Plays.
     Vol. III." Cited in NUC (1970.B14), p. 595.

B SHORTER WRITINGS

1 COLLIER, JEREMY. A Short View of the Profaneness and Immorality
     of the English Stage.... London: Samuel Birt, [etc.].
          Reissue of 1730.B1.

1739

A BOOKS

1 CONGREVE, WILLIAM. The Double Dealer. London: for the Book-
     sellers in Town & Country, 95 pp.

2 _____. The Mourning Bride. London: for the Booksellers in
        Town & Country, pp. 289-358.
            Bound with The Old Bachelor. Cited in NUC (1970.B14),
        p. 590. See 1739.A3.

3 _____. The Old Bachelor. London: for the Booksellers in Town
        & Country.
            Bound with The Mourning Bride. See 1739.A2.

B SHORTER WRITINGS--NONE

1740

A BOOKS

1 CONGREVE, WILLIAM. The Judgement of Paris, 66 pp.
            Music by Thomas Augustine Arne. Cited in National Union
        Catalog: Pre 1956 Imprints, vol. 21. London: Mansell,
        p. 672.

B SHORTER WRITINGS

1 CIBBER, COLLEY. An Apology for the Life of Mr. Colley Cibber.
        London: by John Watts for the author, 346 pp., passim.
            Many references to Congreve's private and professional life.

1742

A BOOKS

1 ANON. [Adaptation of scenes from The Old Bachelor], "The
        Braggadochio," in The Stroller's Pacquet Open'd. London:
        n.p.
            Cited in BM (1966.B2), vol. 25, col. 689.

2 CONGREVE, WILLIAM. The Mourning Bride. London: for J. and R.
        Tonson, 71 pp.

B SHORTER WRITINGS--NONE

1743

1743

A BOOKS

1 CONGREVE, WILLIAM. Incognita. Dublin: by M. Rhames for
      J. Rhames, 62 pp.

B SHORTER WRITINGS--NONE

1744

A BOOKS

1 CONGREVE, WILLIAM. The Double Dealer. Dublin: for Philip
      Crampton, 78 pp.

2 _____. "An Essay Concerning Humour in Comedy." In An Essay
      Towards Fixing the True Standards of Wit, Humour, Raillery,
      Satire, and Ridicule, by Corbyn Morris. London: J. Roberts,
      [etc.], pp. 66-75.
         Reprinted 1947.A2.

3 _____. The Story of Semele. Altered from the Semele of
      Mr. William Congreve, and set to Music by Mr. George Frederick
      Handel. London: for J. and R. Tonson, 28 pp.
         Text only.

B SHORTER WRITINGS--NONE

1746

A BOOKS

1 CONGREVE, WILLIAM. Amour pour amour. In Le théâtre anglois.
      Tom 7. Londres, 1746-49.
         French translation of Love for Love.

2 _____. L'épouse en deuil. In Le théâtre anglois. Tom 6.
      Londres, 1746-49.
         French translation of The Mourning Bride.

B SHORTER WRITINGS--NONE

<u>1747</u>

A BOOKS

1 CONGREVE, WILLIAM. <u>Love for Love</u>. London: for J. and R. Tonson and S. Draper, 106 pp.

2 _____, trans. [Book III of the <u>Art of Love</u>]. In <u>Ovid's Art of Love...Together with his Remedy of Love</u>. London: for J. and R. Tonson and S. Draper.

B SHORTER WRITINGS--NONE

<u>1748</u>

A BOOKS

1 CONGREVE, WILLIAM. <u>Love for Love</u>. Dublin: for George Risk, [etc.], 106 pp.

B SHORTER WRITINGS--NONE

<u>1749</u>

A BOOKS--NONE

B SHORTER WRITINGS

1 MELMOTH, WILLIAM, ed. "Letter LXX. To Euphronius. Aug. 20, 1722." In <u>Letters on Several Subjects. By the late Sir Thomas Fitzosborne</u>. Vol. 2. London: for R. Dodsley, pp. 176-202.
   Compares passages of Pope's translation of <u>The Iliad</u> with those by Congreve. Congreve's is "languid and inelegant," his prose "unaffecting," the rhymes "tasteless."

<u>1750</u>

A BOOKS

1 CONGREVE, WILLIAM. <u>The Double Dealer</u>. In <u>A Select Collection of the Best Modern English Plays</u>. Vol. 8 [no. 1]. The Hague: for H. Scheurleer, Jr.

1750

2 _____. The Mourning Bride. Dublin: James Dalton, 70 pp.

3 _____. The Mourning Bride. London: for J. & R. Tonson and
       S. Draper, 71 pp.

4 _____, trans. [Book III of the Art of Love]. In Ars Amandi; or,
       Ovid's Art of Love...Together with his Remedy of love.
       Dublin: for James Dalton.

B SHORTER WRITINGS

1 "CONGREVE (WILLIAM)." Biographia Britannica; or, The Lives of
       the Most eminent Persons. Vol. 3. London: for W. Innys,
       [etc.], pp. 1439–49.
         Numerous references to earlier comments on Congreve.

1751

A BOOKS

1 CONGREVE, WILLIAM. The Dramatic Works. 2 vols. Glasgow: by
       Robert and Andrew Foulis.

2 _____. The Double Dealer. Glasgow: R. & A. Foulis, 97 pp.

3 _____. The Mourning Bride. Glasgow: by Robert and Andrew
       Foulis, 82 pp.

4 _____. The Old Bachelor. Glasgow: by Robert and Andrew Foulis,
       126 pp.

5 _____, trans. "The Story of Orpheus and Eurydice" and part of
       "The Tale of Cyparissus." In Ovid's Metamorphoses. Trans-
       lated by the most eminent hands. 2 vols. London: J. and R.
       Tonson and S. Draper.

B SHORTER WRITINGS--NONE

1752

A BOOKS

1 CONGREVE, WILLIAM. Works. 3 vols. The fifth edition. London:
       for Tonson.

2 _____. <u>Poems Upon Several Occasions</u>. Glasgow: by R. and A. Foulis, 189 pp.

3 _____. <u>The Dramatic Works</u>. 2 vols. Glasgow: R. Urie.

4 _____. <u>The Old Bachelor</u>. Dublin: for James Dalton, 72 pp.

B SHORTER WRITINGS--NONE

1753

A BOOKS

1 CONGREVE, WILLIAM. <u>Works</u>. 3 vols. The sixth edition. London: for J. and R. Tonson and S. Draper.

2 _____. <u>The Mourning Bride</u>. Dublin: for G. Risk, [etc.], 70 pp.

3 _____. <u>The Mourning Bride</u>. London: for J. and R. Tonson and S. Draper, 71 pp.

B SHORTER WRITINGS

1 CIBBER, THEOPHILUS. "William Congreve, Esq." In his <u>The Lives of the Poets of Great Britain and Ireland</u>. Vol. 4. London: for R. Griffiths, pp. 83-98.
  Includes Congreve's "Of Improving the Present Time" and concludes with Pope's postscript to his translation of Homer, in which he praises Congreve.

1754

A BOOKS

1 CONGREVE, WILLIAM, trans. [Juvenal's Eleventh Satire]. In <u>The Satyrs of Decimus Junius Juvenalis: and of Aulus Persius Flaccus</u>. London: J. and R. Tonson and S. Draper.

2 _____. <u>The Mourning Bride</u>. Edinburgh: for James Reid, 54 pp.

3 _____. <u>The Old Bachelor</u>. London: for J. and R. Tonson and S. Draper, 80 pp.

1754

4 _____. "The Power of Harmony, an ode, wrote in honour of
St. Cecilia." London, 12 pp.
Cited in <u>NUC</u> (1970.B14), p. 594.

B SHORTER WRITINGS--NONE

1755

A BOOKS

1 CONGREVE, WILLIAM. <u>Love for Love</u>. Edinburgh: for G. Hamilton
and J. Balfour, 116 pp.

2 _____. <u>The Mourning Bride</u>. Edinburgh: for G. Hamilton and
J. Balfour, 70 pp.

3 _____. <u>The Mourning Bride</u>. In <u>Select Collection of English
Plays</u>. Vol. 2. Edinburgh: for G. Hamilton and J. Balfour.

4 _____. <u>The Way of the World</u>. Edinburgh: for G. Hamilton and
J. Balfour, 106 pp.

B SHORTER WRITINGS--NONE

1756

A BOOKS

1 CONGREVE, WILLIAM. <u>Love for Love</u>. London: for J. and R.
Tonson, 98 pp.

2 _____. <u>Love for Love</u>. London: for J. and R. Tonson, 106 pp.

3 _____. <u>The Way of the World</u>. London: for J. and R. Tonson,
82 pp.

B SHORTER WRITINGS--NONE

1757

A BOOKS

1 CONGREVE, WILLIAM. Love for Love. Dublin: for Peter Wilson,
   94 pp.

2 _____. The Mourning Bride. Dublin: for Peter Wilson, 71 pp.

3 _____. The Mourning Bride. London: for the Proprietors, 71 pp.

4 _____. The Mourning Bride. London: for J. and R. Tonson,
   71 pp.

5 _____, trans. [Book III of the Art of Love]. In Ovid's Art of
   Love...Together with his Remedy of love. London: Jacob and
   Richard Tonson.

B SHORTER WRITINGS--NONE

1758

A BOOKS

1 CONGREVE, WILLIAM. The Mourning Bride. Glasgow: n.p., 64 pp.

B SHORTER WRITINGS--NONE

1759

A BOOKS

1 CONGREVE, WILLIAM. The Double Dealer. Dublin: for G. and A.
   Ewing, [etc.], 95 pp.

2 _____. Love for Love. Glasgow, 94 pp.
   Cited in NUC (1970.B14), p. 588.

3 _____. Le Train du Monde. Précédée d'une dissertation sur la
   comédie angloise. [Paris?], 134 pp.
   Cited in NUC (1970.B14), p. 594.

4 _____. The Way of the World. Dublin: for G. and A. Ewing,
   [etc.], 94 pp.

1760

B SHORTER WRITINGS--NONE

<u>1760</u>

A BOOKS

1 CONGREVE, WILLIAM. <u>Love for Love</u>. Dublin: for G. and A. Ewing,
   [etc.], 106 pp.

2 _____. <u>The Old Bachelor</u>. Dublin: for G. and A. Ewing, [etc.],
   71 pp.

B SHORTER WRITINGS--NONE

<u>1761</u>

A BOOKS

1 CONGREVE, WILLIAM. <u>Works</u>. 3 vols. Birmingham: by
   J. Baskerville for J. and R. Tonson.

2 _____. <u>Dramatic Works</u>. 2 vols. Glasgow: for R. Urie.

3 _____. <u>The Double Dealer</u>.
   Cited in <u>NUC</u> (1970.B14), p. 585.

B SHORTER WRITINGS--NONE

<u>1762</u>

A BOOKS

1 CONGREVE, WILLIAM, ed. <u>The Dramatic Works of John Dryden</u>.
   6 vols. London: for J. and R. Tonson, 1762-63.

2 _____, trans. "The Impossible Thing" and "The Lout Looking for
   his Heifer." In <u>Tales and Novels in Verse</u>. Edinburgh: by
   Samuel Humphreys.
   From two tales by La Fontaine.

3 _____. <u>The Mourning Bride</u>. Dublin: by Cusack Greene, 70 pp.

4 _____. The Mourning Bride. In The English Theatre. Vol. 6
[no. 4]. London: for T. Lownds [sic].

5 _____. Semele. Altered from the Semele of Congreve and music
by Handel. London: for J. and R. Tonson, 24 pp.
Without the music.

B SHORTER WRITINGS

1 KAMES, LORD (HENRY HOME). "The three Unities." In his Elements
of Criticism. Vol. 3. Edinburgh: for A. Millar, [etc.],
pp. 259-93.
Touches upon the structural weaknesses and strengths of
Congreve's plays.

1763

A BOOKS

1 CONGREVE, WILLIAM. The Mourning Bride. London: for J. and R.
Tonson, 71 pp.

B SHORTER WRITINGS--NONE

1764

A BOOKS

1 CONGREVE, WILLIAM. The Mourning Bride. London: for J. and R.
Tonsom [sic], 71 pp.

2 _____, trans. [Book III of the Art of Love]. In Ovid's Art of
Love...Together with his Remedy of love. London: for Jacob
and Richard Tonson.

B SHORTER WRITINGS--NONE

1765

A BOOKS

1 CONGREVE, WILLIAM. Love for Love. In The English Theatre.
Vol. 5 [no. 2]. London: for T. Lowndes, 106 pp.

1765

2   _____.   The Mourning Bride.   In The English Theatre.   Vol. 6.
         London: for T. Lowndes.

B SHORTER WRITINGS--NONE

1766

A BOOKS

1   CONGREVE, WILLIAM.   Liebe für Liebe.   Leipzig: bey Joh. Gottl.
         Rothe, Kopenhagen, 232 pp.
              "No. 8 in a volume labeled on spine: Komisches Theater."
         Cited in NUC (1970.B14), p. 587.

2   _____.   The Mourning Bride.   London: for J. and R. Tonson,
         71 pp.

B SHORTER WRITINGS--NONE

1767

A BOOKS

1   CONGREVE, WILLIAM.   The Way of the World.   London: for
         T. Davies, [etc.], 82 pp.
              "No. 4 in a volume of plays with binder's title: Plays.
         Vol. X."   Cited in NUC (1970.B14), p. 595.

B SHORTER WRITINGS--NONE

1768

A BOOKS

1   CONGREVE, WILLIAM.   The Double Dealer.   Edinburgh: by and for
         Martin and Wotherspoon, 83 pp.

2   _____.   Love for Love.   In The Theatre; or, Select Works of the
         British Dramatic Poets.   Vol. 11 [no. 3].   Edinburgh:
         Martin & Wotherspoon, 107 pp.

3   _____.   The Mourning Bride.   Edinburgh: by and for Martin and
         Wotherspoon, 69 pp.

16

4 ____. <u>The Mourning Bride</u>. London: for T. Lowndes, [etc.], 71 pp.

5 ____. <u>The Mourning Bride</u>. In <u>The Theatre; or, Select Works of the British Dramatic Poets</u>. Vol. 10. Edinburgh: Martin & Wotherspoon.

6 ____. <u>The Old Bachelor</u>. Edinburgh: by and for Martin & Wotherspoon, 83 pp.

B SHORTER WRITINGS--NONE

1769

A BOOKS

1 CONGREVE, WILLIAM. <u>Love for Love</u>. In <u>The English Theatre</u>. Vol. 5 [no. 3]. London: for T. Lowndes.

2 ____. <u>The Mourning Bride</u>. In <u>The English Theatre</u>. Vol. 6 [no. 2]. London: for T. Lowndes.

3 ____, trans. [Book III of the <u>Art of Love</u>]. In <u>Ovid's Art of Love...Together with his Remedy of love</u>. London: for Jacob Tonson.

B SHORTER WRITINGS--NONE

1770

A BOOKS

1 CONGREVE, WILLIAM. <u>Love for Love</u>. London: for T. Davies, [etc.], 81 pp.

2 [____. <u>The Way of the World</u>]. [London: T. Lowndes, 1770?], 84 pp.
    "Title-page wanting." Cited in <u>NUC</u> (1970.B14), p. 595.

B SHORTER WRITINGS

1 GENTLEMAN, FRANCIS. "<u>The Mourning Bride</u>. Essay." In his <u>The Dramatic Censor; or, Critical Companion</u>. Vol. 2. London: for J. Bell and C. Etherington, pp. 399-417.

1771

> The play is one of the "worst living tragedies; it is
> apparently laboured, the sentiments in general strained, the
> versification in many places monotonous, and the plot
> equivocal."

1771

A BOOKS

1 CONGREVE, WILLIAM. Der Arglistige. Hamburg, 136 pp.
      German translation of The Double Dealer.

B SHORTER WRITINGS--NONE

1772

A BOOKS

1 CONGREVE, WILLIAM. The Double Dealer. London: Davies, 77 pp.
      "(In: Plays, v.10)." Cited in NUC (1970.B14), p. 585.

B SHORTER WRITINGS--NONE

1773

A BOOKS

1 CONGREVE, WILLIAM. Works. 3 vols. Dublin: Thomas Ewing.

2 _____. The Dramatic Works. 2 vols. London: for S. Crowder.
      [etc.].

3 _____. The Mourning Bride. Glasgow, 72 pp.
      Cited in NUC (1970.B14), p. 591.

4 _____, trans. [Ovid's] Metamorphoses [Part of Book 10]. Trans-
      lated by the most eminent hands. 2 vols. The fourth edition.
      London: for T. Davies, T. Becket, [etc.].

5 _____. The Way of the World. Dublin: W. Wilson, 84 pp.

B SHORTER WRITINGS--NONE

<u>1774</u>

A BOOKS

1 CONGREVE, WILLIAM. <u>The Works</u>. 2 vols. The seventh edition.
    London: for T. Lowndes, [etc.].

2 _____. [<u>Dramatic Works</u>]. London: for W. Fox.
    Bound with <u>Jane Shore</u> and <u>The Fair Penitent</u>.

3 _____. <u>Plays</u>.
    Cited in <u>NUC</u> (1970.B14), p. 583.

4 _____. <u>The Double Dealer</u>. Edinburgh: [by J. Robertson?].
    Cited in <u>NUC</u> (1970.B14), p. 585.

5 _____. <u>Love for Love</u>. Edinburgh: by J. Robertson, 99 pp.

6 _____. <u>Love for Love</u>. London: for W. Fox, 103 pp.

7 _____. <u>The Mourning Bride</u>. London: for W. Fox, 67 pp.

8 _____. <u>The Old Bachelor</u>. Edinburgh: John Robertson, 79 pp.

9 _____. <u>The Old Bachelor</u>. London: for W. Fox, 82 pp.

10 _____. <u>The Way of the World</u>. Edinburgh: J. Robertson, 79 pp.

11 _____. <u>The Way of the World</u>. London: for W. Fox, 92 pp.

B SHORTER WRITINGS--NONE

<u>1775</u>

A BOOKS

1 CONGREVE, WILLIAM. [<u>Works</u>]. [Vol. 1]. London, 1775-76.
    Includes <u>The Old Bachelor</u>, <u>The Double Dealer</u>, <u>Love for
    Love</u>, and <u>The Mourning Bride</u>. Cited in <u>NUC</u> (1970.B14),
    p. 588.

2 _____. <u>Plays</u>. [London, 1775-].
    Contains <u>The Old Bachelor</u>, <u>The Double Dealer</u>, <u>Love for Love</u>,
    <u>The Way of the World</u>, and <u>The Mourning Bride</u>. Cited in <u>NUC</u>
    (1970.B14), p. 583.

1775

3 _____. Le Fourbe. Londres. Et se trouve à Paris chez Ruault,
Libraire.
French translation of The Double Dealer. Cited in BM
(1966.B2), col. 982.

4 _____. Love for Love. In The English Theatre. Vol. 5 [no. 2].
London: T. Lowndes, 1775- .
Cited in NUC (1970.B14), vol. 160, p. 385.

5 _____. The Mourning Bride. London: by W. Oxlade, 58 pp.

6 _____. The Mourning Bride. In The English Theatre. Vol. 6
[no. 1]. London: T. Lowndes, 1775- .
Cited in NUC (1970.B14), vol. 160, p. 385.

B SHORTER WRITINGS--NONE

1776

A BOOKS

1 CONGREVE, WILLIAM. The Double Dealer. In Bell's British Theatre.
Vol. 13 [no. 2]. London: for John Bell, 1776-78, 82 pp.

2 _____. The Double Dealer. In The New English Theatre. Vol. 9.
London, 1776-77, 77 pp., 8vo.

3 _____. The Double Dealer. In The New English Theatre. Vol. 9
[no. 2]. London: for J. Rivington, [etc.], 1776-77, 77 pp.,
12mo.

4 _____. Le Fourbe. Paris: Ruault, 80 pp.
French translation of The Double Dealer. "[Collection de
pièces françaises; comédies, v.42, no.4]." Cited in NUC
(1970.B14), p. 586.

5 _____. Love for Love. London: for J. Bell, 96 pp.

6 _____. Love for Love. London: for T. Davies, 95 pp.

7 _____. Love for Love. In Bell's British Theatre. Vol. 8 [no. 2].
London: for John Bell, 1776-78, 96 pp.

8 _____. Love for Love. In The New English Theatre. Vol. 5.
London, 1776-77, 95 pp., 8vo.

9 _____. Love for Love. In The New English Theatre. Vol. 5
[no. 5]. London: for J. Rivington, [etc.], 1776-77, 90 pp.,
12mo.

10 _____. The Mourning Bride. London: for J. Bell, 63 pp.

11 _____. The Mourning Bride. London: for T. Davies, [etc.],
67 pp.

12 _____. The Mourning Bride. In Bell's British Theatre. Vol. 3
[no. 3]. London: for John Bell, 1776-78, 63 pp.

13 _____. The Mourning Bride. In The New English Theatre. Vol. 4
London, 1776-77, 67 pp., 8vo.

14 _____. The Mourning Bride. In The New English Theatre. Vol. 4
[no. 3]. London: for J. Rivington, [etc.], 1776-77, 59 pp.,
12mo.

15 _____. The Old Bachelor. London: for John Bell and
C. Etherington at York, 81 pp.

16 _____. The Old Bachelor. London: for T. Davies, [etc.], 80 pp.

17 _____. The Old Bachelor. In Bell's British Theatre. Vol. 2
[no. 4]. London: for John Bell, 1776-78, 81 pp.

18 _____. The Old Bachelor. In The New English Theatre. Vol. 3.
London, 1776-77, 80 pp., 8vo.

19 _____. The Old Bachelor. In The New English Theatre. Vol. 3
[no. 2]. London: for J. Rivington, [etc.], 1776-77, 70 pp.
12mo.

20 _____. The Old Bachelor. In The New English Theatre. Vol. 3
[no. 2]. London [1776-], 80 pp., 16mo.

21 _____, trans. [Book III of the Art of Love]. In Ovid's Art of
Love...Together with his Remedy of love. London: W. Strahan,
[etc.].

22 _____. The Way of the World. In Bell's British Theatre.
Vol. 11 [no. 2]. London: for John Bell, 1776-78, 87 pp.

23 _____. The Way of the World. In The New English Theatre.
Vol. 5. London, 1776-77, 84 pp., 8vo.

1776

24 _____. The Way of the World. In The New English Theatre.
   Vol. 5 [no. 1]. London: for J. Rivington, [etc.], 1776-77,
   83 pp., 12mo.

B SHORTER WRITINGS—NONE

1777

A BOOKS

1 CONGREVE, WILLIAM. Die braut in trauer. Danzig: D. L. Wedeln,
   95 pp.
      German translation of The Mourning Bride.

2 _____. The Double Dealer. London: for John Bell, 82 pp.

3 _____. The Double Dealer. In Bell's Theatre. 5 nos. in 1 vol.
   Vol. 2 [no. 4]. London: J. Bell, 1777-80.

4 _____. The Mourning Bride. London: for J. Wenman, 16 pp.

5 _____. The Old Bachelor. In Bell's Theatre. 5 nos. in 1 vol.
   Vol. 2 [no. 1]. London: J. Bell, 1777-80.

6 _____, trans. [Book III of the Art of Love]. In Ovid's Art of
   Love...Together with his Remedy of Love. London: for
   T. Caslon and W. Davenhill.

7 _____. The Way of the World. 8vo.
      Cited in Summers, 1934.B4.

8 _____. The Way of the World. London: for John Bell, 87 pp.,
   12mo.

9 _____. The Way of the World. In Bell's British Theatre; Comedies.
   [no. 2]. London: J. Bell.

B SHORTER WRITINGS—NONE

1778

A BOOKS

1 CONGREVE, WILLIAM. The Works. 2 vols. London: for the Editor
   and sold by J. Wenman.

2 _____. <u>The Poetical Works of Will. Congreve</u>. With the Life of
the Author. In <u>The Poets of Great Britain Complete from
Chaucer to Churchill</u>. Edinburgh: for John Bell at the
Apollo Press, 216 pp.

3 _____. <u>The Judgment of Paris</u>. [London]: J. Wenman, 3 pp.
"(In Plays. London, 1778). Title page wanting; caption
title." Cited in <u>NUC</u> (1970.B14), p. 587.

4 _____. <u>The Judgment of Paris</u>. In <u>Theatrical Magazine</u>. Vol. 2.
[London? 1778?], 3 pp.
Cited in <u>NUC</u> (1970.B14), p. 587.

5 _____. <u>The Old Bachelor</u>. London: for John Bell, 73 pp.

6 _____. <u>The Old Bachelor</u>. London: J. Bell, 81 pp.

B SHORTER WRITINGS--NONE

<u>1779</u>

A BOOKS

1 CONGREVE, WILLIAM. <u>Poems</u>. In <u>Works of the English Poets</u>.
Edited by Samuel Johnson. Vol. 29. London: by H. Hughes
for C. Cathurst.

2 _____. <u>The Mourning Bride</u>. London: by the Etheringtons for
J. Bell, 63 pp.

B SHORTER WRITINGS--NONE

<u>1780</u>

A BOOKS

1 CONGREVE, WILLIAM. <u>The Judgment of Paris</u>. [London?: Harrison?
178- ?], 3 pp.
"No. 16 in a volume lettered: English plays, 1771-1781."
Cited in <u>NUC</u> (1970.B14), p. 587.

2 _____. <u>Love for Love</u>. London: J. Bell, 81 pp.

1780

3 _____. Love for Love. In British Theatre. Vol. 8 [no. 2].
     London: for John Bell, 1780-81, 99 pp.

4 _____. The Mourning Bride. In Bell's British Theatre. Vol. 3
     [no. 3]. London: John Bell, 63 pp.

5 _____. The Old Bachelor. In British Theatre. Vol. 2 [no. 4].
     London: for John Bell, 1780-81, 73 pp.

6 _____. The Way of the World. London: for John Bell, 79 pp.

7 _____. The Way of the World. In British Theatre. Vol. 11
     [no. 2]. London: for John Bell, 1780-81, 79 pp.

B SHORTER WRITINGS--NONE

1781

A BOOKS

1 CONGREVE, WILLIAM. [Three Plays]. London: W. Fox.
     Contains the 1774 editions of The Old Bachelor, The Double
     Dealer, and Love for Love.

2 _____. The Old Bachelor. In Theatrical Magazine. Vol. 5.
     London: for Harrison, and sold by J. Wenman, 22 pp.
          Cited in NUC (1970.B14), p. 593.

B SHORTER WRITINGS

1 JOHNSON, SAMUEL. "Congreve." In his Lives of the Most Eminent
     English Poets. Vol. 3. London: for C. Bathurst, [etc.],
     pp. 43-69.
          Praises Congreve's achievements as a young dramatist, add-
     ing that the comedies are works of a mind "replete with images,
     and quick in combination." Yet "the perusal of his works will
     make no man better; and...their ultimate effect is to repre-
     sent pleasure in alliance with vice, and to relax those obli-
     gations by which life ought to be regulated."

1782

A BOOKS

1 CONGREVE, WILLIAM, trans. [Book III of the Art of Love]. In
  Ovid's Art of Love...together with his Remedy of love.
  London: for T. Caslon, [etc.].

B SHORTER WRITINGS--NONE

1783

A BOOKS

1 CONGREVE, WILLIAM. The Mourning Bride. London: for T. and W.
  Lowndes, [etc.], 67 pp.

2 _____. The Mourning Bride. London: by H. Whitworth [ca.1783?],
  59 pp.

3 _____. A noiva de luto. Lisboa: Na. Offic. Patr. de
  F. L. Ameno, 141 pp.
  Portuguese translation of The Mourning Bride. "Bound with
  Martinelli, C. A. mái indiscreta. Lisboa, 1795." Cited in
  NUC (1970.B14), p. 592.

4 _____. Die vaeterliche Rache; oder, Liebe für Liebe. Wien:
  Logenmeister, 120 pp.

B SHORTER WRITINGS--NONE

1784

A BOOKS

1 CONGREVE, WILLIAM. Poems upon Several Occasions. Lisburn: by
  T. Ward, 189 pp.

2 _____. The Poetical Works. In The Poets of Great Britain complete from Chaucer to Churchill. 2nd ed. Vol. 56. Edinburg
  [sic]: Apollo Press, 216 pp.

3 _____. Love for Love. London: by R. Butters, 60 pp.

1784

B SHORTER WRITINGS

1 DAVIES, THOMAS. <u>Dramatic Miscellanies</u>. Vol. 3. London: for
the Author, pp. 311–82.
Critical biography. "Congreve formed himself upon
Wycherly [sic]; but his wit is more flowing; his fancy more
exuberant, his knowledge more extensive, and his judgement
more profound..."

<u>1785</u>

A BOOKS

1 CONGREVE, WILLIAM. <u>Love for Love</u>. London: J. Nichols, 96 pp.

B SHORTER WRITINGS--NONE

<u>1787</u>

A BOOKS

1 CONGREVE, WILLIAM. <u>Der Lauf der Welt</u>. [Translated by J. J. C.
Bode from Congreve's <u>The Way of the World</u>]. Leipzig, 192 pp.

2 _____. <u>The Mourning Bride</u>. London: Lister, 24 pp.

3 _____. <u>The Mourning Bride</u>. London: for the Proprietors and
sold by R. Randall, 45 pp.

4 _____. <u>The Way of the World</u>. London: for W. Lowndes, [etc.],
83 pp.

B SHORTER WRITINGS--NONE

<u>1788</u>

A BOOKS

1 CONGREVE, WILLIAM. <u>The Works</u>. 2 vols. A new edition. London:
for W. Lowndes, [etc.].

2 _____. <u>The Double Dealer</u>. London: for W. Lowndes, 79 pp.

3 ____. <u>Love for Love</u>. London: for W. Lowndes, [etc.], 90 pp.

4 ____. <u>The Mourning Bride</u>. London: for W. Lowndes, [etc.],
    59 pp.

5 ____. <u>A Noiva de luto</u>. Translated by J. A. C. Lisboa, 40 pp.
    Portuguese translation of <u>The Mourning Bride</u>.

6 ____. <u>The Old Bachelor</u>. London: for W. Lowndes, [etc.], 70 pp.

<u>B SHORTER WRITINGS--NONE</u>

<u>1789</u>

<u>A BOOKS</u>

1 CONGREVE, WILLIAM. <u>Letters</u>. In <u>Literary Relics</u>, by George-
    Monck Berkeley. London: for C. Elliot and T. Kay, pp. 317-83.
        Contains forty-three letters from Congreve to Joseph Keally.

<u>B SHORTER WRITINGS</u>

1 CAMPBELL, JOHN. "William Congreve." In <u>Biographia Britannica</u>.
    Vol. 4. London: by Rivington and Marshall for J. Rivington,
    [etc.], pp. 68-82.
        Survey of life and works with many references to and quota-
    tions from earlier criticism.

<u>1790</u>

<u>A BOOKS</u>

1 CONGREVE, WILLIAM. <u>Poems</u>. In <u>The Works of the English Poets</u>.
    Edited by Samuel Johnson. Vol. 34. London: for J. Buckland,
    [etc.], pp. [125]-323.

<u>B SHORTER WRITINGS--NONE</u>

1791

1791

A BOOKS

1 CONGREVE, WILLIAM. The Double Dealer. Dublin: G. Burnet,
   78 pp.

2 _____. The Double Dealer. In British Theatre. Vol. 26 [no. 3].
   London: J. Bell, [etc.], 1791–1802, 120 pp.

3 _____. The Double Dealer. In British Theatre. Vol. 36 [no. 2].
   [London: J. Bell, 1791–99].

4 _____. Love for Love. London: for the Proprietors under the
   Direction of John Bell, 114 pp., 4to.

5 _____. Love for Love. London: J. Bell, 114 pp., 8vo.

6 _____. Love for Love. London: for J. Bell, 142 pp., 12mo.

7 _____. Love for Love. London: John Bell, 142 pp., 18mo.

8 _____. Love for Love. In British Theatre. Vol. 4 [no. 3].
   London: J. Bell, [etc.], 1791–1802, 142 pp.

9 _____. Love for Love. In British Theatre. Vol. 20 [no. 3].
   [London: J. Bell, 1791–99], 142 pp.

10 _____. Love for Love. In British Theatre. [no. 2]. London:
   for the Proprietors under the Direction of John Bell, 114 pp.
   The play has "stronger diversities of character than any
   other written by Congreve, and those characters have a closer
   approximation to life."

11 _____. The Mourning Bride. Dublin: W. Jones, 96 pp., 12mo.

12 _____. The Mourning Bride. Dublin: W. Jones, 96 pp., 16mo.

13 _____. The Mourning Bride. London: J. Bell, 96 pp., 8vo.

14 _____. The Mourning Bride. London: for the Proprietors under
   the Direction of John Bell, 96 pp., 12mo.

15 _____. The Mourning Bride. London: J. Bell, 96 pp., 24mo.

16 _____. The Mourning Bride. In Bell's British Theatre. Vol. 18.
   London: John Bell, 96 pp.

17 ____. The Mourning Bride. In British Theatre. Vol. 1 [no. 4].
[London: J. Bell, 1791–99].

18 ____. The Mourning Bride. In British Theatre. Vol. 3 [no. 4].
London: J. Bell, [etc.], 1791–1802, 96 pp.

19 ____. The Mourning Bride. In British Theatre. [no. 4].
London: for the Proprietors under the Direction of John Bell,
86 pp.

20 ____. The Old Bachelor. In British Theatre. Vol. 26 [no. 4].
London: J. Bell, 1791–1802, 103 pp.

21 ____. The Old Bachelor. In British Theatre. Vol. 28 [no. 3].
[London: J. Bell, 1791–99], 103 pp.

22 ____. The Way of the World. In Bell's British Theatre.
Vol. 2. London: J. Bell, 1791–1802.
    Cited in Drury's Guide to Best Plays by James M. Salem.
2nd ed. Metuchen, N. J.: Scarecrow Press, 1969, p. 89.

23 ____. The Way of the World. In British Theatre. Vol. 25
[no. 3]. [London: J. Bell, 1791–99].

24 ____. The Way of the World. In British Theatre. Vol. 32
[no. 4]. London: J. Bell, 1791–1802, 128 pp.

B SHORTER WRITINGS--NONE

1792

A BOOKS

1 CONGREVE, WILLIAM. The Double Dealer. In English Theatre.
Vol. 2 [no. 4]. London: for J. Bell.

2 ____, trans. [Juvenal's Eleventh Satire]. In The Works of
Juvenal. Translated by John Dryden and others. A Complete
Edition of the Poets of Great Britain. Edited by Robert
Anderson. Vol. 12. London: J. & A. Arch, [etc.].

3 ____. The Old Bachelor. In English Theatre. Vol. 2 [no. 1].
London: for J. Bell, 81 pp.

B SHORTER WRITINGS--NONE

1793

<u>1793</u>

<u>A BOOKS</u>

1 CONGREVE, WILLIAM. <u>The Poetical Works</u>. Edinburgh: by Mundell
   and Son, 1793. In <u>The Works of the British Poets</u> by Robert
   Anderson. Vol. 7. London: John and Arthur Arch. Edinburgh:
   for Bell and Bradfute and J. Mundell, 1795.

2 _____, trans. [Book III of the <u>Art of Love</u>]. In <u>Ovid's Art of
   Love...together with his Remedy of love</u>. London: for the
   Booksellers.

<u>B SHORTER WRITINGS--NONE</u>

<u>1794</u>

<u>A BOOKS</u>

1 CONGREVE, WILLIAM, trans. <u>Ovid's Metamorphoses</u> [Part of Book
   10]. Translated by Dryden...and other eminent persons.
   4 vols. London: for Martin and Bain.

<u>B SHORTER WRITINGS--NONE</u>

<u>1795</u>

<u>A BOOKS</u>

1 CONGREVE, WILLIAM. <u>The Double Dealer</u>. London: for John Bell,
   98 pp.

2 _____. <u>The Double Dealer</u>. London: for J. Bell, 120 pp., 12mo.

3 _____. <u>The Double Dealer</u>. London: J. Bell, 120 pp., 24mo.

4 _____. <u>The Mourning Bride</u>. In <u>Jones's British Theatre</u>. Vol. 2.
   Dublin: by John Chambers for William Jones, 96 pp., 12mo.

5 _____. <u>The Mourning Bride</u>. In <u>Jones's British Theatre</u>. Vol. 2
   [no. 2]. Dublin: W. Jones, 96 pp., 16mo.

6 _____. <u>The Old Bachelor</u>. London: for J. Bell, 87 pp., 8vo.

7 _____. The Old Bachelor. London: J. Bell, 87 pp., 12mo.

8 _____. The Old Bachelor. London: J. Bell, 103 pp.

9 _____. The Old Bachelor. In Early British Comedies. [no. 1].
   London: for the Proprietors under the Direction of John Bell,
   103 pp.

10 _____, trans. [Book III of the Art of Love]. In Ovid's Art of
    Love...Together with his Remedy of love. London: for the
    booksellers.

B SHORTER WRITINGS--NONE

1796

A BOOKS

1 CONGREVE, WILLIAM. The Poetical Works. Cooke's Pocket Edition
   of Select British Poets. London: for C. Cooke [1796], 136 pp.

2 _____. The Mourning Bride. London: for the Proprietors, 96 pp.
   In "Miscellaneous bound collection of plays, v.17." Cited
   in NUC (1970.B14), p. 591.

3 _____. The Way of the World. London: G. Cawthorn, 107 pp.

4 _____. The Way of the World. London: George Cawthorn, 128 pp.,
   12mo.

5 _____. The Way of the World. London: George Cawthorn, 128 pp.,
   24mo.

B SHORTER WRITINGS--NONE

1797

A BOOKS

1 CONGREVE, WILLIAM. The Double Dealer. London: George Cawthorn,
   120 pp.

2 _____. The Double Dealer. In Bell's British Theatre. Vol. 28
   [no. 1]. London: for George Cawthorn, 98 pp., 8vo.

1797

3 _____. The Double Dealer. In <u>Bell's British Theatre</u>. Vol. 28
[no. 1]. London: J. Bell, 120 pp., 24mo.

4 _____. The Double Dealer. In <u>Bell's British Theatre</u>. Vol. 28
[no. 3]. London: G. Cawthorn, 120 pp.

5 _____. The Double Dealer. In <u>Early British Comedies</u>. [no. 4].
London: for and under the Direction of G. Cawthorn, 120 pp.
Binding spine gives date of 1791; imprint, that of 1797.

6 _____. Love for Love. In <u>Bell's British Theatre</u>. Vol. 1
[no. 3]. London: George Cawthorn, 114 pp.

7 _____. The Mourning Bride. In <u>Bell's British Theatre</u>. Vol. 19
[no. 1]. London: for and under the Direction of George
Cawthorn, 96 pp., 8vo.

8 _____. The Mourning Bride. In <u>Bell's British Theatre</u>. Vol. 19
[no. 1]. London: J. Bell, 96 pp., 24mo.

9 _____. The Old Bachelor. London: George Cawthorn, 103 pp.

10 _____. The Old Bachelor. In <u>Bell's British Theatre</u>. Vol. 28
[no. 2]. London: George Cawthorn, 87 pp., 8vo.

11 _____. The Old Bachelor. In <u>Bell's British Theatre</u>. Vol. 28
[no. 2]. London: George Cawthorn, 87 pp., 12mo.

12 _____. The Old Bachelor. In <u>Bell's British Theatre</u>. Vol. 28
[no. 2]. London: G. Cawthorn, 103 pp., 12mo.

13 _____. The Old Bachelor. In <u>British Theatre</u>. Vol. 28 [no. 4].
London: for J. Bell [1791-1803?], 103 pp.

14 _____. The Way of the World. In <u>Bell's British Theatre</u>. Vol. 8
[no. 1]. London: for and under the Direction of George
Cawthorn, 128 pp.

15 _____. The Way of the World. In <u>Bell's British Theatre</u>. Vol. 33.
London: George Cawthorn, 107 pp., 8vo.

16 _____. The Way of the World. In <u>Bell's British Theatre</u>. Vol. 33
[no. 3]. London: G. Cawthorn, 107 pp., 12mo.

17 _____. The Way of the World. In <u>Bell's British Theatre</u>. Vol. 33
[no. 3]. London: J. Bell, 128 pp., 24mo.

B SHORTER WRITINGS--NONE

A BOOKS--NONE

B SHORTER WRITINGS

1 WALPOLE, HORACE. "Thoughts on Comedy." In his The Works.
   Vol. 2. London: for G. G. and J. Robinson and J. Edwards,
   pp. 315-22.
       Written in 1775 and 1776. We are so charmed by and approv-
   ing of the wit that "our passions cannot be engaged.... No
   man would be corrected, if sure that his wit would make his
   vices or ridicules overlooked."

A BOOKS

1 CONGREVE, WILLIAM. Poems. In The Works of the English Poets.
   Edited by Samuel Johnson. Vol. 4. London: A. Miller.

2 _____. Love for Love. Reduced to three acts by John Hollinghead.
   [London, 18--?], 46 pp.
       Cited in NUC (1970.B14), p. 589.

3 _____. The Mourning Bride. Glasgow [18--?], 64 pp.
       Cited in NUC (1970.B14), p. 591.

4 _____. The Way of the World. London: C. Lowndes [1800], 83 pp.
       Cited in BM (1966.B2), col. 988.

B SHORTER WRITINGS

1 MALONE, EDMOND, ed. The Critical and Miscellaneous Prose Works
   of John Dryden. Vol. 1, pt. 1. London: H. Baldwin & Son,
   pp. 222-30.
       Traces Dryden's friendship with Congreve.

A BOOKS

1 CONGREVE, WILLIAM. The Mourning Bride. Dublin: William and
   John Martin, 66 pp.

1801

2 _____. The Mourning Bride. London, 12mo.
   Cited in Protopopesco, 1924.A6.

B SHORTER WRITINGS--NONE

1802

A BOOKS

1 CONGREVE, WILLIAM. The Poetical Works. In The Literary Cabinet.
   Vol. 19. London: Charles Taylor, 136 pp.

2 _____. The Double Dealer. London: C. Lowndes, 83 pp.

3 _____. The Mourning Bride. In Select Plays, From Celebrated
   Authors. Vol. 4. Baltimore: by Warner & Hannah [1802]-1804,
   61 pp.

B SHORTER WRITINGS--NONE

1803

A BOOKS

1 CONGREVE, WILLIAM. The Mourning Bride. Baltimore: Warner and
   Hanna [sic], 61 pp.

2 _____, trans. [Book III of the Art of Love]. In Ovid's Art of
   Love...Together with his Remedy of love. London: J. Jones.

B SHORTER WRITINGS--NONE

1804

A BOOKS

1 CONGREVE, WILLIAM. The Double Dealer. London: George Cawthorn,
   120 pp.

2 _____. The Double Dealer. In Bell's Select British Theatre.
   Vol. 11. London: George Cawthorn, 120 pp.

34

3 _____. The Double Dealer. In The British Drama. Vol. 2, pt. 1. Edinburgh: by James Ballantyne; London: by William Miller, pp. [168]-194.

4 _____. Love for Love. In The British Drama. Vol. 2, pt. 1. Edinburgh: by James Ballantyne; London: by William Miller, pp. [282]-314.

5 _____. Love for Love. In Sharpe's British Theatre. Vol. 10 [no. 1]. London: for C. Whittingham for J. Sharpe, 1804-05, 100 pp.

6 _____. The Mourning Bride. Dublin: by William & John Martin, 66 pp.

7 _____. The Mourning Bride. In The British Drama. Vol. 1, pt. 1. Edinburgh: by James Ballantyne; London: by William Miller, pp. [271]-293.

8 _____. The Old Bachelor. In Bell's Select British Theatre. Vol. 15. London: George Cawthorn, 103 pp.

9 _____, trans. [Book III of the Art of Love]. In [Ovid's] The Art of love...The remedy of love, The art of beauty, and Amours. London: for B. Crosby by J. Swan.

10 _____. The Way of the World. In The British Drama. Vol. 2, pt. 1. Edinburgh: by James Ballantyne; London: by William Miller, pp. [251]-281.

B SHORTER WRITINGS

1 ANON. "Of the Character of Congreve as a Writer of Comedy." The Scots Magazine, and Edinburgh Literary Miscellany, 66 (January), 9-14.
  The characters are not individualized and the wit brings attention to the author, but the incidents please and the plots are original. Concludes that Congreve may serve as a model for dramatists and as a purifier of the public taste.

1805

A BOOKS

1 CONGREVE, WILLIAM. The Mourning Bride. In Sharpe's British Theatre. Vol. 12 [no. 3]. London: by C. Whittingham for J. Sharpe, 1804-05, 65 pp.

1806

B SHORTER WRITINGS—NONE

<u>1806</u>

A BOOKS

1 CONGREVE, WILLIAM. <u>The Mourning Bride</u>. London: Harrison,
   79 pp.
          "No. 1 in vol. lettered: Plays. Congreve and others."
   Cited in <u>NUC</u> (1970.B14), p. 591.

B SHORTER WRITINGS—NONE

<u>1807</u>

A BOOKS

1 CONGREVE, WILLIAM. <u>Poetical Works</u>. With the life of the author
   by Samuel Johnson. In <u>Poets of Great Britain</u>. Vol. 28.
   London: for Cadell and Davies.

2 ____. <u>Select Poems</u>. In <u>The Works of the British Poets</u>.
   Collated by T. Park. Vol. 41 [pt. 1]. London: for J. Sharpe,
   1807-15, pp. [91]-127.

3 ____, trans. [Book III of the <u>Art of Love</u>]. In <u>Ovid's Art of</u>
   <u>love; together with his Remedy of love</u>. London: S. Bagster.

4 ____, trans. <u>Ovid's Metamorphoses</u> [Part of Book 10], by John
   Dryden, esq. and other translators. London: S. Bagster,
   1807- .

5 ____, trans. <u>Ovid's Metamorphoses</u> [Part of Book 10]. Originally
   published by Sir Samuel Garth. Translated into English verse
   by various authors. London: by Bretell.
          Another edition was published by W. Suttaby and B. Crosby,
   [etc.], 1807.

B SHORTER WRITINGS—NONE

<u>1808</u>

A BOOKS

1 CONGREVE, WILLIAM. <u>Love for Love</u>. In <u>The British Theatre</u>. With
  remarks by Mrs. Inchbald. Vol. 13 [no. 1]. London: for
  Longman, Hurst, Rees, and Orme, 90 pp.

2 _____. <u>The Mourning Bride</u>. In <u>The British Theatre</u>. With
  remarks by Mrs. Inchbald. Vol. 13 [no. 2]. London: for
  Longman, Hurst, Rees, and Orme, 56 pp.

B SHORTER WRITINGS

*1 WATKINS, JOHN. <u>Characteristic Anecdotes of Men of Learning and
  Genius, etc</u>. London, pp. 420–25.
        Cited in Gosse, 1888.A3.

<u>1809</u>

A BOOKS

1 CONGREVE, WILLIAM. <u>Select Poems</u>. In <u>The Works of the British
  Poets</u>. Supplement to <u>The British Poets</u>. Vol. 2. London:
  for J. Sharpe.

B SHORTER WRITINGS--NONE

<u>1810</u>

A BOOKS

1 CONGREVE, WILLIAM. <u>The Poems</u>. In <u>The Works of the English
  Poets</u>. Edited by Alexander Chalmers. Vol. 10. London:
  for J. Johnson, [etc.], pp. [255]–309.

2 _____, trans. <u>Ovid's Metamorphoses</u> [Part of Book 10]. In <u>The
  Works of the English Poets</u>. Edited by Alexander Chalmers.
  Vol. 20. London: J. Johnson.

3 _____. <u>The Way of the World</u>. London, 8vo.
        Cited in Protopopesco, 1924.A6.

B SHORTER WRITINGS--NONE

1811

1811

A BOOKS

1 CONGREVE, WILLIAM. <u>The Double Dealer</u>. In <u>The Modern British Drama</u>. Vol. 3. London: for William Miller by James Ballantyne, Edinburgh, pp. 336-63.

2 ____. <u>Love for Love</u>. In <u>The Modern British Drama</u>. Vol. 3. London: for William Miller by James Ballantyne, Edinburgh, pp. 364-98.

3 ____. <u>The Mourning Bride</u>. In <u>The Modern British Drama</u>. Vol. 1. London: for William Miller by James Ballantyne, Edinburgh, pp. 513-35.

4 ____. <u>The Old Bachelor</u>. In <u>The Modern British Drama</u>. Vol. 3. London: for William Miller by James Ballantyne, Edinburgh, pp. 309-35.

5 ____. <u>The Way of the World</u>. In <u>The Modern British Drama</u>. Vol. 3. London: for William Miller by James Ballantyne, Edinburgh, pp. 399-429.

B SHORTER WRITINGS--NONE

1812

A BOOKS

1 CONGREVE, WILLIAM, trans. [Juvenal's Eleventh Satire]. In <u>The Satires of Decimus Junius Juvenalis; and of Aulus Persius Flaccus</u>. London: Suttaby, Evance, and Fox, [etc.], 1812. Rpt. in <u>The Works of the British Poets</u>. Collated by T. Park. Vol. 61. 1828.

B SHORTER WRITINGS

1 BAKER, DAVID ERSKINE, comp. "William Congreve." In <u>Biographia Dramatica; or, a Companion to the Playhouse</u>. Vol. 1, pt. 1. London: for Longman, Hurst, [etc.], pp. 141-44.
      Cites Johnson's appraisal of Congreve to conclude a brief survey of Congreve's life.

2 NICHOLS, JOHN. <u>Literary Anecdotes of the Eighteenth Century</u>.
   London: Nichols, Son, and Bentley, vol. 1, pp. 299, 341–42;
   vol. 2, pp. 194, 372; vol. 3, p. 452; vol. 4, p. 373.
      Refers to Congreve's portrait owned by Tonson, the Collier
   controversy, verses to Congreve by Miss Trotter, Peter Daval's
   dedication of his <u>Memoirs of Cardinal de Retz</u> to Congreve,
   Baskerville's edition of <u>The Works</u>, and John Locker's translation into Greek of one of Congreve's comedies.

1814

A BOOKS

1 CONGREVE, WILLIAM. <u>The Mourning Bride</u>. In <u>The London Theatre</u>,
   by Thomas Dibdin. Vol. 11. London: for Whittingham and
   Arliss [1814]–1816.

2 _____, trans. [Book III of the <u>Art of Love</u>]. In <u>Ovid's Art of
   love, and, Art of beauty</u>. London: F. Noble.

B SHORTER WRITINGS--NONE

1815

A BOOKS

1 CONGREVE, WILLIAM. <u>The Double Dealer</u>. London: for John Miller,
   82 pp.

2 _____. <u>The Double Dealer</u>. In <u>The London Theatre</u>, by Thomas
   Dibdin. Vol. 3 [no. 6]. London: for Whittingham and
   Arliss, 79 pp.

3 _____. <u>The Double Dealer</u>. In <u>The London Theatre</u>, by Thomas
   Dibdin. Vol. 20 [no. 2]. London: for Whittingham and Arliss,
   1815–18, 79 pp.

4 _____. <u>Love for Love</u>. In <u>The London Theatre</u>, by Thomas Dibdin.
   Vol. 6 [no. 7]. London: for Whittingham and Arliss, 79 pp.

5 _____. <u>Love for Love</u>. In <u>The London Theatre</u>, by Thomas Dibdin.
   Vol. 16 [no. 2]. London: for Whittingham and Arliss,
   1815–18, 79 pp.

1815

6 _____. The Mourning Bride. In The London Theatre, by Thomas
Dibdin. Vol. 8 [no. 1]. London: for Whittingham and Arliss,
59 pp.

7 _____. The Mourning Bride. In The London Theatre, by Thomas
Dibdin. Vol. 11 [no. 2]. London: Whittingham and Arliss,
1815-18, 59 pp.

8 _____, trans. [Book III of the Art of Love]. In [Ovid's] The Art
of Love...The Remedy of Love...The Art of Beauty; and Amours.
London: Neely and Jones.

9 _____, trans. "The Story of Orpheus and Eurydice" and part of
"The Tale of Cyparissus." In Ovid's Metamorphoses. Trans-
lated by the most eminent hands. 2 vols. New York:
R. M'Dermut and D. D. Arden.

10 _____. The Way of the World. London: for John Miller, 81 pp.

11 _____. The Way of the World. In The London Theatre, by Thomas
Dibdin. Vol. 12 [no. 4]. London: for Whittingham and Arliss,
91 pp.

12 _____. The Way of the World. In The London Theatre, by Thomas
Dibdin. Vol. 24 [no. 1]. London: for Whittingham and Arliss,
1815-18, 91 pp.

B SHORTER WRITINGS--NONE

1816

A BOOKS

1 CONGREVE, WILLIAM. The Poetical Works. In Cooke's Pocket Edition of Select British Poets. Vol. 35. London: C. Cooke,
136 pp.

2 _____. Love for Love. New York: by David Longworth, 72 pp.

B SHORTER WRITINGS--NONE

<u>1817</u>

A BOOKS

1 CONGREVE, WILLIAM. <u>Love for Love</u>. In <u>The British Drama</u>, by
R. Cumberland. Vol. 5 [no. 3]. London: for C. Cooke, 96 pp.
Despite its bright and sparkling characters, the play lacks
one "pure and perfect model of simple nature."

2 _____. <u>The Mourning Bride</u>. Lisboa, 119 pp., 8vo.
Cited in <u>BM</u> (1966.B2), col. 985.

3 _____. <u>The Mourning Bride</u>. In <u>The British Drama</u>, by
R. Cumberland. Vol. 5. London: for C. Cooke, 59 pp.

4 _____. <u>The Mourning Bride</u>. In <u>The British Drama</u>, by
R. Cumberland. Vol. 12 [no. 3]. London: for C. Cooke,
59 pp.
The play is a defective specimen of tragedy because it
lacks those properties essential to tragedy.

5 _____. <u>The Way of the World</u>. In <u>The British Drama</u>, by
R. Cumberland. Vol. 3 [no. 2]. London: for C. Cooke,
86 pp.
Plot, character, and dialogue do not combine in the construction of the play.

B SHORTER WRITINGS--NONE

<u>1818</u>

A BOOKS

1 CONGREVE, WILLIAM. <u>The Poetical Works</u>. In <u>Cooke's Pocket Edition of the Original and Complete Works of Select British
Poets</u>. Vol. 19. London: Charles Taylor, 136 pp.

2 _____. <u>The Old Bachelor: a tale</u>. 2 vols. Baltimore, 24mo.
Cited in <u>NUC</u> (1970.B14), p. 593.

B SHORTER WRITINGS

1 HAZLITT, WILLIAM. "Love for Love." In his <u>A View of the English
Stage; or, A Series of Dramatic Criticisms</u>. London: for
Robert Stodart, [etc.], pp. 226-29.

1819

Reviews the Drury Lane production (January 1816). Although inferior in "wit and elegance" to The Way of the World, Love for Love is "unquestionably the best-acting of all of his plays."

1819

A BOOKS

1 CONGREVE, WILLIAM. Select Poems. In The Works of the British Poets. With a life of the author by Ezekiel Sanford. Vol. 14. Philadelphia, 1819-23, pp. [361]-383.

B SHORTER WRITINGS

1 HAZLITT, WILLIAM. "On Wycherley, Congreve, Vanbrugh, and Farquhar." Lecture IV in his Lectures on the English Comic Writers. London: Taylor and Hessey, pp. 133-76.
    Congreve's "forte was the description of actual manners, whether elegant or absurd"; his style is the "highest model of comic dialogue."

1820

A BOOKS

1 CONGREVE, WILLIAM. The Mourning Bride. Edinburgh: Oliver and Boyd [ca. 1820], 44 pp.

B SHORTER WRITINGS

1 SPENCE, JOSEPH. Anecdotes, Observations, and Characters, of Books and Men. London: W. H. Carpenter; Edinburgh: Archibald Constable, xxxix + 501 pp., passim.
    Numerous references to Congreve and his relationship to his contemporaries.

1822

A BOOKS

1 CONGREVE, WILLIAM, trans. [Juvenal's Eleventh Satire]. In The Satires of Decimus Junius Juvenalis. In The British Poets. Vol. 97. Chiswick: C. Whittingham [1822].

2 _____, trans. <u>Ovid's Metamorphoses</u> [Part of Book 10]. In <u>The British Poets</u>. Vols. 94–95. Chiswick: C. Whittingham [1822].

B SHORTER WRITINGS--NONE

1823

A BOOKS--NONE

B SHORTER WRITINGS

1 LAMB, CHARLES. "On the Artificial Comedy of the Last Century." In his <u>Elia</u>. Essays which have appeared under that signature in the <u>London Magazine</u>. London: for Taylor and Hessey, pp. 323–37.
   The characters do not offend the "moral sense" because they exist in a "Utopia of gallantry" that has no "reference whatever to the world that is."

1824

A BOOKS

1 CONGREVE, WILLIAM. <u>The Double Dealer</u>. In <u>The London Stage</u>. Vol. 4 [no. 14]. London: for the Proprietors by Sherwood, Jones [1824–27], 20 pp.

2 _____. <u>Love for Love</u>. In <u>The British Drama</u>. Vol. 2. London: Jones.

3 _____. <u>Love for Love</u>. In <u>The London Stage</u>. Vol. 3 [no. 7]. London: for the Proprietors by Sherwood, Jones [1824–27], 20 pp.

4 _____. <u>The Mourning Bride</u>. In <u>The British Drama.</u> Vol. 1. London: by Jones, pp. [709]–729.

5 _____. <u>The Mourning Bride</u>. In <u>The British Drama</u>. Vol. 1. London: by Jones, 1824–25.

6 _____. <u>The Mourning Bride</u>. In <u>The British Theatre</u>, by Mrs. Inchbald. Vol. 4. London: for Hurst, Robinson.

1824

7 _____. The Mourning Bride. In The London Stage. Vol. 3
   [no. 20]. London: for Sherwood, Jones.

8 _____. The Mourning Bride. In The London Stage, Vol. 4
   [no. 48?]. London: By Sherwood, Jones [1824-27], 16 pp.

9 _____. The Way of the World. In The London Stage. Vol. 2
   [no. 27]. London: Sherwood, Jones.

10 _____. The Way of the World. In The London Stage. Vol. 4
   [no. 17]. London: for the Proprietors by Sherwood, Jones
   [1824-27], 20 pp.

B SHORTER WRITINGS--NONE

1825

A BOOKS

1 CONGREVE, WILLIAM. Love for Love. In Cumberland's British
   Theatre. Edited by George Daniel. Vol. 19 [no. 2]. London:
   John Cumberland, 1825-55.
       Cited in The Drama Scholars' Index to Plays and Filmscripts,
   by Gordon Samples. Metuchen, N. J.: Scarecrow Press, 1974,
   p. 79.

2 _____. Love for Love. In Cumberland's British Theatre.
   Vol. 19 [no. 4]. London: J. Cumberland [ca.1825-55], 75 pp.

B SHORTER WRITINGS--NONE

1826

A BOOKS

1 CONGREVE, WILLIAM. Love for Love. In The British Drama. Vol. 2
   London: Jones, pp. [1190]-1220.

2 _____, trans. Ovid's Metamorphoses [Part of Book 10]. Translated by various authors. London: for the Proprietors of
   the English classics by J. F. Dove.

B SHORTER WRITINGS--NONE

1828

A BOOKS

1 CONGREVE, WILLIAM. <u>The Mourning Bride</u>. In <u>The British Drama</u>.
     Vol. 1. London: Jones, 1828–29.

B SHORTER WRITINGS--NONE

1829

A BOOKS

1 CONGREVE, WILLIAM. <u>Love for Love</u>. London: J. Cumberland
     [1829?], 75 pp.

2 _____. <u>The Mourning Bride</u>. In <u>The British Theatre</u>, by an
     Englishman. Leipsic: Frederick Fleischer.

B SHORTER WRITINGS--NONE

1830

A BOOKS

1 CONGREVE, WILLIAM. <u>The Old Bachelor</u>. [London? 1830?], 100 pp.
     Cited in <u>NUC</u> (1970.B14), p. 593.

B SHORTER WRITINGS--NONE

1831

A BOOKS

1 CONGREVE, WILLIAM. <u>The Mourning Bride</u>. In <u>The British Theatre</u>,
     by Owen Williams. Leipsic: for Frederick Fleischer.

B SHORTER WRITINGS--NONE

1832

1832

A BOOKS

1 CONGREVE, WILLIAM. <u>Love for Love</u>. In <u>The British Drama</u>. Vol. 2.
Philadelphia: J. J. Woodward.

2 _____. <u>The Mourning Bride</u>. In <u>The British Drama</u>. Vol. 1.
Philadelphia: J. J. Woodward.

B SHORTER WRITINGS

1 GENEST, JOHN. <u>Some account of the English Stage from the Restoration in 1660 to 1830</u>. Vol. 2. Bath: for H. E. Carrington,
pp. 44-228, passim.
Cast lists of first performances of, together with his own
and others' comments on, Congreve's plays. "Shakespeare ex-
cepted, Congreve is certainly our best comic writer..."

1833

A BOOKS

1 CONGREVE, WILLIAM. <u>Love for Love</u>. In <u>The British Drama</u>. Vol. 2.
Philadelphia: M. Wallis.

2 _____. <u>The Mourning Bride</u>. In <u>The British Drama</u>. Vol. 1.
Philadelphia: I. Bird.

3 _____, trans. [Book III of the <u>Art of Love</u>]. In <u>Ovid</u>. Translated by Dryden, Pope, Congreve, Addison, and others. London:
by A. J. Valpy.

4 _____, trans. <u>Ovid</u> [Part of Book 10 of the <u>Metamorphoses</u>].
Translated by Dryden, Pope, Congreve, Addison, and others.
2 vols. London: by A. J. Valpy.

B SHORTER WRITINGS

1 COLERIDGE, HARTLEY. "William Congreve." In his <u>Biographia
Borealis; or, Lives of Distinguished Northerns</u>. London:
Whitaker, Treacher; Leeds: F. E. Bingley, pp. [665]-693.
Biographical and critical. "The darkest--at least the
most enduring--stain on [Congreve's] memory, is the immoral-
ity of his writings; but this was the vice of the time, and

his comedies are considerably more decorous than those of his predecessors."

1834

A BOOKS

1 CONGREVE, WILLIAM. The Double Dealer. In The Acting Drama. London: Mayhew, Isaac, and Mayhew.

2 ____. Love for Love. In The Acting Drama. London: Mayhew, Isaac, and Mayhew.

B SHORTER WRITINGS--NONE

1836

A BOOKS

1 CONGREVE, WILLIAM, trans. Ovid [Part of Book 10 of the Metamorphoses]. Translated by Dryden, Pope, Congreve, Addison, and others. 2 vols. New York: Harper.

B SHORTER WRITINGS--NONE

1837

A BOOKS

1 CONGREVE, WILLIAM. Love for Love. In The British Drama. Vol. 2. Philadelphia: DeSilver, Thomas.

2 ____. The Mourning Bride. In The British Drama. Vol. 1. Philadelphia: DeSilver, Thomas.

B SHORTER WRITINGS--NONE

<u>1838</u>

A BOOKS

1   CONGREVE, WILLIAM. <u>Love for Love</u>. In <u>The British Drama</u>.
      Vol. 2. Philadelphia: Thomas, Cowperthwait.

2   _____. <u>The Mourning Bride</u>. In <u>The British Drama</u>. Vol. 1.
      Philadelphia: Thomas, Cowperthwait.

3   _____, trans. <u>Ovid</u> [Part of Book 10 of the <u>Metamorphoses</u>].
      Translated by Dryden, Pope, Congreve, Addison, and others.
      2 vols. New York: Harper.

B SHORTER WRITINGS

1   LARDNER, DIONYSIUS, cond. "William Congreve." In <u>Eminent</u>
      <u>Literary and Scientific Men of Great Britain and Ireland</u>.
      Vol. 3 of <u>The Cabinet of Biography</u>. London: Longman, Orme,
      [etc.], pp. 232-51.
         Congreve's comedies claim our admiration and demonstrate a
      "perpetual vein of wit," but nothing would be lost if the
      plays were totally banished because "whatever may be their
      merits, it is impossible to disguise their immorality."

<u>1840</u>

A BOOKS

1   CONGREVE, WILLIAM. <u>The Dramatic Works of Wycherley, Congreve,</u>
      <u>Vanbrugh, and Farquhar</u>. Biographical and critical notices by
      Leigh Hunt. London: Edward Moxon, pp. xxii-xlvi, 143-298.
         Contains the five plays together with <u>The Judgment of Paris</u>
      and <u>Semele</u>. <u>See</u> 1840.B1. Subsequent editions 1849.A1;
      1851.A1; 1860.A1; 1864.A1; 1866.A1; 1875.A1; 1880.A1.

B SHORTER WRITINGS

1   HUNT, LEIGH. <u>The Dramatic Works of Wycherley, Congreve, Vanbrugh,</u>
      <u>and Farquhar</u>. London: Edward Moxon, pp. xxii-xlvi.
         The plays demonstrate that Congreve's "love is spare and
      sorry; his belief in nothing, abundant," his plots "over-
      ingenious," the wit "tiresome," and the fine ladies and
      gentlemen "heartless."

2 MACAULAY, T. B. "Comic Dramatists of the Restoration." The
   Edinburgh Review, 72, 514-28.
         Reviews Leigh Hunt's The Dramatic Works (1840.A1).
   "Congreve's offences against decorum, though highly culpable,
   were not as gross as those of Wycherley. In fact, in every
   point Congreve maintained his superiority to Wycherley."

1842

A BOOKS

1 CONGREVE, WILLIAM. Love for Love. In The British Drama.
   Vol. 2. Philadelphia: M'Carty and Davis.

2 _____. The Mourning Bride. In The British Drama. Vol. 1.
   Philadelphia: M'Carty and Davis.

3 _____, trans. Ovid [Part of Book 10 of the Metamorphoses].
   Translated by Dryden, Pope, Congreve, Addison, and others.
   2 vols. New York: n.p.

B SHORTER WRITINGS--NONE

1844

A BOOKS

1 CONGREVE, WILLIAM, trans. Ovid [Part of Book 10 of the
   Metamorphoses]. Translated by Dryden, Pope, Congreve, Addison,
   and others. 2 vols. New York: Harper.

B SHORTER WRITINGS--NONE

1848

A BOOKS

1 CONGREVE, WILLIAM, trans. Ovid [Part of Book 10 of the
   Metamorphoses]. Translated by Dryden, Pope, Congreve, Addison,
   and others. 2 vols. New York: Harper [1848].

B SHORTER WRITINGS--NONE

1849

1849

A BOOKS

1 CONGREVE, WILLIAM. <u>The Dramatic Works of Wycherley, Congreve,</u>
      <u>Vanbrugh, and Farquhar</u>, by Leigh Hunt. London: Edward Moxon,
      pp. xix-xxxviii, 143-298.
         New edition of 1840.A1. <u>See</u> 1840.B1.

B SHORTER WRITINGS--NONE

1850

A BOOKS

1 CONGREVE, WILLIAM. <u>Love for Love</u>. In <u>The British Drama</u>.
      Vol. 2. Philadelphia: T. Davies, pp. 382-412.

2 ____. <u>The Mourning Bride</u>. In <u>The British Drama</u>. Vol. 1.
      Philadelphia: T. Davies, pp. 709-29.

B SHORTER WRITINGS--NONE

1851

A BOOKS

1 CONGREVE, WILLIAM. <u>The Dramatic Works of Wycherley, Congreve,</u>
      <u>Vanbrugh, and Farquhar</u>, by Leigh Hunt. London: Edward Moxon,
      pp. xix-xxxviii, 143-298.
         <u>See</u> 1840.A1 and 1840.B1.

B SHORTER WRITINGS--NONE

1852

A BOOKS

1 CONGREVE, WILLIAM. <u>Poems upon Several Occasions</u>. Dublin: for
      Peter Wilson.

B SHORTER WRITINGS--NONE

1853

A BOOKS--NONE

B SHORTER WRITINGS

1 THACKERAY, W. M. "Charity and Humour." Lecture no. 7 in his
   The English Humourists of the Eighteenth Century. London:
   Smith, Elder.
       Congreve was "immensely liked--more so than any man of his
   age," yet there is "no more feeling in his comedies, than in
   as many books of Euclid."

2 _____. "Congreve and Addison." Lecture no. 2 in his The
   English Humourists of the Eighteenth Century. London:
   Smith, Elder, pp. 55-104.
       "Congreve's theatre is a temple of Pagan delights, and
   mysteries not permitted except among heathens."

1854

A BOOKS

1 CONGREVE, WILLIAM. Love for Love. Revised, curtailed, and
   altered by James W. Wallack and correctly marked as acted by
   Henry B. Phillips, prompter. New York, London: D. Appleton,
   88 pp.

2 _____. Love for Love. In The British Drama. Vol. 2.
   Philadelphia: M. Polock.

3 _____. The Mourning Bride. In The British Drama. Vol. 1.
   Philadelphia: M. Polock.

4 _____. [Selections]. In Songs from the Dramatists. Edited by
   Robert Bell. London: J. W. Parker, pp. 254-56.

B SHORTER WRITINGS--NONE

1859

A BOOKS

1 CONGREVE, WILLIAM. Love for Love. In The British Drama.
   Vol. 2. Philadelphia: J. B. Lippincott.

1859

2 _____. The Mourning Bride. In The British Drama. Vol. 1.
      Philadelphia: J. B. Lippincott.

B SHORTER WRITINGS--NONE

1860

A BOOKS

1 CONGREVE, WILLIAM. The Dramatic Works of Wycherley, Congreve,
      Vanbrugh, and Farquhar, by Leigh Hunt. London: Routledge,
      Warne, and Routledge.
      New edition. See 1840.A1 and 1840.B1.

B SHORTER WRITINGS--NONE

1864

A BOOKS

1 CONGREVE, WILLIAM. The Dramatic Works of Wycherley, Congreve,
      Vanbrugh, and Farquhar, by Leigh Hunt. London.
      Cited in Summers, 1934.B4. See 1840.A1 and 1840.B1.

2 _____. The Double Dealer. In The British Drama. Vol. 9.
      London: by John Dicks, 1864-72.

3 _____. Love for Love. In The British Drama. Vol. 10. London:
      by John Dicks, 1864-72.

4 _____. The Mourning Bride. In The British Drama. Vol. 3.
      London: by John Dicks, 1864-65.

5 _____. The Mourning Bride. In The British Drama. Vol. 3.
      London: by John Dicks, 1864-72.

6 _____, trans. Ovid [Part of Book 10 of the Metamorphoses].
      Translated by Dryden, Pope, Congreve, Addison, and others.
      2 vols. New York: Harper.

7 _____. The Way of the World. In The British Drama. Vol. 11.
      London: by John Dicks, 1864-72.

B SHORTER WRITINGS--NONE

1865

A BOOKS

1 CONGREVE, WILLIAM. The Mourning Bride [Excerpt from II.i.-iii].
    In Golden Leaves from the British and American Dramatic Poets.
    Collected and arranged by John W. S. Hows. New York: Bunce
    and Huntington, pp. 239-48.

B SHORTER WRITINGS--NONE

1866

A BOOKS

1 CONGREVE, WILLIAM. The Dramatic Works of Wycherley, Congreve,
    Vanbrugh, and Farquhar, by Leigh Hunt. London and New York:
    George Routledge.
       A new edition. See 1840.A1 and 1840.B1.

2 _____. The Mourning Bride. In The British Drama. Vol. 3.
    London: by John Dicks, 1866-67.

3 _____. The Mourning Bride. In The British Drama. Vol. 3.
    London: by John Dicks, 1866-68.

B SHORTER WRITINGS--NONE

1869

A BOOKS--NONE

B SHORTER WRITINGS

*1 ZINCK, AUGUST G. L. Congreve, Vanbrugh og Sheridan. En
     Skildring til Belysning af de sociale Forhold og det
     aandelige Liv i England fra Carl den Andens Tid og til
     henimod den franske Revolution. Kjøbenhavn.
        Cited in BM (1966.B2), vol. 263, col. 628.

1871

A BOOKS--NONE

1871

B SHORTER WRITINGS

1 CLARKE, CHARLES COWDEN. "On the Comic Writers of England.
No. IX.--Wycherley and Congreve." Gentleman's Magazine,
7 NS, 823-45.
"...setting aside the single quality of his diamond-like wit,
Congreve is a much less heart-to-heart writer...and far less
moral than Wycherley, and this arises purely from his want of
faith in single-mindedness and truth." As such, Congreve
accurately records the "spirit, morals, and manners of...the
aristocratic society of the boasted Revolution of 'Glorious
Memory' of 1688."

2 WHARTON, GRACE and PHILIP. "William Congreve." In their
The Wits and Beaux of Society. London: George Routledge,
pp. 106-26.
Mainly biographical. The remembrance of Congreve's plays
is likened to a "horrible nightmare."

1872

A BOOKS

1 CONGREVE, WILLIAM, trans. "Hymn to Venus." In The Minor Poems
of Homer. New York: A. Denham.

2 _____, trans. Ovid [Part of Book 10 of the Metamorphoses].
Translated by Dryden, Pope, Congreve, Addison, and others.
2 vols. New York: Harper.

B SHORTER WRITINGS--NONE

1874

A BOOKS

1 CONGREVE, WILLIAM. The Mourning Bride. [Dicks' Standard Plays,
no. 99]. London [1874?].

B SHORTER WRITINGS--NONE

<u>1875</u>

A BOOKS

1 CONGREVE, WILLIAM. <u>The Dramatic Works of Wycherley, Congreve,</u> <u>Vanbrugh, and Farquhar</u>, by Leigh Hunt. London and New York: G. Routledge.
   <u>See</u> 1840.A1 and 1840.B1.

B SHORTER WRITINGS

*1 WARD, ADOLPHUS WILLIAM. <u>A History of English Dramatic Literature</u> <u>to the death of Queen Anne</u>. Vol. 2. London: Macmillan, pp. 582–89.
   Cited in Gosse, 1888.A3.

<u>1877</u>

A BOOKS

1 CONGREVE, WILLIAM. <u>The Double Dealer</u>. [Dicks' Standard Plays, no. 199]. London: [1877?].

2 _____. <u>Love for Love</u>. [Dicks' Standard Plays, no. 149]. London: [1877?].

B SHORTER WRITINGS

1 SWINBURNE, ALGERNON C. "William Congreve." In <u>The Encyclopaedia</u> <u>Britannica</u>. Vol. 6. London: A. & C. Black, pp. 271–72.
   Congreve is inferior to Molière, but superior to Vanbrugh, Farquhar, and Sheridan. Reprinted 1886.B2.

<u>1878</u>

A BOOKS

1 CONGREVE, WILLIAM. <u>Works</u>. 2 vols. London: for the Editor.
   Cited in <u>NUC</u> (1970.B14), p. 582.

1878

B SHORTER WRITINGS

*1 GRISY, AMBROISE ROMAINE de. Histoire de la Comédie Anglaise
      (1672-1707). Paris: Didier, pp. 151-257.
          Cited in Gosse, 1888.A3.

 2 L'ESTRANGE, A. G. "Congreve--Lord Dorset." In his History of
      English Humour. Vol. 1. London: Hurst and Blackett,
      pp. 355-58.
          The humor of Congreve is to be found not in the plot, but
      in the dialogue. Reprinted New York: Burt Franklin, 1970.

                              1880

A BOOKS

 1 CONGREVE, WILLIAM. The Dramatic Works of Wycherley, Congreve,
      Vanbrugh, and Farquhar, by Leigh Hunt. London and New York:
      G. Routledge.
          See 1840.A1 and 1840.B1.

 2 _____. [Selected Poems]. In The English Poets. Edited by
      Thomas Humphry Ward. Vol. 3. London: Macmillan, pp. 10-12.

B SHORTER WRITINGS--NONE

                              1881

A BOOKS

 1 CONGREVE, WILLIAM. "On Mrs. Arabella Hunt's Singing." In
      English Odes. Selected by E. W. Gosse. London: C. K. Paul;
      New York: Appleton.
          Reprinted 1884.A1; 1889.A1; 1890.A3.

B SHORTER WRITINGS

 1 BELJAME, ALEXANDRE. Le Public et les Hommes de Lettres en
      Angleterre au Dix-huitième Siècle 1660-1744. Paris:
      Hachette, 506 pp., passim.
          Brief references to the plays and to Congreve's relation-
      ship with his literary contemporaries. English edition:
      Kegan Paul, [etc.], 1948.

1883

A BOOKS

1 CONGREVE, WILLIAM. The Double Dealer. [Dicks' Standard Plays,
      no. 199]. London: J. Dicks; New York: Samuel French [1883?],
      pp. [129]–152.

2 _____. Love for Love. [Dicks' Standard Plays, no. 149]. London:
      J. Dicks [1883?], pp. [225]–249.

3 _____. The Mourning Bride. [Dicks' Standard Plays, no. 99].
      London: J. Dicks [ca.1883], pp. [879]–894.

4 _____. The Way of the World. [Dicks' Standard Plays, no. 86].
      London: J. Dicks [1883?], 8vo.

5 _____. The Way of the World. [Dicks' Standard Plays, no. 86].
      London: J. Dicks [1883?], 26 pp., 12mo.

6 _____. [Scenes from] The Way of the World and The Double Dealer.
      In English Comic Dramatists. Edited by Oswald John Frederick
      Crawfurd. London: Kegan Paul, Trench, pp. 129–60.
        Despite Congreve's consummate wit, style, and marvelous
      characterization, his "sympathies are narrow, his morality
      on the wrong side of tolerable." Reprinted 1889.A2.

B SHORTER WRITINGS--NONE

1884

A BOOKS

1 CONGREVE, WILLIAM. "On Mrs. Arabella Hunt's Singing." In
      English Odes. Selected by Edmund W. Gosse. London: K. Paul,
      Trench.
        Reprint of 1881.A1.

2 _____, trans. [Book III of the Art of Love]. In Ovid's Art of
      love; Remedy of love; and Art of beauty. London: for the
      booksellers, [1884?].

B SHORTER WRITINGS--NONE

1885

1885

A BOOKS--NONE

B SHORTER WRITINGS

1 HUTTON, LAURENCE. "William Congreve." In his <u>Literary Landmarks of London</u>. Boston: James R. Osgood, pp. 63-64.
       Identifies various parts of London with phases in
   Congreve's life.

1886

A BOOKS--NONE

B SHORTER WRITINGS

1 MOLLOY, JOSEPH FITZGERALD. "Congreve's <u>Love for Love</u>." In his
   <u>Famous Plays</u>. London: Ward and Downey, pp. [3]-35.
       Discusses the background to Restoration drama and the
   literary context in which <u>Love for Love</u> was written and
   produced. Reprinted 1888.B3.

2 SWINBURNE, ALGERNON CHARLES. "Congreve." In his <u>Miscellanies</u>.
   London: Chatto and Windus; New York: Worthington,
   pp. 50-55.
       Reprint of 1877.B1.

1887

A BOOKS

1 CONGREVE, WILLIAM. [Complete Plays]. In <u>William Congreve</u>.
   Edited by Alex. Charles Ewald. Mermaid Series. London:
   Vizetelly, xli + 486 pp.
       Includes Macaulay's essay on the "Comic Dramatists of the
   Restoration" (1840.B2). With the exception of <u>Love for Love</u>,
   Congreve's comedies are "better to read than to act...[but as]
   a painter of contemporary life and manners, studied from the
   vantage point of fashion, [Congreve] has no equal." Reprinted
   1888.A1; 1903.A1; 1923.A2; 1930.A2; 1947.A1; 1948.A1;
   1949.A1. New Mermaid Dramabook editions 1956.A1; 1961.A1;
   1963.A1; 1966.A1.

B SHORTER WRITINGS

1 STEPHEN, LESLIE. "William Congreve." Dictionary of National
   Biography. Vol. 12. London: Smith, Elder, pp. 6-9.
      Congreve's "wit is saturnine, and a perpetual exposition
   of the baser kind of what passes for worldly wisdom. The
   atmosphere of his plays is asphyxiating."

1888

A BOOKS

1 CONGREVE, WILLIAM. [Complete Plays]. In William Congreve.
   Edited by Alex. Charles Ewald. Unexpurgated ed. Mermaid
   Series. London: Vizetelly, xli + 486 pp.
      Reprint of 1887.A1.

2 _____, trans. [Book III of the Art of Love]. In Ovid's Art of
   Love, Remedy of Love, and Art of Beauty [etc.]. London:
   Macdonald [1888].

3 GOSSE, EDMUND. Life of William Congreve. London: Walter Scott;
   New York: Thomas Whittaker; Toronto: W. J. Gage, 192 + ix pp.
      First attempt at a detailed biography of Congreve. Collates
   and examines existing sources of information, which show
   Congreve "more amiable and much less cynical than he had been
   depicted" earlier. Reprinted 1972.A6; revised edition 1924.A4.

B SHORTER WRITINGS

1 DORAN, J. Annals of the English Stage from Thomas Betterton to
   Edmund Kean. Edited and revised by Robert W. Lowe. Vol. 1.
   London: John C. Nimmo, [xiii] + 436 pp., passim.
      If it is true that Congreve copied from nature, "it is
   also true that he laughs with his vicious and brilliant bad
   men and women, makes a joke of vice, and never attempts to
   correct it."

2 MERYDEW, J. T., ed. "William Congreve." In Love Letters of the
   Past and Present Century. Vol. 1. London: Remington,
   pp. [44]-58.
      Only one letter, to Mrs. Arabella Hunt, seems to be authen-
   tic. The other six, having neither salutations nor signatures,
   are probably fabricated by the editor.

1888

3 MOLLOY, J. FITZGERALD. "Congreve's <u>Love for Love</u>." In his
   <u>Famous Plays: Their Histories and their Authors</u>. London:
   Ward & Downey, pp. [3]-35.
      New edition of 1886.B1.

1889

A BOOKS

1 CONGREVE, WILLIAM. "On Mrs. Arabella Hunt's Singing." In
   <u>English Odes</u>. Selected by Edmund W. Gosse. London: Kegan
   Paul, Trench; New York: Appleton.
      Reprint of 1881.A1.

2 _____. [Scenes from] <u>The Way of the World</u> and <u>The Double Dealer</u>.
   In <u>English Comic Dramatists</u>. Edited by Oswald John Frederick
   Crawfurd. New York: D. Appleton, pp. 129-60.
      Reprint of 1883.A6.

B SHORTER WRITINGS--NONE

1890

A BOOKS

*1 BENNEWITZ, ALEXANDER. "Molières Einfluss auf Congreve." Diss.,
    Leipzig.
       Cited in McNamee, 1968.B10. <u>See</u> 1890.A2.

2 _____. <u>Congreve und Molière</u>. Leipzig: H. Haessel, 159 pp.
      Argues that Congreve was greatly indebted to Molière.
   <u>See</u> Ph.D. dissertation, 1890.A1.

3 CONGREVE, WILLIAM. "On Mrs. Arabella Hunt's Singing." In
   <u>English Odes</u>. Selected by Edmund W. Gosse. New York:
   D. Appleton.
      Reprint of 1888.A1.

B SHORTER WRITINGS

1 HENLEY, W. E. "Congreve. His Biographers and Critics: The
   Real Congreve: The Dramatist: The Writer." In his <u>Views and
   Reviews: Essays in Appreciation</u>. London: David Nutt,
   pp. 201-07.

1897

"Congreve's plays are...as dull in action as they are
entertaining in print.... they are marked by such a deliber-
ate and immitigable baseness of morality as makes them impossible to man." American edition 1902.B1.

1894

A BOOKS

1 CONGREVE, WILLIAM. <u>The Way of the World</u>. Edited with an introduction and explanatory notes by W. P. Barrett. Temple Dramatists. London: Dent, xii + 145 pp.
       The central theme is the relationships between men and
   women in marriage. The style differentiates the characters.
   Reprinted 1933.A2; 1934.A3; 1949.A4; 1951.A5; 1967.A5.

B SHORTER WRITINGS--NONE

1895

A BOOKS

1 CONGREVE, WILLIAM. <u>The Comedies</u>. Introduction by G. S. Street.
   English Classics. 2 vols. London: Methuen; Chicago: Stone
   and Kimball.
       Defends Congreve's choice of material and affirms that his
   attitude toward it is the "amusing pose of the boyish cynic
   turned into an artistic convention."

B SHORTER WRITINGS--NONE

1897

A BOOKS

1 CONGREVE, WILLIAM. <u>The Mourning Bride</u>. London.
            Cited in <u>NUC</u> (1970.B14), p. 592.

2 SCHMID, D. <u>William Congreve, sein Leben und seine Lustspiele</u>.
       Wien und Leipzig: Wilhelm Braumüller, viii + 179 pp.
          Reviews criticism of and analyzes each comedy and dis-
   cusses Congreve's significance and position as dramatist.
   Concludes that although Congreve is often highly immoral, his
   code of morals is not ours. Reprinted 1964.A9.

1897

B SHORTER WRITINGS

1   MEREDITH, GEORGE. <u>An Essay on Comedy, and the Uses of the Comic</u>
       <u>Spirit</u>. Westminster: A. Constable, 105 pp.
          Congreve "hits the mean of a fine style and a natural in
       dialogue. He is at once precise and voluble.... In this he
       is a classic, is worthy of treading a measure with Molière."

                        <u>1900</u>

A BOOKS

1   CONGREVE, WILLIAM. <u>Incognita</u>.
          A musical composition [by Egon Wellesz] based on Congreve's
       work. Cited in <u>NUC</u> (1970.B14), p. 586.

B SHORTER WRITINGS--NONE

                        <u>1902</u>

A BOOKS--NONE

B SHORTER WRITINGS

1   HENLEY, W. E. "Congreve. His Biographers and Critics: The Real
       Congreve: The Dramatist: The Writer." In his <u>Views and Re-</u>
       <u>views: Essays in Appreciation</u>. New York: Charles Scribner's,
       pp. 201-07.
          American edition of 1890.B1.

                        <u>1903</u>

A BOOKS

1   CONGREVE, WILLIAM. [Complete Plays]. In <u>William Congreve</u>.
       Edited by Alex. Charles Ewald. Mermaid Series. London:
       T. Fisher Unwin; New York: Charles Scribner's, xli + 486 pp.
          Reprint of 1887.A1.

B SHORTER WRITINGS--NONE

1904

A BOOKS--NONE

B SHORTER WRITINGS

1   CRAWFORD, J. P. WICKERSHAM. "On the Relation of Congreve's
    Mourning Bride to Racine's Bajazet." Modern Language Notes,
    19, no. 7 (November), pp. 193–94.
        A comparison between the two plays reveals Congreve's debt
    to Racine.

1906

A BOOKS--NONE

B SHORTER WRITINGS

1   COLLINS, CHARLES W. "Great Love Stories of the Theatre.
    No. VIII--Anne Bracegirdle and William Congreve." The Green
    Book Album, 6: 129–37.
        Traces the development of the relationship between the
    actress and the dramatist. Reprinted 1911.B1.

1907

A BOOKS--NONE

B SHORTER WRITINGS

*1 KERBY, WILLIAM MOSELEY. "Molière and the Restoration Comedy in
    England." Diss., London University.
        Traces the influence of the "French comic drama upon those
    dramatists who shared in the foundation of a classic or regu-
    lar drama in England...as well as...Congreve." Cited in
    Stratman, 1971.B16.

2   WALKLEY, A. B. "Way of the World (Mermaid Society, April 1904)."
    In his Drama and Life. London: Methuen; New York:
    Brentano's, pp. 304–08.
        Collection of essays from The London Times. Reviews the
    Mermaid Society production, affirming that the play still
    evokes a "vivid sense of reality." Reprinted 1967.B12.

1908

1908

A BOOKS--NONE

B SHORTER WRITINGS

1 THORNDIKE, ASHLEY H. <u>Tragedy</u>. Boston and New York: Houghton
   Mifflin, pp. 3, 273-77, passim.
      <u>The Mourning Bride</u> is representative of various features
   of Restoration tragedy. Reprinted 1965.B11.

1909

A BOOKS

1 CONGREVE, WILLIAM. "Concerning Humour in Comedy." In <u>Critical</u>
   <u>Essays of the Seventeenth Century</u>. Edited by J. E. Spingarn.
   Vol. 3. Oxford: Clarendon Press, pp. 242-52.

B SHORTER WRITINGS--NONE

1910

A BOOKS--NONE

B SHORTER WRITINGS

1 ARCHER, WILLIAM. "The Comedies of Congreve." <u>The Forum</u>, 43,
   no. 3 (March), pp. 276-82; no. 4 (April), pp. 343-46.
      Surveys Congreve's life and works, arguing that the success
   of <u>The Old Bachelor</u> and <u>Love for Love</u> and the relative failure
   of <u>The Double Dealer</u> and <u>The Way of the World</u> were due to the
   structural strengths and weaknesses of the respective plays.

2 MILES, DUDLEY HOWE. <u>The Influence of Molière on Restoration</u>
   <u>Comedy</u>. New York: Columbia University Press, xi + 272 pp.,
   passim.
      Includes references to all of Congreve's comedies.
   Appendix lists those parts of Congreve's plays that indicate
   "direct borrowings from Molière."

1911

A BOOKS--NONE

B SHORTER WRITINGS

1 COLLINS, CHARLES W. "Anne Bracegirdle and William Congreve."
   In his Great Love Stories of the Theatre. New York:
   Duffield, pp. 85–107.
      Reprint of 1906.B1.

1912

A BOOKS

1 CONGREVE, WILLIAM. [The Plays]. In William Congreve. Introduction by William Archer. Masterpieces of the English Drama.
   New York: American Book Company, v + 466 pp.
      Does not include The Old Bachelor. Congreve regards life
   from a "standpoint of complete ethical indifference; and it
   is in moods of indifference that we relish his comedies."
   Congreve is the "last of the ancients" rather than the "first
   of the moderns."

2 _____. The Way of the World. In Restoration Plays from Dryden
   to Farquhar. Introduction by Edmund Gosse. Everyman's
   Library. London: J. M. Dent; New York: E. P. Dutton,
   pp. vii–xvii, [163]–235.
      Congreve's "first merit resides in his style." Reprinted
   1922.A2; 1925.A6; 1929.A9; enlarged edition 1932.A1; paperback edition 1962.A9; reprint of 1932 edition 1974.A6.

B SHORTER WRITINGS

1 STUART, DONALD CLIVE. "The Source of Gresset's Méchant." Modern
   Language Notes, 27, no. 2 (February), pp. 42–45.
      The "principal characters, the motives actuating them, the
   main plot, [and] the cool double dealing of the two so-called
   villains are so strikingly similar" that Gresset must have
   been influenced to a very great extent by Congreve's The
   Double Dealer.

2 WHIBLEY, CHARLES. "The Restoration Drama. II." In The Age of
   Dryden. Edited by A. W. Ward and A. R. Waller. Vol. 8 of
   The Cambridge History of English Literature. Cambridge,
   England: University Press; New York: G. P. Putnam's,
   pp. 166–201.
      Congreve manifested his true genius in his interpretation
   of gallantry, and his style is "still unmatched in the literature of England." Separate entries not made for subsequent
   reprints: 1920, 1932, 1934, 1949, 1952, 1964.

<u>1913</u>

A BOOKS--NONE

B SHORTER WRITINGS

1 ARMSTRONG, CECIL FERARD. "William Congreve." In his <u>Shakespeare</u>
<u>to Shaw: Studies in the Life's Work of Six Dramatists of the</u>
<u>English Stage</u>. London: Mills and Boon, pp. 128-46.
   Although Congreve was "a follower rather than a leader,"
his "polished wit, style and epigram...have never been sur-
passed, and seldom equalled." His plays are "perfect specimens of their kind." Reprinted 1969.B2.

2 CANBY, HENRY SEIDEL. "Congreve as Dramatist." <u>The Sewanee</u>
<u>Review</u>, 21, no. 4 (October), pp. 421-27.
   A "better romanticist than moralist," Congreve left "the
coarse and brutal still unlovely...the noble he disengaged
and perfected." <u>See</u> 1916.B1.

3 HEUSS, ALFRED. "Das Semele-Problem bei Congreve und Händel."
<u>Zeitschrift der Internationalen Musikgesellschaft</u>, Heft 6
(1913-14), 143-56.
   Discusses the dramatic, psychological, and idealistic
aspects of the Congreve-Händel <u>Semele</u> and the inadequate
German translations of the libretto.

4 PALMER, JOHN. "William Congreve." In his <u>The Comedy of Manners</u>.
London: G. Bell, pp. 141-200.
   "Congreve was mildly driven to fashion an image of existence observed at ease, incuriously, with no ambition to pursue
the spirit of truth into the dark." <u>See</u> 1914.B3.

<u>1914</u>

A BOOKS

1 CONGREVE, WILLIAM. <u>The Way of the World</u>. In <u>Representative</u>
<u>English Dramas from Dryden to Sheridan</u>. Edited by Frederick
Tupper and James W. Tupper. New York: Oxford University
Press, pp. 117-55, 439-42.
   The characterization, the flash of wit, and the perfection
of speech give <u>The Way of the World</u> its enduring place in
English literature. New and enlarged edition 1934.A4.

B SHORTER WRITINGS

1 COURTNEY, W. L. "The Idea of Comedy--II. Comedy of Manners.
      High Comedy, or Comedy of Character." The Fortnightly Review,
      NS 95 (1 June), 1063-80.
         Wycherley and Congreve did not "intend ostensibly to be
      critics....all that [they] intend to do is to present the
      gentlemen and ladies of their time with a mirror in which
      they can see some of their worst follies reflected."

2 NETTLETON, GEORGE HENRY. "Congreve, Vanbrugh, and Farquhar."
      In his English Drama of the Restoration and Eighteenth
      Century (1642-1780). New York: Macmillan, pp. 120-40.
         Congreve is the descendant of Etherege and the ancestor of
      Sheridan. In Congreve's hands, "the comedy of society is
      touched with rare literary skill. It is artificial comedy,
      but the art is masterly." Reprinted 1921.B3; 1923.B5;
      1928.B5; 1932.B5; 1968.B11.

3 PALMER, JOHN. Comedy. London: M. Secker; New York: George H.
      Doran, pp. 30-64, passim.
         "In Congreve there is neither feeling nor morality. There
      is only wit, issuing from the rub of intellect and manner."
      See 1913.B4.

4 SCHELLING, FELIX E. English Drama. London: J. M. Dent; New
      York: E. P. Dutton, pp. 266-69.
         Although his style has no parallel in English, Congreve was
      perverse in his moral indifference to the "foul and glittering
      Utopia" depicted in the plays.

1915

A BOOKS--NONE

B SHORTER WRITINGS

1 BERNBAUM, ERNEST. The Drama of Sensibility. A Sketch of the
      History of English Sentimental Comedy and Domestic Tragedy
      1696-1780. London and Boston: Ginn, ix + 288 pp., passim.
         Cites Congreve's comedies to demonstrate that his comic
      spirit is antithetical to that of sentimental comedy.
      Reprinted 1958.B1.

1916

A BOOKS

1   CONGREVE, WILLIAM. The Way of the World. In Representative
    English Plays: From the Middle Ages to the End of the Nine-
    teenth Century. Edited with introductions and notes by
    John S. P. Tatlock and Roger G. Martin. New York: Century
    Company, pp. 502-42.
         "There is nothing brutal or repulsive in the ethics of
    The Way of the World..." The play is one of the most "charac-
    teristic specimens of the type on his best side..." Reprinted
    1917.A1; new edition, revised and enlarged, 1938.A4.

B SHORTER WRITINGS

1   CANBY, HENRY SEIDEL. "Congreve as a Romanticist." Publications
    of the Modern Language Association, 31, NS 24, no. 1 [March],
    pp. 1-23.
         In presenting his own conception of the life of the fash-
    ionable world, Congreve transforms the real world into a
    Utopia of gallantry. See also 1913.B2.

2   MILES, DUDLEY. "Morals of the Restoration." The Sewanee Review,
    24, no. 1 (January), pp. 105-14.
         Restoration dramatists, including Congreve, use their wit
    to reflect "their clear consciousness of the traditional
    belief that love and faithfulness accompany marriage..."

1917

A BOOKS

1   CONGREVE, WILLIAM. The Way of the World. In Representative
    English Plays. Edited with introductions and notes by
    John S. P. Tatlock and Robert G. Martin. New York: Century
    Company, pp. 502-42.
         Reprint of 1916.A1.

B SHORTER WRITINGS--NONE

1919

A BOOKS--NONE

B SHORTER WRITINGS

1 WHIBLEY, CHARLES. "Congreve and Some Others." In his <u>Literary
   Studies</u>. London: Macmillan, pp. 240–97.
       Congreve displays his genius in his interpretation of
   gallantry and his art in the rhythm and cadence of his speech.

1920

A BOOKS

1 CONGREVE, WILLIAM. <u>Love for Love</u>. Abridged by Robert Edmond
   Jones. [n.p., 192–?].
       "Prompt book made from type script....cast, light plot,
   and ground plan" of the production at Greenwich Village
   Theatre, New York, 31 March, 1925. Cited in <u>NUC</u> (1970.B14),
   p. 589.

B SHORTER WRITINGS

1 MATHEWSON, LOUISE. <u>Bergson's Theory of the Comic in the Light
   of English Comedy</u>. Univ. of Nebraska Studies in Lang., Lit.
   and Crit., No. 5. Lincoln, Neb.: Motor Publishing Co.,
   28 pp.
       Restoration comedy, including that by Congreve, has "no
   power to bring about self-correction in the spectator. Indeed
   [it] fulfills Bergson's definition in but one particular, the
   entire absence of feeling."

2 REYNOLDS, MYRA. "Satiric Representations of the Learned Lady in
   Comedy." In her <u>The Learned Lady in England, 1650–1760</u>.
   Vassar Semi-Centennial Series. Boston and New York:
   Houghton Mifflin, pp. 384–86.
       Lady Froth in <u>The Double Dealer</u> is Congreve's contribution
   to the learned lady in comedy.

1921

A BOOKS--NONE

B SHORTER WRITINGS

1 BALL, F. ELRINGTON. "Congreve as a Ballad-Writer." <u>Notes and
   Queries</u>, 12th ser., 8 (16 April), 301–03.

1921

>   Attributes six occasional ballads (two of which Sir Walter
> Scott had earlier attributed to Swift) to Congreve. <u>See</u>
> 1933.B3.

2 GOSSE, EDMUND. "Note on Congreve." <u>London Mercury</u>, 3, no. 18
   (April), pp. 638-43.
>   Comments upon Congreve's version of two tales by
> La Fontaine and enlarges upon several biographical facts and
> Congreve's minor works dealt with in his <u>Life of William
> Congreve</u> (1888.A3). Reprinted, with extra concluding
> paragraph, 1922.B1.

3 NETTLETON, GEORGE HENRY. "Congreve, Vanbrugh, and Farquhar."
   In his <u>English Drama of the Restoration and Eighteenth Century
   1642-1780</u>. New York: Macmillan, pp. 120-40.
>   Reprint of 1914.B2.

*4 SUMMERS, MONTAGUE. <u>The Double Dealer: Theatrical History</u>.
   [1921].
>   Cited in <u>BM</u> (1966.B2), vol. 232, col. 553. This may have
> been incorporated into the Nonesuch edition of <u>The Complete
> Works</u> (1923.A1).

*5 ____. <u>Love for Love. Theatrical History</u>. [1921], 8 pp.
   <u>See</u> 1921.B4.

*6 ____. <u>The Way of the World. Theatrical History</u>. [1921], 8 pp.
   <u>See</u> 1921.B4.

7 WOODBERRY, GEORGE EDWARD. "A Biography of Congreve." In his
   <u>Studies of a Litterateur</u>. New York: Harcourt, Brace,
   pp. 107-12.
>   Reviews Gosse's biography of Congreve (1888.A3), adding
> that Congreve's style has a quality as unique as Shakespeare's
> prose.

<u>1922</u>

A BOOKS

1 CONGREVE, WILLIAM. <u>Incognita</u>. Edited by H. F. B. Brett-Smith.
   Percy Reprints. No. 5. Oxford: Basil Blackwell; New York
   and Boston: Houghton Mifflin, xviii + 71 pp.
>   "The merits of <u>Incognita</u> are...more considerable than has
> commonly been allowed."

2 _____. The Way of the World. In Restoration Plays from Dryden to Farquhar. Introduction by Edmund Gosse. Everyman's Library. London: J. M. Dent; New York: E. P. Dutton, pp. vii-xvii, [163]-235.
  Reprint of 1912.A2.

B SHORTER WRITINGS

1 GOSSE, EDMUND. "A Note on Congreve." In his Aspects and Impressions. New York: Charles Scribner's, pp. 77-86.
  Reprint, with extra concluding paragraph, of 1921.B2.

2 MORSE, CHARLES. "A Great Comic Dramatist." Dalhousie Review, 2: 335-48.
  In examining the works within the context of the "apostate" world of Restoration England, is surprised that Congreve was as "clean a man...and writer as he proved to be."

3 _____. "The Plays of William Congreve." The Canadian Magazine, 58, no. 6 (April), pp. 473-80.
  Congreve, a man of "decent instincts," described life as he saw it in a period "when England was drinking the lees in the profligate cup of the Restoration." Although the unexpurgated muse offends decorum, the plays illustrate the "beauty of literary expression as disengaged from the thought it reveals."

4 ROBBINS, ALFRED. "Shakespeare's Sonnets and Congreve." Notes and Queries. 12th ser., 11 (19 August), 145-46.
  An advertisement in The Post Boy (24-27 February, 1710/11) refers to Congreve's copy of an "Old Edition" of Shakespeare's poetry.

1923

A BOOKS

1 CONGREVE, WILLIAM. The Complete Works. Edited by Montague Summers. 4 vols. Soho [London]: Nonesuch Press.
  Includes biography, critical and textual notes. "Comedy has never been touched by more delicate and more unfaltering fingers than those of Congreve." Reprinted 1964.A1.

2 _____. [Complete Plays]. In William Congreve. Edited by Alex. Charles Ewald. Mermaid Series. London: T. F. Unwin; New York: C. Scribner's, xli + 486 pp.
  Reprint of 1887.A1.

1923

3 _____. [Selected Poems]. In A Sheaf of Poetical Scraps. Edited
by Dragosh Protopopesco. Academia Română; Memoriile Secţiunei
Leterare, ser. III, tom. I, mem. 5 (June, 1923).
Several unknown or neglected pieces by Congreve. Second
edition, enlarged, 1925.A2.

4 _____. Love for Love. In Types of English Drama 1660-1780.
Edited with notes and biographical sketches by David Harrison
Stevens. Boston: Ginn, pp. 276-328.

5 _____. The Way of the World. In Types of English Drama 1660-
1780. Edited with notes and biographical sketches by David
Harrison Stevens. Boston: Ginn, pp. 329-74.

B SHORTER WRITINGS

1 ANON. "William Congreve." The Times Literary Supplement
(4 October), pp. 641-42.
Congreve has become the dramatist of the library rather
than of the stage.

2 ARCHER, WILLIAM. The Old Drama and the New: An Essay in Re-
Valuation. Boston: Small, Maynard, pp. 169-202, passim.
Discusses the technical differences between the four
comedies and asserts that although Millamant is a great
creation, Congreve is not as witty as Sheridan.

3 HELDT, W. "A Chronological and Critical Review of the Appreciation and Condemnation of the Comic Dramatists of the Restoration and Orange Periods." Neophilologus, 8 no. 3 (July),
pp. 197-204.
The moral aim in Congreve's plays is easily discernible.

*4 MOORE, JOHN BROOKS. "The Comic and the Realistic in English
Drama." Diss., University of Wisconsin, 231 pp.
Cited in Comprehensive Dissertation Index 1861-1972.
Vol. 36. Ann Arbor: Xerox University Microfilms, 1973,
p. 144.

5 NETTLETON, GEORGE HENRY. "Congreve, Vanbrugh, and Farquhar."
In his English Drama of the Restoration and Eighteenth Century
1642-1780. New York: Macmillan, pp. 120-40.
Reprint of 1914.B2.

6 NICOLL, ALLARDYCE. A History of Restoration Drama 1660-1700.
Cambridge, England: University Press, vi + 397 pp., passim.

Survey includes references to all of Congreve's plays.
"The atmosphere of the school of manners...in its most perfect form, is to be found in the works of Congreve." Separate
entries not made for subsequent reprints: 2nd edition revised
1928; third edition revised 1940; 4th edition revised 1952;
reprinted 1961 and 1965.

7 _____. An Introduction to Dramatic Theory. London: George G.
Harrap, pp. 186-97.
Refers to The Double Dealer and The Way of the World to
illustrate the comedy of manners. Revised and enlarged edition called The Theory of Drama (1931.B3).

8 PROTOPOPESCO, D. "Congreve." The Times Literary Supplement
(8 November), p. 751.
Letter regarding several omissions in Summers's edition of
Congreve's works (1923.A1). Reproduces text of "A Satyr
Against Love," cites further proof of Congreve's authorship
of several ballads, and refers to three letters from Congreve
to Pope.

9 STRACHEY, LYTTON. "Congreve, Collier, Macaulay, and
Mr. Summers." The Nation and The Athenaeum, 34 (13 October),
56-58.
Reviews Summers's edition of The Complete Works (1923.A1)
and defends Congreve against Collier and Macaulay. Rpt. in
Portraits in Miniature and other Essays. London: Chatto and
Windus, 1931, pp. 40-49; and in his Literary Studies. New
York: Harcourt, Brace and World, 1969, pp. 53-57.

1924

A BOOKS

1 CONGREVE, WILLIAM. The Way of the World. Foyle's Dramatic
Library. London: W. & G. Foyle, 95 pp.

2 _____. The Way of the World. Holerth Library. No. 57. London:
Holerth Press [1924], 104 pp.

3 _____. The Way of the World. In The Chief British Dramatists,
Excluding Shakespeare. Edited by Brander Matthews and Paul
Robert Leider. Boston: Houghton Mifflin, pp. [607]-[652].
Reprinted 1925.A5.

4 GOSSE, EDMUND. Life of William Congreve. New York: Charles
Scribner's, xi + 181 pp.
Revised and enlarged version of 1888.A3.

1924

*5 KROHNE, WILHELM. "Congreves Novelle Incognita." Diss.,
    Muenster University.
        Cited in McNamee, 1968.B10.

6 PROTOPOPESCO, DRAGOSH. Un Classique Moderne. William Congreve,
   sa vie, son oeuvre. Lettre-préface de M. Louis Cazamian.
   Paris: Les éditions de "La Vie Universitaire," 434 pp.
       Discusses Congreve's art with reference to all five plays,
   Congreve's influence, as well as the most significant earlier
   criticism dealing with Congreve.

B SHORTER WRITINGS

1 DOBRÉE, BONAMY. "Congreve." In his Restoration Comedy: 1660-
   1720. Oxford: Clarendon Press, pp. [121]-150.
       Detailed examination of the relationship between style and
   thought. Concludes that while Congreve was too "much of a
   poet to accept the surface of life, he was too little a poet
   to find beauty in the bare facts of existence..." Reprinted
   1938.B1; 1946.B1; 1951.B2; 1955.B3; 1958.B4; 1962.B3; 1966.B7;
   1970.B5; also reprinted in 1966.B8.

2 FALLS, CYRIL. "William Congreve." In his The Critics Armoury.
   London: R. Cobden-Sanderson, pp. 79-95.
       Argues that the reason for Congreve's exclusion from the
   stage is that he "follows a tradition that...is un-English."
   To appreciate Congreve, therefore, it is necessary for us to
   "set ourselves in the dramatist's place and to view comedy
   rather through his eyes than through our own."

3 KRUTCH, JOSEPH WOOD. Comedy and Conscience after the Restoration.
   New York: Columbia University Press, xi + 300 pp., passim.
       Examines and traces "the various influences which led to
   the decline of the Restoration comedy and the rise of the
   Sentimental Comedy by considering the general social and
   literary history of the times." Includes references to
   Congreve's plays and to his part in the Collier controversy.
   Reprinted with two additions (index and bibliography of relevant modern discussions prepared by G. S. Alleman) 1949.B5;
   1961.B3.

*4 LYNCH, KATHLEEN M. "English Sources of Restoration Comedy of
    Manners." Diss., University of Michigan.
        Cited in Comprehensive Dissertation Index 1861-1972.
    Vol. 35. Ann Arbor: Xerox University Microfilms, 1973,
    p. 817. Enlarged and altered into book 1926.B3.

5 STOLL, E[LMER] E[DGAR]. "Literature No 'Document.'" <u>Modern</u>
   <u>Language Review</u>, 19, no. 2 (April), pp. 141-57.
        Restoration comedy reflects the tastes rather than the
   life of the time. Refers to Congreve. Altered, enlarged,
   and reprinted 1927.B4; 1942.B5. <u>See also</u> 1928.B4, B6, B7,
   B9; 1934.B3; 1943.B6.

<u>1925</u>

<u>A BOOKS</u>

1 CONGREVE, WILLIAM. <u>Comedies</u>. Edited by Bonamy Dobrée. World's
   Classics. No. 276. London & New York: Humphrey Milford,
   Oxford University Press, xxviii + 441 pp.
        Also includes "Concerning Humour in Comedy." It is the
   "aesthetic pleasure we get from Congreve [not the moral or
   philosophic] that earns him his high place." Reprinted
   1929.A2; 1934.A1; 1939.A1; 1944.A1; 1949.A2; 1951.A2;
   1957.A1; 1959.A1; 1963.A2; 1966.A2.

2 _____. [Selected Poems]. In <u>A Sheaf of Poetical Scraps:</u>
   <u>Together with a "Satyr Against Love," Prose Miscellanies</u>
   <u>and Letters</u>. Edited by Dragosh Protopopesco. [Bucharest]:
   Cultura Naţională, 70 pp.
        Second and enlarged edition of 1923.A3.

3 _____. "Character of Dryden." In <u>Dryden: Poetry and Prose</u>.
   Introduction and notes by David Nichol Smith. Oxford:
   Clarendon Press, pp. 1-3.
        Taken from Congreve's dedication to his edition of <u>The</u>
   <u>Dramatic Works of John Dryden</u>, 1717. Reprinted 1946.A1;
   1951.A3; 1955.A2.

4 _____. <u>Semele</u>. Alterations adopted by Handel. Cambridge:
   University Press, 47 pp.
        As performed at the New Theatre, Cambridge, 10-14
   February, 1925.

5 _____. <u>The Way of the World</u>. In <u>The Chief British Dramatists,</u>
   <u>Excluding Shakespeare</u>. Edited by Brander Matthews and Paul
   Robert Leider. Boston and New York: Houghton Mifflin,
   pp. [607]-[652].
        Reprint of 1924.A3.

6 _____. <u>The Way of the World</u>. In <u>Restoration Plays from Dryden</u>
   <u>to Farquhar</u>. Introduction by Edmund Gosse. Everyman's

1925

Library. London: J. M. Dent; New York: E. P. Dutton,
pp. vii–xvii, [163]–235.
Reprint of 1912.A2.

B SHORTER WRITINGS

1 AGATE, JAMES. "'The Way of the World' by William Congreve.
Lyric Theatre, Hammersmith." In his The Contemporary Theatre,
1924. With an introduction by Noel Coward. London: Chapman
and Hall, pp. 81–85.
    The review emphasizes Edith Evans' portrayal of Millamant.
Reprinted 1945.B1; 1969.B1.

2 ANON. "Congreve's Love for Love." Theatre Arts Monthly, 9,
no. 6 (June), pp. 358–59.
    Plates: Costume designs for Mrs. Frail and Valentine and
stage setting.

3 ____. "Continuity in English Drama." The Times Literary
Supplement (29 October), pp. 705–06.
    Congreve's plays, while deriving from the past, also point
forward to sentimental comedy.

4 ARUNDELL, DENNIS. "The Gordian Knot Untied." The Times Literary
Supplement (4 June), p. 384.
    Suggests that The Gordian Knot Untied was written by Walsh
and was an earlier version of Squire Trelooby, written by
Walsh, Congreve, and Vanbrugh. See 1925.B7.

5 DUKES, ASHLEY. "Congreve as a Modernist." Theatre Arts Monthly,
9, no. 1 (January), pp. 53–59.
    The "patient, thoughtful creation of character...links the
author's spirit with our own." Plate: costume designs for
Foible and Petulant.

6 J.[ENNINGS], R.[ICHARD]. "The Theatre: Ibsen and Congreve."
Spectator, 135 (28 November), 967.
    In reviewing the New Scala production of The Mourning Bride,
Jennings affirms that the play reveals Congreve's poverty of
invention.

7 LAWRENCE, W. J. "The Gordian Knot Untied." The Times Literary
Supplement (11 June), p. 400.
    Disagrees with Arundell's suggestion (1925.B4) regarding
the identification of The Gordian Knot Untied with Squire
Trelooby.

8 NICOLL, ALLARDYCE. <u>British Drama: An Historical Survey from</u>
   <u>the Beginnings to the Present Time</u>. London: G. G. Harrap;
   New York: Thomas Y. Crowell, pp. 254-55.
   Congreve's comedies return to the path established by
   Etherege, but Congreve's "whole power is centered on an
   airiness of fancy and a delicacy of pointed style..." Separate
   entries not made for subsequent reprints: 1932, 1933, 1946,
   1947, 1949, 1955, 1958, 1962, 1963.

9 PERRY, HENRY TEN EYCK. "William Congreve." In his <u>The Comic</u>
   <u>Spirit in Restoration Drama: Studies in the Comedy of</u>
   <u>Etherege, Wycherley, Congreve, Vanbrugh, and Farquhar</u>.
   New Haven: Yale University Press, pp. 56-81.
   Analyzes the situations, characters and dialogue, and
   general atmosphere of the plays, which are seen as the
   "supreme expression...of a very special and a very conspic-
   uous phase of the Comic Spirit."

10 WALKLEY, A. B. "Congreve" and "<u>The Way of the World</u>." In his
   <u>Still More Prejudice</u>. London: William Heinemann,
   pp. 34-38, 39-43.
   Reviews Gosse's biography of Congreve (revised and enlarged
   edition 1929.A4) and the production of the play at the Hammersmith Lyric Theatre. Praises the play's "stark reality."

1926

A BOOKS

1 CONGREVE, WILLIAM. <u>The Way of the World</u>. Edited by Lloyd Edwin
   Smith. Girard, Kan.: Haldeman-Julius, 95 pp.
   Includes Macaulay's essay and extracts from those by Lamb,
   Swift, and Hazlitt, together with the commendatory verses by
   Steele.

B SHORTER WRITINGS

1 DOBRÉE, BONAMY. "Young Voltaire: A Conversation between William
   Congreve and Alexander Pope, Twickenham, September, 1726."
   <u>The Nation and The Athenaeum</u>, 40, no. 5 (6 November),
   pp. 179-80.
   An imaginary conversation that focuses primarily upon
   Voltaire and his visit to Congreve. Reprinted 1933.B1;
   1967.B4.

1926

2   LAWRENCE, W. J.   "A Congreve Holograph."   Review of English
       Studies, 2, no. 7 (July), p. 345.
           Document in which Congreve requests that his dividend on
       South Sea stock be payed to Mr. Thomas Snow.

3   LYNCH, KATHLEEN M.   "Congreve."   In her The Social Mode of
       Restoration Comedy.   Univ. of Michigan Pub. in Lang. and
       Lit., Vol. 3.   New York: Macmillan, pp. 182–213.
           "The plays of Congreve present a brief, authentic record
       of the précieuse movement in comedy."   See Ph.D. dissertation,
       1924.B4.

4   PEARSON, RALPH.   "Prints and the Theatre."   Theatre Arts Monthly,
       10, no. 10 (October), pp. 689–94.
           Lithograph: Robert Edmond Jones directing Love for Love.

5   READ, HERBERT.   "The Definition of Comedy."   In his Reason and
       Romanticism: Essays in Literary Criticism.   London: Faber
       and Gwyer, pp. 127–38.
           Defends Congreve against earlier critics and affirms that
       it is Congreve's "psychological observation" that sets his
       comedies apart from those of his contemporaries.

                                1927

A BOOKS

1   CONGREVE, WILLIAM.   The Comedies.   Edited with an introduction
       by Joseph Wood Krutch.   New York: Macmillan, xv + 392 pp.
           Congreve on the whole "softened rather than intensified"
       the current of the age.   "Amused and detached, he was content
       to let the world wag as it would...but his attitude was never
       any more harsh or corrupt than that appropriate to a man of
       the world."   Reprinted 1929.A3.

B SHORTER WRITINGS

*1 ASHBY, STANLEY ROYAL.   "The Treatment of the Themes of Classical
       Tragedy in English Tragedy between 1660 and 1738."   Diss.,
       Harvard University.
           Cited in Stratman, 1971.B16.

2   CAZAMIAN, LOUIS.   "The Transition."   In Modern Times (1660–1914).
       Vol. 2 of A History of English Literature.   London & Toronto:
       J. M. Dent, pp. 72–74.

If Congreve's art does not probe very far below the surface, it does analyze the feminine soul. Yet from all his
art there "emanates...a softened and almost indulgent pessi-
mism.... The only virtue which is held up to us...is
sincerity."

3 ISAACS, J. "Congreve and America." Review of English Studies,
3, no. 9 (January), p. 79.
A quote from the Maryland Gazette (4 February, 1728/9)
taken from the Daily Post (1 October, 1728) describing
Congreve's accident at Bath.

4 STOLL, ELMER EDGAR. "Literature and Life." In his Shakespeare
Studies: Historical and Comparative in Method. New York:
Macmillan, pp. 39-89, passim.
Altered and enlarged version of 1924.B5; reprinted 1942.B5.

5 WILSON, JOHN HAROLD. "The Influence of Beaumont and Fletcher on
Restoration Drama." Diss., Ohio State University, 156 pp.
Cited in Comprehensive Dissertation Index 1861-1972.
Vol. 37. Ann Arbor: Xerox University Microfilms, 1973,
p. 924. See book, 1928.B8.

1928

A BOOKS

1 CONGREVE, WILLIAM. The Mourning Bride, Poems and Miscellanies.
Edited by Bonamy Dobrée. World's Classics. No. 277. London:
Humphrey Milford, Oxford University Press, xxvi + 540 pp.
Includes a brief biographical and critical introduction to
the works in this volume. Reprinted 1929.A1.

2 _____. The Way of the World. Boston: W. H. Baker, ix + 94 pp.
Acting edition of the Repertory Theatre of Boston.

3 _____. The Way of the World. "An unexpurgated Edition, including original signed Etching by A. R. Middleton Todd...and a
Foreword by M. C. Salaman." London: Haymarket Press, xxi +
79 pp.
Includes Steele's dedicatory epistle. The play is "per-
meated with reality."

4 _____. The Way of the World. In Great English Plays. Twenty-
three Masterpieces from the Mysteries to Sheridan (excluding
Shakespeare) with Three Representative Plays of the Nineteenth
Century. Edited with a running commentary by H. F. Rubinstein.
London: Victor Gollancz; New York: Harper, pp. 835-82.

1928

5   . The Way of the World. In <u>Types of Social Comedy</u>. Edited
   by Robert Metcalf Smith. World Drama Series. New York:
   Prentice-Hall, pp. [169]-266.
      Congreve's play reflects a world in which "nothing is good
   or bad, in which there is neither morality nor feeling, but
   in which men and women are pretending to be civilized; in
   which sex is a battle of wits rather than of emotions, and
   manners are the prime consideration."

B SHORTER WRITINGS

1 ANON. "Two Hundred Years Ago." <u>Notes and Queries</u>, 155
   (6 October), 236.
      Reprinted notice on performance and cast of <u>The Mourning
   Bride</u> from the <u>Daily Post</u> (5 October, 1728).

2 ELWIN, MALCOLM. "Congreve." In his <u>The Playgoer's Handbook to
   Restoration Drama</u>. London: Jonathan Cape, pp. 164-79.
      Short study of Congreve's plays, concluding that Congreve
   is the "chief exponent of the comedy of manners <u>par
   excellence</u>..." Reprinted 1966.B11.

3 HODGES, JOHN C. "The Authorship of <u>Squire Trelooby</u>." <u>Review of
   English Studies</u>, 4, no. 16 (October), pp. 404-13.
      It is doubtful whether the <u>Squire Trelooby</u> published anon-
   ymously in 1704 represents the acted version written by
   Congreve, Vanbrugh, and Walsh. <u>See</u> 1968.B15; 1970.B8.

4 LACEY, T. A. "'Artificial' Comedy." <u>The Times Literary Supple-
   ment</u> (15 March), p. 188.
      Restoration stage marriage law need not be seen as a
   travesty upon fact. <u>See</u> 1924.B5; 1928.B6, B7, B9; 1934.B3;
   1943.B6.

5 NETTLETON, GEORGE HENRY. "Congreve, Vanbrugh, and Farquhar." In
   his <u>English Drama of the Restoration and Eighteenth Century
   1642-1780</u>. New York: Macmillan, pp. 120-40.
      Reprint of 1914.B2.

6 STOLL, ELMER EDGAR. "'Artificial' Comedy." <u>The Times Literary
   Supplement</u> (1 March), p. 150.
      Restoration comedy reflects the tastes and not the life of
   the time. <u>See</u> 1924.B5; 1928.B4, B7, B9; 1934.B3; 1943.B6.

7 TREVELYAN, G. M. "'Artificial' Comedy." <u>The Times Literary
   Supplement</u> (5 January), p. 12.

A recent production of The Way of the World suggests that Restoration comedy is as "artificial" as real men and women. See 1924.B5; 1928.B4, B6, B9; 1934.B3; 1943.B6.

8 WILSON, JOHN HAROLD. The Influence of Beaumont and Fletcher on Restoration Drama. Columbus: Ohio State University Press, pp. 21-100, passim.

Includes references to all of Congreve's comedies and to the influence of Beaumont and Fletcher upon them. See Ph.D. dissertation, 1927.B5; reprinted 1968.B20.

9 WILLIAMS, BASIL. "'Artificial' Comedy." The Times Literary Supplement (12 January), p. 28.

The characters in The Way of the World, and especially Millamant's love for Mirabell, are implausible. See 1924.B5; 1928.B4, B6, B7; 1934.B3; 1943.B6.

1929

A BOOKS

1 CONGREVE, WILLIAM. The Mourning Bride, Poems and Miscellanies. Edited by Bonamy Dobrée. World's Classics. No. 277. London: Oxford University Press, xxvi + 540 pp.
    Reprint of 1928.A1.

2 _____. Comedies. Edited by Bonamy Dobrée. World's Classics. No. 276. London and New York: Oxford University Press, xxviii + 441 pp.
    Reprint of 1925.A1.

3 _____. The Comedies. Edited with an introduction by Joseph Wood Krutch. New York: Book League of America, xv + 392 pp.
    Reprint of 1927.A1.

4 _____. The Way of the World and Love for Love. With illustrations and decorations by John Kettelwell. London: John Lane, Bodley Head; New York: Dodd, Mead, v + 222 pp.

5 _____. Love for Love. In A Book of Dramas, an Anthology of Nineteen Plays. Compiled by Bruce Carpenter. New York: Prentice-Hall, pp. 323-99.
    Congreve's play "sparkles with a hard brilliancy."
    Reprinted 1934.A2; new edition 1949.A3.

6 _____. The Way of the World. London: for J. Tonson, 1700 [Cambridge, Mass.: 1929].

1929

Photostat copy of the original in the Harvard Library.
Cited in <u>NUC</u> (1970.B14), p. 596.

7 _____. <u>The Way of the World</u>. In <u>British Drama. Ten Plays from</u>
<u>the Middle of the Fourteenth Century to the end of the Nine-</u>
<u>teenth</u>. Edited by Paul Robert Leider, Robert Morss Lovett,
and Robert Kilburn Root. Boston: Houghton Mifflin,
pp. [235]-[283].

8 _____. <u>The Way of the World</u>. In <u>British Plays from the Restora-</u>
<u>tion to 1820</u>. Edited with introductions and bibliographies
by Montrose J. Moses. Vol. 1. Boston: Little, Brown,
pp. 237-82.
Reprinted 1931.A1.

9 _____. <u>The Way of the World</u>. In <u>Restoration Plays from Dryden</u>
<u>to Farquhar</u>. Introduction by Edmund Gosse. Everyman's
Library. London: J. M. Dent; New York: E. P. Dutton,
pp. vii-xvii, [163]-235.
Reprint of 1912.A2.

B SHORTER WRITINGS

1 ANON. "Two Hundred Years Ago." <u>Notes and Queries</u>, 156
(26 January), 56.
Reprinted account from the <u>Flying Post</u> (Saturday, 25
January, 1728/9) of Congreve's death.

2 ANON. "William Congreve." <u>The Times Literary Supplement</u>
(17 January), pp. 33-34.
Critical appreciation of the plays, concluding that the
audience's tastes prevented Congreve from fully expressing his
most cherished ideas: the "form proved too fine...the ideas
too new."

3 CRAWFORD, BARTHOLOW V. "High Comedy in Terms of Restoration
Practice." <u>Philological Quarterly</u>, 8, no. 4 (October),
pp. 339-47.
As applied to the Restoration, high comedy "must be
defined in the light of a special sort of social environment,
flowering in a special sort of dramatic product." Draws nine
conclusions regarding the "Artificial Comedy" of Etherege,
Congreve, and their contemporaries.

4 DALE, HARRISON. "The Comedies of William Congreve." <u>Fortnightly</u>
<u>Review</u>, NS 125 (1 January), 55-64.

Survey of Congreve's life and writings to commemorate the Congreve bicentenary. Acknowledges <u>Love for Love</u> and <u>The Way of the World</u> as Congreve's two greatest comedies and Congreve as one of the world's greatest comic dramatists.

5   DOBRÉE, BONAMY. "<u>The Mourning Bride</u> and <u>Cato</u>." In his <u>Restoration Tragedy: 1660–1720</u>. Oxford: Clarendon Press, pp. 167–78.
    Sees <u>The Mourning Bride</u> as a thriller rather than a tragedy, but Congreve's blank verse as "the best instrument for the drama of his age, better even than Dryden's." Refers also to Congreve's analysis of the Pindaric ode and to his comments on operatic recitative. Reprinted and corrected 1950.B1; 1954.B2; re-corrected 1959.B3; 1963.B2; 1966.B9.

6   _____. <u>William Congreve: A Conversation between Jonathan Swift and John Gay, at the house of the Duke of Queensbury near London, June, 1730</u>. Univ. of Washington Chapbooks, no. 26. Seattle: University of Washington Book Store, 24 pp.
    Fictional dialogue that refers to several aspects of Congreve's life, including his personal attributes, his friendship with Anne Bracegirdle, and his handling of the Jeremy Collier controversy. Reprinted 1933.B1; 1935.B1; 1967.B4; 1969.B3; 1973.B3; 1976.B3.

7   HODGES, JOHN C. "William Congreve in the Government Service." <u>Modern Philology</u>, 27, no. 1 (November), pp. 183–92.
    Materials at the Public Records Office in London used to ascertain the terms of and income derived from the four government posts held by Congreve. Concludes that Congreve's "literary effort varied in inverse proportion to his governmental aid."

8   MONTGOMERY, GUY. "The Challenge of Restoration Comedy." In <u>University of California Publications in English</u>. Vol. 1. Berkeley: University of California Press, pp. 133–51.
    The human significance of Restoration comedy lies "in its representation of one of those recurring efforts of individuality to maintain its integrity in a world threatened by the confining limitations of law." Refers to Millamant as the apotheosis of Restoration women. Reprinted 1966.B24.

*9 MUESCHKE, PAUL. "Prototypes of Restoration Wits and Would-Bees in Ben Jonson's Realistic Comedy." Diss., University of Michigan.
    Cited in <u>Comprehensive Dissertation Index 1861–1972</u>. Vol. 36. Ann Arbor: Xerox University Microfilms, 1973, p. 198.

1929

10 THORNDIKE, ASHLEY H. <u>English Comedy</u>. New York: Macmillan,
      pp. 314-28.
          Although inferior to Molière, "especially in the range and
      depth of his humour," Congreve may compare with the master of
      comedy in "style and wit and in the treatment of such comic
      situations as come within his range..." Incorporates all four
      of Congreve's comedies.

<u>1930</u>

A BOOKS

1 CONGREVE, WILLIAM. <u>The Works</u>. Edited by F. W. Bateston.
      London: P. Davies; New York: Minton, Balch, xxviii + 507 pp.
          Includes the four comedies, <u>Incognita</u>, and selected poems.
      Although Congreve's characters are "without a background,
      without roots....the idiosyncrasies of his creations seem to
      control and inform the manner of their speech."

2 _____. [Complete Plays]. In <u>William Congreve</u>. Edited by
      Alexander C. Ewald. Mermaid Series. London: Benn, xli +
      486 pp.
          Reprint of 1887.A1.

3 _____. <u>Incognita</u>. In <u>Shorter Novels: Seventeenth Century</u>.
      Edited by Philip Henderson. Everyman's Library. No. 841.
      London: J. M. Dent, pp. [237]-303.
          The "complete detachment from the romantic attitude...is
      struck with a deliberate irony." Reprinted 1962.A1.

B SHORTER WRITINGS

1 EATON, WALTER PRICHARD. "Congreve's 'Love for Love.'" In his
      <u>The Drama in English</u>. New York, [etc.]: Charles Scribner's,
      pp. 165-70.
          The play represents what was "best and most enduring [style,
      elegance, and intellectual neatness] in a strange and fasci-
      nating epoch of English history..."

2 SMITH, WILLARD. <u>The Nature of Comedy</u>. Boston: R. G. Badger,
      pp. 151-53.
          Cites all of Congreve's comedies, stating that Congreve
      "carried to its height the distinctive quality of Restoration
      comedy; its emphasis on dialogue."

3 WILLIAMS, GEORGE G. "Did Thomson write the poem <u>To The Memory</u>
   <u>of Mr. Congreve?</u>" <u>Publications of the Modern Language Asso-</u>
   <u>ciation</u>, 45, no. 4 (December), pp. 1010–13.
       "The style and structure of the poem...throw further light
   on the problem of its authorship." <u>See</u> 1729.B1; 1939.B4;
   1973.B1.

1931

A BOOKS

1 CONGREVE, WILLIAM. <u>The Way of the World</u>. In <u>British Plays from</u>
   <u>the Restoration to 1820</u>. Edited with introductions and
   bibliographies by Montrose J. Moses. Vol. 1. Boston:
   Little, Brown, pp. 237–82.
       Reprint of 1929.A8.

2 _____. <u>The Way of the World</u>. In <u>From Beowulf to Thomas Hardy</u>.
   Edited by Robert Shafer. Vol. 1. New York: Doubleday,
   Doran, pp. 474–515.

3 _____. <u>The Way of the World</u>. In <u>Plays of the Restoration and</u>
   <u>Eighteenth Century</u>. Edited by Dougald MacMillan and Howard
   Mumford Jones. New York: Henry Holt, pp. 400–44.
       The play, illustrating a world of "wit and pleasure....
   instructs us in the way of the world." Enlarged editions
   1938.A3; 1959.A5; 1962.A8; 1964.A7.

4 TAYLOR, D. CRANE. <u>William Congreve</u>. London: Humphrey Milford,
   Oxford University Press, xii + 252 pp.
       Critical biography. "Through Congreve the comedy of man-
   ners reached a plane of high artistic achievement, and his
   genius, working within its narrow limits, places him as much
   above his contemporaries as Shakespeare towers above his."
   Reprinted 1963.A7.

B SHORTER WRITINGS

1 ALLEN, ROBERT J. "The Kit-Kat Club and the Theatres." <u>Review</u>
   <u>of English Studies</u>, 7, no. 25 (January), pp. 56–61.
       Traces the influence of the club, of which Congreve was
   a prominent member, upon the theater, especially its role in
   establishing the Queen's Theatre in the Haymarket.

1931

2 GRAY, CHARLES HAROLD. <u>Theatrical Criticism in London to 1795</u>.
      New York: Columbia University Press, vii + 333 pp., passim.
         Refers to the reception of Congreve's plays between 1730
      and 1795. Reprinted 1964.B5.

3 NICOLL, ALLARDYCE. <u>The Theory of Drama</u>. New York: Thomas Y.
      Crowell, pp. 222–26.
         Revised and enlarged edition of <u>An Introduction to Dramatic</u>
      <u>Theory</u> (1923.B7).

*4 WILCOX, JOHN. "The Relation of Molière to Restoration Comedy."
      Diss., University of Michigan.
         Cited in <u>Comprehensive Dissertation Index 1861–1972</u>.
      Vol. 37. Ann Arbor: Xerox University Microfilms, 1973,
      p. 879. <u>See</u> book 1938.B4.

1932

A BOOKS

1 CONGREVE, WILLIAM. <u>The Way of the World</u>. In <u>Restoration Plays</u>
      <u>from Dryden to Farquhar</u>. Introduction by Edmund William
      Gosse. Everyman's Library. London: Dent, pp. xiii–xiv,
      [163]–235.
         Enlarged edition of 1929.A9. <u>See</u> 1912.A2.

B SHORTER WRITINGS

1 DE BEER, E. S. "Congreve's <u>Incognita</u>: The Source of its Setting,
      with a Note on Wilson's <u>Belphegor</u>." <u>Review of English Studies</u>,
      8, no. 29 (January), pp. 74–77.
         Topographical passages in <u>Incognita</u> may have been influ-
      enced by John Raymond's <u>An Itinerary contayning a Voyage made</u>
      <u>through Italy, in the yeare 1646 and 1647</u> (London, 1648).

2 DOBRÉE, BONAMY. "William Congreve: I. His Life.... II. His
      Work." In his <u>Variety of Ways: Discussions on Six Authors</u>.
      Oxford: Clarendon Press, pp. 46–85.
         Biographical and critical survey. Congreve should be
      appreciated for his aesthetic rather than for his moral and
      philosophical achievements. Reprinted 1967.B5; 1973.B4;
      1976.B4.

3 EMPEROR, JOHN BERNARD. "The Juvenalian and Persian Element in
      English Literature from the Restoration to Dr. Johnson."
      Diss., Cornell University, pp. 191–208, 467–69.

Although the "influence of Persius upon Congreve is very
slight," that of Juvenal is more direct and prevalent.

4 JACKSON, ALFRED. "London Playhouses, 1700-1705." Review of
   English Studies, 8, no. 31 (July), pp. 291-302.
      Cites references from the London Post to a benefit per-
   formance of Love for Love, from the English Post to a canceled performance of The Old Bachelor, and from the London
   Gazette to Queen Anne's request to Vanbrugh and Congreve to
   establish "a New Company of Comedians" to combat the "Abuse
   and Immorality of the Stage..."

5 NETTLETON, GEORGE HENRY. "Congreve, Vanbrugh, and Farquhar."
   In his English Drama of the Restoration and Eighteenth Century
   (1642-1780). New York: Macmillan, pp. 120-40.
      Reprint of 1914.B2.

                            1933

A BOOKS

1 CONGREVE, WILLIAM. Love for Love. In Twelve Famous Plays of
   the Restoration and Eighteenth Century. Introduction by
   Cecil A. Moore. New York: Modern Library, pp. vii-xxiii,
   [255]-342.
      Congreve gave the comedy of manners its "final perfection
   of epigrammatic splendor and delicate artistry..."
   Reprinted 1960.A2.

2 _____. The Way of the World. Edited with an introduction and
   explanatory notes by W. P. Barrett. The Temple Dramatists.
   London: J. M. Dent, xii + 145 pp.
      Reprint of 1894.A1.

3 _____. The Way of the World. In Twelve Famous Plays of the
   Restoration and Eighteenth Century. Introduction by Cecil A.
   Moore. New York: Modern Library, pp. vii-xxiii, [419]-497.
      See 1933.A1. Reprinted 1960.A4.

4 FUKUHARA, RINTARO. William Congreve. Tokyo: Kenkyusha, [x] +
   154 pp.
      In Japanese. Includes sketch of Congreve's life, chapters
   on Incognita, the poetry, the five plays, and miscellaneous
   works.

1933

B SHORTER WRITINGS

1 DOBRÉE, BONAMY. "William Congreve: A Conversation between
   Jonathan Swift and John Gay, at the house of the Duke of
   Queensbury near London. June, 1720." and "Young Voltaire:
   A Conversation between William Congreve and Alexander Pope.
   Twickenham. September, 1726." In his As Their Friends Saw
   Them: Biographical Conversations. London: Jonathan Cape,
   pp. 63-72, 73-92.
       Reprint of 1926.B1 and 1929.B6; reprinted 1967.B4.

2 ELLEHAUGE, MARTIN. English Restoration Drama: Its Relation to
   Past English and Past and Contemporary French Drama. From
   Jonson via Molière to Congreve. Copenhagen: Levin &
   Munksgaard, pp. 185-310, passim.
       Concentrates on the "evolutionistic significance" of
   Restoration drama, analyzing its form and spirit. Refers
   to The Old Bachelor, Love for Love, and The Way of the World.
   Reprinted 1970.B7 and 1974.B5.

3 HODGES, JOHN C. "The Ballad in Congreve's Love for Love."
   Publications of the Modern Language Association, 48, no. 3
   (September), pp. 953-54.
       Suggests that Ben's song in Love for Love was written by
   Congreve. See 1921.B1.

*4 LUND, SERENA M. "The Comedy of Manners in the Eighteenth Century,
   1700-1780." Diss., London University.
       Cited in McNamee, 1968.B10.

<u>1934</u>

A BOOKS

1 CONGREVE, WILLIAM. The Comedies. Edited by Bonamy Dobrée.
   World's Classics. No. 276. London and New York: Oxford
   University Press, xxviii + 441 pp.
       Reprint of 1925.A1.

2 _____. Love for Love. In A Book of Dramas. Edited by Bruce
   Carpenter. New York: Prentice-Hall, pp. 323-99.
       Reprint of 1929.A5.

3 _____. The Way of the World. Edited with an introduction and
   explanatory notes by W. P. Barrett. The Temple Dramatists.
   New York: Dutton, xii + 145 pp.
       Reprint of 1894.A1.

4 _____. The Way of the World. In Representative English Dramas
from Dryden to Sheridan. Edited by Frederick Tupper and
James W. Tupper. New York: Oxford University Press,
pp. 295-333, 695-98.
New and enlarged edition of 1914.A1.

B SHORTER WRITINGS

1 HARASZTI, ZOLTÁN. "Early Editions of Congreve's Plays." More
Books, 9, no. 3 (March), pp. 81-95.
Brief account of Congreve's critical reputation up to
Macaulay and a survey of Congreve's life and works. Mentions
several early editions of works by and related to Congreve
located in the Boston (Mass.) Public Library.

2 NORRIS, EDWARD T. "A Possible Source of Congreve's Sailor Ben."
Modern Language Notes, 49, no. 1 (January), pp. 334-35.
Contends that the characterization of Sailor Ben was in-
fluenced not by Thomas D'Urfey's Captain Porposs, but by
Edward Ravenscroft's Captain Durzo.

3 STOLL, ELMER EDGAR. "The Beau Monde at the Restoration." Modern
Language Notes, 49, no. 7 (November), pp. 425-32.
Restoration comedy is the image not of the beau monde
itself but of its tastes; the comedy "refracts instead of
reflecting." Cites The Way of the World. See 1924.B5;
1928.B4, B6, B7, B9; 1943.B6.

4 SUMMERS, MONTAGUE. A Bibliography of the Restoration Drama.
London: Fortune Press [1934], pp. 42-44.
Gives first production dates, first editions of printed
plays, editions that appeared during Congreve's lifetime, and
important subsequent reprints up to 1923. Another edition,
n.d., pp. 26-28.

5 _____. The Restoration Theatre. New York: Macmillan, xxi +
352 pp., passim.
Study of such aspects as announcements and advertisements,
systems of admission, the audience, scenery and costumes, and
epilogues. Includes references to all of Congreve's plays.

*6 WHITEMAN, SAMUEL ALFRED. "Literary Criticism from the Restoration
Dramatists." Diss., New York University.
Cited in Comprehensive Dissertation Index 1861-1972.
Vol. 37. Ann Arbor: Xerox University Microfilms, 1973,
p. 859.

1935

1935

A BOOKS

1 CONGREVE, WILLIAM. The Way of the World. In English Plays
   1660–1820. Compiled by A. E. Morgan. New York and London:
   Harper, pp. [407]–457.
   The purpose of the play is to "give scope to...bright stars
   to shoot meteor-wise across the artificial firmament of fine
   society."

2 _____. The Way of the World. In A Treasury of the Theatre: An
   Anthology of Great Plays from Aeschylus to Eugene O'Neill.
   Edited by Burns Mantle and John Gassner. New York: Simon and
   Schuster, pp. 1015–66.
   "Though less consistently sprightly than Love for Love,
   [The Way of the World] excels in...scintillating, audacious
   conversation...and contains Congreve's most brilliant charac-
   terizations." Reprinted 1939.A5; revised editions 1940.A4;
   1951.A8; 1963.A5; third edition 1967.A8.

B SHORTER WRITINGS

1 DOBRÉE, BONAMY. "William Congreve: A Conversation between
   Jonathan Swift and John Gay, at the house of the Duke of
   Queensbury near London. June, 1730." In Modern Short Biog-
   raphies. Edited by Marston Balch. New York: Harcourt, Brace,
   pp. 348–58.
   Reprint of 1929.B6.

2 HODGES, JOHN C. "On the Date of Congreve's Birth." Modern
   Philology, 33, no. 1 (August), pp. 83–85.
   Congreve was born not in 1669, as stated by Taylor
   (1931.A4), but in February 1670.

*3 JOHNSON, FRANK L. "The Conventions of Restoration Comedy."
    Diss., University of Wisconsin.
    Cited in Comprehensive Dissertation Index 1861–1972.
    Vol. 35. Ann Arbor: Xerox University Microfilms, 1973,
    p. 236.

4 MACAULAY, T. C. "French and English Drama in the Seventeenth
   Century: Some Contrasts and Parallels." Essays and Studies.
   Vol. 20. Oxford: Clarendon Press, pp. 45–74.
   The Double Dealer exemplifies the way in which English
   dramatists tended to violate the dramatic unities: "...the
   action becomes too closely packed and the spasmodic effect
   of the changes of scene is heightened."

5 SWAEN, A. E. H. "The authorship of 'A soldier and a sailor.'"
   <u>Archiv für das Studium der Neuren Sprachen und Literaturen</u>,
   NS 168: 237–40.
      Congreve may well be the author of the three-stanza song
   that appears in <u>Love for Love</u>, but the ballad of Buxom Joan
   is an extension by a balladist of Congreve's song.

1936

A BOOKS

1 CONGREVE, WILLIAM. <u>Love for Love</u>. In <u>The Play's the Thing: An
   Anthology of Dramatic Types</u>. Edited by Fred B. Millet and
   Gerald Eades Bentley. New York: Appleton-Century-Crofts,
   pp. 247–87.
      Congreve's "dual interests in dialogue and character are
   masterfully fused." Reprinted 1964.A4.

2 _____. <u>The Way of the World</u>. In <u>Dryden and His Contemporaries:
   Cowley to Farquhar</u>. Vol. 4 of <u>Representative English Comedies</u>.
   Edited by Charles Mills Gayley and Alwin Thaler, with critical
   notes by George Rapall Noyes. New York: Macmillan,
   pp. 561–665.
      <u>See</u> 1936.B6.

B SHORTER WRITINGS

1 HODGES, JOHN C. "Congreve's Will and Personal Papers." <u>Notes
   and Queries</u>, 171 (15 August), 117.
      Some problems arising from the loss of Congreve's original
   will and a request for help in tracing its location. <u>See</u>
   1964.A3.

2 _____. "The Dating of Congreve's Letters." <u>Publications of the
   Modern Language Association</u>, 51, no. 1 (March), pp. 153–64.
      A new chronological arrangement of sixty-eight letters
   written by Congreve, which clears up obscure references and
   gives insight into the character of the writer. <u>See</u> 1964.A3.

3 _____. "William Congreve: Confused Signatures." <u>The Times
   Literary Supplement</u> (15 August), p. 664.
      Differentiates the signature of Colonel William Congreve
   from that of the dramatist.

4 HOWARTH, R. G. "The Date of 'The Old Bachelor.'" <u>The Times
   Literary Supplement</u> (13 June), p. 500.

1936

Contends that <u>The Old Bachelor</u> was written early in 1689.
<u>See</u> 1943.B2; 1946.B2.

5 MAU, HEDWIG. "Das 'junge Mädchen'. Ein Beitrag zu dem Thema:
Die Frau in der Komödie der Restauration." <u>Britannica</u>.
Herausgegeben vom Seminar für englische Sprache und Kultur
an der Hansischen Universität. Heft 13. Hamburg, pp. 67-89.
The love battle between the gay couple is resolved because
the heroine succeeds in her demands and creates a favorable
basis for harmony. References to <u>The Way of the World</u>.

6 NOYES, GEORGE RAPALL. "William Congreve: <u>The Way of the World</u>."
In <u>Dryden and His Contemporaries: Cowley to Farquhar</u>. Vol.
4 in <u>Representative English Comedies</u>. Edited by Charles Mills
Gayley and Alwin Thaler. New York: Macmillan, pp. 533-60.
Congreve's first three comedies manifest "increased attention to formal rules, more independent study of character and
increased emphasis on it rather than intrigue, and a transfer
of attention from 'humor' to 'manners.'" <u>The Way of the World</u>
is "true comedy of manners, dealing primarily with social
affectations and habits..." Congreve's comic spirit is "that
of a sense which is neither elevated nor enlightened, nor even
common." <u>See</u> 1936.A2.

*7 TEETER, LOUIS B. "I. Political Themes in Restoration Tragedy.
II. The Dramatic Use of Hobbes' Political Ideas. A Chapter
from Political Themes in Restoration Tragedy." Diss., Johns
Hopkins University.
Cited in <u>Comprehensive Dissertation Index 1861-1972</u>.
Vol. 37. Ann Arbor: Xerox University Microfilms, 1973,
p. 469.

<u>1937</u>

A BOOKS--NONE

B SHORTER WRITINGS

1 CLARK, WILLIAM S. "Corpses, Concealments, and Curtains on the
Restoration Stage." <u>Review of English Studies</u>, 13, no. 52
(October), pp. 438-48.
Refers to the traverse device in the second scene of Act IV
in <u>The Double Dealer</u>.

2 KNIGHTS, L. C. "Restoration Comedy: The Reality and the Myth."
<u>Scrutiny</u>, 6, no. 2 (September), pp. 122-43.

Congreve's comedies are included in this study, which affirms that Restoration comedy is "trivial, gross and dull." Reprinted 1946.B3; 1947.B3; 1964.B8; 1966.B15.

3 ROSE ANTHONY, SISTER. The Jeremy Collier Stage Controversy: 1698-1726. Milwaukee: Marquette University Press, xv + 328 pp., passim.
    Includes Congreve's role in the controversy, stating that his vindication is "disappointing in that it betrays very little of the wit and genius one might expect from the lauded playwright." Reprinted 1966.B26.

4 SNIDER, ROSE. "William Congreve." In her Satire in the Comedies of Congreve, Sheridan, Wilde, and Coward. Univ. of Maine Studies, Ser. 2, no. 42. Orono: University of Maine Press, pp. 1-40.
    Congreve, a Restoration gentleman par excellence wished not to reform but merely to point out the superficiality of his artificial society. Reprinted 1972.B26.

5 WILSON, J. DOVER. "Shakespeare, Milton and Congreve." The Times Literary Supplement (16 January), p. 44.
    Congreve's description of Millamant may have been influenced by Milton's Dalila, who in turn owes something to Shakespeare's Cleopatra.

6 [WOOLF, VIRGINIA]. "Congreve's Comedies: Speed, Stillness and Meaning." The Times Literary Supplement (25 September), pp. 681-82.
    The skillful use of language ("conveyed by the curl of a phrase on the ear, by speed; by stillness") and characterization disprove Johnson's negative criticism. We "learn as writers of books and as livers of life." Reprinted in her The Moment and Other Essays, 1947.B6; 1948.B8.

1938

A BOOKS

1 CONGREVE, WILLIAM. The Double Dealer. Adapted by William, Lord Lebanon for the Jacobite Club in 1937. Foreword by W. A. Aiken. College Comedies, no. 4. New Haven: by C. R., at the Printing House...for the Players.
    Congreve was a "realist, who saw beneath the surface of reality with extraordinary penetration; yet he was so fastidious that he could not bear to uncover the truth in its nakedness, but preferred rather to clothe his observations upon life in the ribald and fantastic garments of another world."

1938

2 _____. Love for Love (employing certain portions of The Way of
the World). Acting version by Lawrence Langner. [New York:
Rialto Service Bureau].
Cited in NUC (1970.B14), p. 589.

3 _____. The Way of the World. In Plays of the Restoration and
Eighteenth Century. Edited by Dougald MacMillan and Howard
Mumford Jones. New York: Holt, pp. 400-44.
Enlarged edition of 1931.A3. Reprinted 1959.A5; 1962.A8;
1964.A7.

4 _____. The Way of the World. In Representative English Plays
from the Miracle Plays to Pinero. Edited with introductions
and notes by J. S. P. Tatlock and the late R. G. Martin.
New York: Appleton-Century-Crofts, pp. 502-42.
Second edition, revised and enlarged, of 1917.A1; see
1916.A1.

B SHORTER WRITINGS

1 DOBRÉE, BONAMY. "Congreve." In his Restoration Comedy: 1660-
1720. London: Oxford University Press, H. Milford,
pp. [121]-150.
Reprint of 1924.B1.

2 LYNCH, KATHLEEN M. "Congreve's Irish Friend, Joseph Keally."
Publications of the Modern Language Association, 53, no. 4
(December), pp. 1076-87.
A biography of Congreve's closest friend that concludes
with a detailed analysis of their relationship up until
Keally's death.

3 POOL, E. MILLICENT. "A Possible Source of 'The Way of the
World.'" Modern Language Review, 33, no. 2 (April),
pp. 258-60.
Some of the conditions laid down in the proviso scene
recall a similar scene in Nolant de Fatouville's Arlequin
Jason ou Le Toison d'or (1684). See 1946.B6; 1959.B8.

4 WILCOX, JOHN. "Congreve, Vanbrugh, and Farquhar." In his The
Relation of Molière to Restoration Comedy. New York:
Columbia University Press, pp. 154-77.
There is "no demonstrable borrowing from Molière in any
of [Congreve's] comedies.... Congreve exploited English
prototypes. He developed them to their highest expression
because he was a comic genius..." See Ph.D. dissertation,
1931.B4; reprinted 1964.B14.

1939

A BOOKS

1 CONGREVE, WILLIAM. Comedies. Edited by Bonamy Dobrée. World's
   Classics. No. 276. London and New York: Oxford University
   Press, xxviii + 441 pp.
        Reprint of 1925.A1.

2 _____. "A Soldier, and a Sailor." Song from Act III of Love
   for Love. In From Beowulf to Thomas Hardy. New edition with
   period introductions by Robert Shafer. New York: Odyssey
   press, p. 801.

3 _____. The Way of the World. In British Dramatists from Dryden
   to Sheridan. Edited by George H. Nettleton. Boston:
   Houghton Mifflin; London: George G. Harrap, pp. 151-54,
   [309]-[347].
        Congreve himself achieved that poise which was the goal of
   the Restoration gentleman. Revised edition 1969.A5.

4 _____. The Way of the World. In English Literature and its
   backgrounds. Vol. 1. Edited by Bernard D. N. Grebanier and
   Stith Thompson. New York: Cordon, pp. 578-615.
        The play may "justly be called not only Congreve's finest
   play, but the finest English comedy of manners as well."
   Revised edition 1949.A6.

5 _____. The Way of the World. In A Treasury of the Theatre: An
   Anthology of Great Plays from Aeschylus to Eugene O'Neill.
   Edited by Burns Mantle and John Gassner. New York: Simon
   and Schuster, pp. 1015-66.
        Reprint of 1935.A2.

B SHORTER WRITINGS

1 HODGES, JOHN C. "Fresh Manuscript Sources for a Life of William
   Congreve." Publications of the Modern Language Association,
   54, no. 2 (June), pp. 432-38.
        Newly discovered manuscripts shed further light on the life
   of Congreve. See 1941.A2.

2 ISAACS, J. "Congreve's Library." Library, 4th ser., 20, no. 1
   (June), pp. 41-42.
        List includes thirteen volumes bearing Congreve's signature
   (eleven of which were located in the library of the Duke of
   Leeds) and eight books containing Congreve's name in the lists
   of subscribers.

1939

3 JAGGARD, WM. "'The Way of the World': Stage History." Notes
    and Queries, 177 (12 August), p. 122.
        Short account of the stage history of The Way of the World.

4 McKILLOP, ALAN D. "The Authorship of 'A Poem to the Memory of
    Mr. Congreve.'" Modern Language Notes, 54, no. 8 (December),
    p. 599.
        Although the "internal evidence is naturally inconclusive....
    David Mallet's authorship of the poem is twice certified by
    the bookseller." See 1729.B1; 1930.B3; 1973.B1.

5 WILLIAMS, EDWIN E. "Dr. James Drake and Restoration Theory of
    Comedy." Review of English Studies, 15, no. 58 (April),
    pp. 180-91.
        Explores Drake's "contribution to the theory of Restoration
    comedy" and concludes that his "principles may help to explain
    certain aspects of the works of Wycherley and Congreve."

                            1940

A BOOKS

1 CONGREVE, WILLIAM. [Four Songs]. In English Literature 1650-
    1800. Edited by John C. Mendenhall. Chicago: J. B.
    Lippincott, p. 279.

2 _____. Love for Love. Produced in New York, June 3 to 8, by
    the players under the direction of Robert Edmond Jones. With
    an introduction by Franklin P. Adams. New York: Charles
    Scribner's, [vii] + 88 pp.

3 _____. The Mourning Bride. London: H. Milford, Oxford Univer-
    sity Press [1940], 540 pp.
        Cited in Stratman, 1966.B29. The pagination suggests that
    this may refer to an edition (no source) of Dobrée's The
    Mourning Bride, Poems and Miscellanies, World's Classics,
    no. 277.

4 _____. The Way of the World. In Aeschylus to Hebbel. Vol. 2
    of A Treasury of the Theatre. Revised and adapted for col-
    leges by Philo M. Buck, Jr., John Gassner, [and] H. S.
    Alberson. New York: Simon and Schuster, pp. 1015-66.
        The Way of the World demonstrates Congreve's "adult view
    of men and women." Revised edition of 1935.A2.

                            96

5 ____. The Way of the World. In <u>English Literature 1650-1800</u>.
   Edited by John C. Mendenhall. Chicago: J. B. Lippincott,
   pp. 278-321.
      The play has but one flaw: "its wit is so universal...
   that it somewhat blurs distinction of character, and obscures
   the plot."

6 ____. The Way of the World. In <u>Types of English Drama</u>. Edited
   by John W. Ashton. New York: Macmillan, pp. 385-88, 389-469.
      Survey of the comedy of manners, praising Congreve for his
   style.

B SHORTER WRITINGS

1 BIGELOW, LESLIE PLATT. "The Style and the Wit of the Restoration
   Comedy of Manners." Diss., Ohio State University, 195 pp.,
   passim.
      Examines the briskness and beauty of the style and the
   rhetoric and tone of the wit in six Restoration comedies,
   including <u>The Old Bachelor</u>, <u>Love for Love</u>, and <u>The Way of
   the World</u>.

2 BROWN, JOHN MASON. "Congreve and Bobby Clark." In his <u>Broadway
   in Review</u>. New York: W. W. Norton, pp. 79-83.
      Comments upon the characters and wit of <u>Love for Love</u> and
   then reviews The Players Club's production of the play.

3 GASSNER, JOHN. "From Etherege to Sheridan." In his <u>Masters
   of the Drama</u>. New York: Dover Publications, pp. 304-14.
      Congreve did not have the "slightest interest in reforming
   what he saw." Devoid of "the spirit of meliorism" which seeks
   to convert that which it ridicules, he was content to be a
   "laughing recording angel." Reprinted 1945.B4.

*4 HORNE, MARK DANIEL. "The Villain in Restoration Tragedy."
   Diss., Louisiana State University and Agricultural and
   Mechanical College, 468 pp.
      Cited in <u>Comprehensive Dissertation Index 1861-1972</u>.
   Vol. 35. Ann Arbor: Xerox University Microfilms, 1973, p. 61.

5 HUGHES, LEO. "Attitudes of Some Restoration Dramatists Toward
   Farce." <u>Philological Quarterly</u>, 19, no. 3 (July), pp. 268-87.
      Includes the suggestion that the failure of <u>The Way of the
   World</u> was due to the "Soveraign Sway" of farce, song, and
   dance.

1940

6 PAINE, CLARENCE S. "The Comedy of Manners (1660-1700): A
   Reference Guide to the Comedy of the Restoration, Part II."
   <u>Bulletin of Bibliography</u>, 17, no. 3 (September-December),
   pp. 51-53.
      Cites eighteen items regarding the Collier-Congreve con-
   troversy. <u>See</u> 1941.B3.

<u>1941</u>

A BOOKS

1 CONGREVE, WILLIAM. <u>The Way of the World</u>. In <u>From the Beginnings</u>
   <u>to the Romantic Movement</u>. Vol. 1 of <u>The Literature of England</u>.
   Edited by George B. Woods, Homer A. Watt, and George K.
   Anderson. Chicago: Scott, Foresman, pp. 808-53.
      "Nowhere is there a better picture of the world-weary
   cynical, brittle types of Restoration comedy..." Revised
   edition 1947.A4.

2 HODGES, JOHN. <u>William Congreve the Man: A Biography from New</u>
   <u>Sources</u>. Modern Language Association General Series, no. 11.
   London: Oxford University Press; New York: Modern Language
   Association of America, xvii + 151 pp.
      An attempt "to make possible a more discerning and more
   sympathetic reading of Congreve by bringing from fresh sources
   new information about the boy and the man." Includes index to
   manuscript sources, map of Congreve's London, and genealogical
   tables.

B SHORTER WRITINGS

1 AVERY, EMMETT L. "The Popularity of <u>The Mourning Bride</u> in the
   London Theaters in the Eighteenth Century." <u>Research Studies</u>
   <u>of the State College of Washington</u>, 9, no. 2 (June),
   pp. 115-16.
      Although <u>The Mourning Bride</u> was performed 205 times between
   1702 and 1776, it did not hold the stage so consistently as
   did seven other non-Shakespearean tragedies. <u>See</u> 1951.A1.

2 LANN, EUGENE. ["Forgotten English Comedy"]. [<u>The Theatre</u>,
   <u>U.S.S.R.</u>], 2: 121-31.
      In Russian. Includes references to the reception given to
   Congreve's comedies, including <u>Love for Love</u> and <u>The Way of</u>
   <u>The World</u>.

1942

3 PAINE, CLARENCE S. "The Comedy of Manners (1660-1700): A
   Reference Guide to the Comedy of the Restoration, Part III."
   Bulletin of Bibliography, 17, no. 4 (January-April), pp. 70-72.
       Mentions eleven items, six on different editions of
   Congreve's works and five on biography and criticism. See
   1940.B6.

4 SPASSKY, Y. ["Tragedy in the Seventeenth and Eighteenth Centuries"]. [The Theatre, U.S.S.R.], 5: 89-105.
       In Russian. Cited in Stratman, 1971.B16.

                              1942

A BOOKS

1 CONGREVE, WILLIAM. The Way of the World. In College Survey of
   English Literature. Edited by B. J. Whiting, et al. Vol. 1.
   New York: Harcourt, Brace, pp. 739-73.
       Although the play has hardly its equal for "ease and wit
   and brilliance [and is] refreshingly free from the gross
   obscenities of much of Restoration comedy, [it] does not
   provide an object lesson in moral conduct..." Reprinted
   1946.A2; 1947.A3; 1955.A3.

B SHORTER WRITINGS

*1 ALLEMAN, GELLERT SPENCER. "English Law and the Materials of
    Restoration Comedy." Diss., University of Pennsylvania,
    416 pp.
        Cited in Comprehensive Dissertation Index 1861-1972.
    Vol. 33. Ann Arbor: Xerox University Microfilms, 1973,
    p. 65. See book, 1942.B2.

2 _____ . Matrimonial Law and the Materials of Restoration Comedy.
   Wallingford, Pa.: [n.p.], vii + 155 pp., passim.
       An "analysis of the manner in which Restoration comedy
   (1660-1714) uses materials from matrimonial law," showing
   the relationship between the plays and the life of the time.
   Incorporates all of Congreve's comedies. See Ph.D. dissertation, 1942.B1.

3 AVERY, EMMETT L. "The Première of The Mourning Bride." Modern
   Language Notes, 57, no. 1 (January), pp. 55-57.
       Argues that the first performance was probably given on
   Saturday, 20 February, 1696/7, a week earlier than the date
   cited by Taylor (1931.A4) and Hodges (1941.A2).

1942

4   M., M. "Congreve's Aristophanes." More Books, 17, no. 9
    (November), pp. 437-38.
        A note on Congreve's copy of Comédies Grecques
    d'Aristophanes (Paris, 1692).

5   STOLL, ELMER EDGAR. "Literature and Life." In his Shakespeare
    Studies: Historical and Comparative in Method. New York:
    G. E. Stechert, pp. 39-89, passim.
        Altered and enlarged version of 1924.B5; reprint of
    1927.B4.

                            1943

A BOOKS

1   CONGREVE, WILLIAM. "Three Songs from Love for Love." Music by
    Leslie Bridgewater, written for Gielgud's revival. London:
    Goodwin and Tabb.
        Cited in NUC (1970.B14), p. 594.

2   _____. Le Train du Monde. Préface et Traduction par Aurélien
    Digeon. Paris: Aubier, Éditions Montaigne, 309 + 3 pp.
        French and English texts, together with biographical and
    critical introductions in French.

B SHORTER WRITINGS

1   GIELGUD, JOHN. "Staging 'Love for Love.'" Theatre Arts Monthly,
    27, no. 11 (November), pp. 662-68.
        Discusses his "naturalistic" adaptation of the play. Two
    plates: scenes from Love for Love. See 1945.B3, B5;
    1947.B2; 1948.B1, B4.

2   HODGES, JOHN C. "The Composition of Congreve's First Play."
    Publications of the Modern Language Association, 58, no. 4,
    pt. 1 (December), pp. 971-76.
        Congreve wrote a first draft of The Old Bachelor at
    "Stratton in the spring of 1689 and was still revising the
    play at Ilam as late as August, 1692." See 1936.B4; 1946.B2.

3   HOUGHTON, WALTER E., JR. "Lamb's Criticism of Restoration
    Comedy." English Literary History, 10, no. 1 (March),
    pp. 61-72.
        Defends Lamb's view (1823.B1). Especially refers to the
    influence of Bannister's performance of Ben in Love for Love
    upon Lamb's criticism.

*4 MIGNON, ELISABETH LOUISE. "Old Men and Women in the Restoration
      Comedy of Manners." Diss., Bryn Mawr.
        Cited in Comprehensive Dissertation Index 1861–1972.
      Vol. 36. Ann Arbor: Xerox University Microfilms, 1973,
      p. 58. See book, 1947.B4.

5 POTTER, ELMER B. "The Paradox of Congreve's Mourning Bride."
      Publications of the Modern Language Association, 58, no. 4,
      pt. 1 (December), pp. 977–1001.
        Traces the stage and literary history of the play, explain-
      ing that a paradox arises from the play's theatrical success
      and its critical failure.

6 STOLL, ELMER EDGAR. "The 'Real Society' in Restoration Comedy:
      Hymeneal Pretenses." Modern Language Notes, 58, no. 3
      (March), pp. 175–81.
        Argues that Restoration comedy reflects the taste rather
      than the life of the time, pointing to the dramatists' use of
      trick marriages. Includes references to two masked and one
      deceptive marriage in Congreve's plays. See 1924.B5; 1928.B4,
      B6, B7, B9; 1934.B3.

1944

A BOOKS

1 CONGREVE, WILLIAM. Comedies. Edited by Bonamy Dobrée. World's
      Classics. No. 276. London and New York: Oxford University
      Press, xxviii + 441 pp.
        Reprint of 1925.A1.

B SHORTER WRITINGS

*1 BHUSHAN, V. N. The Hawk Over Heron. Notes on Comedy and the
      Comedy Form with Two Special Chapters on Congreve's Way of
      the World and Barrie's Admirable Crichton. Bombay: Padma
      Publications, 155 pp.
        "Congreve's Way of the World is analyzed according to plot,
      character, theme, and language." Cited in Stratman, 1971.B16.

2 PELTZ, CATHERINE WALSH. "The Neo-classic lyric, 1660–1725."
      Journal of English Literary History, 11, no. 2 (June),
      pp. 92–116.
        "In the verses of Rochester, Congreve, Prior, the neo-
      classic lyric reaches its fullest development..." Refers to
      several of Congreve's lyrics.

1945

A BOOKS

1 CONGREVE, WILLIAM. The Way of the World. In English Comedies.
   Edited with an introduction by John Gassner. Eau Claire,
   Wisc.: E. M. Hale, pp. vii–xix, [79]–153.
   Introduction includes excerpts from Thackeray's essay
   (1853.B2).

2 ____. The Way of the World. In Understanding Drama. Edited
   by Cleanth Brooks and Robert B. Heilman. New York: Henry
   Holt, pp. 389–452.
   Discusses the complexity of plot, the system of values,
   the variations on the theme of love, the use of irony, and
   the relationship of the intrigue plot to the comedy as a
   whole. Also includes questions regarding the play.
   Reprinted 1947.A5.

3 ____. The Way of the World. In Understanding Drama: Eight
   Plays. Edited by Cleanth Brooks and Robert B. Heilman.
   New York: Henry Holt, pp. 389–452.
   See 1945.A2.

B SHORTER WRITINGS

1 AGATE, JAMES. "'The Way of the World' by William Congreve.
   Lyric Theatre, Hammersmith." In Specimens of English Dramatic
   Criticism, XVIII–XX Centuries. Edited by A. C. Ward. World's
   Classics. London: Oxford University Press, pp. 302–306.
   Reprint of 1925.B1.

2 AVERY, EMMETT L. "A Tentative Calendar of Daily Theatrical
   Performances, 1660–1700." Research Studies of the State
   College of Washington, 13, no. 4 (December), pp. 225–83.
   Includes performances of Congreve's plays during this
   period.

3 DUKES, ASHLEY. "Repertory at Last! The English Scene."
   Theatre Arts, 29, no. 1 (January), pp. 22–31.
   Includes a reference to Gielgud's production of Love for
   Love. See 1943.B1; 1945.B5; 1947.B2; 1948.B1, B4.

4 GASSNER, JOHN. "From Etherege to Sheridan." In his Masters of
   the Drama. New York: Dover Publications, pp. 304–14.
   Reprint of 1940.B3.

5 GIELGUD, JOHN. "The Haymarket and the New: London Flocks to
      Repertory." <u>Theatre Arts</u>, 29, no. 3 (March), pp. 166–71.
      Describes his production of <u>Love for Love</u>. <u>See</u> 1943.B1;
      1945.B3; 1947.B2; 1948.B1, B4.

6 SYMONS, JULIAN. "Restoration Comedy (Reconsiderations II)."
      <u>Kenyon Review</u>, 7, no. 2 (Spring), pp. 185–97.
      Examines the moral ideas in Restoration comedy. If
      "Congreve's manner is gentle, his intention is still moral
      and satiric." Refers to <u>Love for Love</u> and <u>The Way of the</u>
      <u>World</u>.

1946

A BOOKS

1 CONGREVE, WILLIAM. "Character of Dryden." In <u>Dryden: Poetry</u>
      <u>and Prose</u>. Introduction and notes by David Nichol Smith.
      Oxford: Clarendon Press, pp. 1–3.
      Reprint of 1925.A3.

2 _____. <u>The Way of the World</u>. In <u>College Survey of English</u>
      <u>Literature</u>. Edited by B. J. Whiting, et al. Vol. 1. New
      York: Harcourt Brace, pp. 739–73.
      Reprint of 1942.A1.

3 _____. <u>The Way of the World</u>. In <u>The Pleasure of their Company.</u>
      <u>An Anthology of Civilized Writing</u>. Edited with an introduc-
      tion by Louis Kronenberger. New York: Alfred A. Knopf,
      pp. 161–233.

B SHORTER WRITINGS

1 DOBRÉE, BONAMY. "Congreve." In his <u>Restoration Comedy: 1660–</u>
      <u>1720</u>. London: Oxford University Press, pp. [121]–150.
      Reprint of 1924.B1.

2 HOWARTH, R. G. "Congreve's First Play: Addendum." <u>Publications</u>
      <u>of the Modern Language Association</u>, 61, no. 2 (June),
      pp. 596–97.
      Discusses the dates of the composition of <u>The Old Bachelor</u>
      and Congreve's departure from Trinity College, Dublin. <u>See</u>
      1936.B4; 1943.B2.

3 KNIGHTS, L. C. "Restoration Comedy: The Reality and the Myth."
      In his <u>Explorations: Essays in Criticism Mainly on the</u>

1946

Literature of the Seventeenth Century. London: Chatto and Windus, pp. 131-49.
Reprint of 1937.B2.

4 SEYLER, ATHENE, and STEPHEN HAGGARD. The Craft of Comedy.
New York: Theatre Arts, pp. 80-95.
Contains an analysis of Love for Love (I.ii.) from the point of view of the players.

*5 SMITH, JOHN H[ARRINGTON]. "Heroes and Heroines in English Comedy, 1660-1750." Diss., Harvard University, 250 pp.
Cited in Comprehensive Dissertation Index 1861-1972.
Vol. 37. Ann Arbor: Xerox University Microfilms, 1973, p. 191. See book, 1948.B6.

6 SMITH, JOHN HARRINGTON. "Thomas Corneille to Betterton to Congreve." Journal of English and Germanic Philology, 45, no. 2 (April), pp. 209-13.
The plot of The Way of the World is a new combination of elements found in two earlier plays, the first of which is Corneille's Le Baron d'Albrikac (1667), influences of which are to be found in the second, Betterton's The Amorous Widow; or, the Wanton Wife (ca. 1670). See 1938.B3; 1959.B8.

1947

A BOOKS

1 CONGREVE, WILLIAM. [Complete Plays]. In William Congreve.
Edited by Alex. Charles Ewald. Mermaid Series. London: E. Benn, xli + 486 pp.
Reprint of 1887.A1.

2 _____. "An Essay Concerning Humour." In An Essay Towards Fixing the True Standards of Wit, Humour, Raillery, Satire and Ridicule, by Corbyn Morris. Ann Arbor: Augustan Reprint Society.
Reprint of 1744.A2.

3 _____. The Way of the World. In The College Survey of English Literature. Edited by B. J. Whiting, et al. Vol. 1.
New York: Harcourt, Brace, 1947-48, pp. 739-73.
Reprint of 1942.A1.

4 _____. The Way of the World. In From the Beginnings to the Romantic Movement. Vol. 1 of The Literature of England.

Edited by George B. Woods, Homer A. Watt, and George K. Anderson. Chicago: Scott, Foresman, pp. 831–76.
Revised edition of 1941.A1.

5 _____. *The Way of the World*. In *Understanding Drama*. Edited by Cleanth Brooks and Robert B. Heilman. London: George G. Harrap, pp. 389–452.
Reprint of 1945.A2.

B SHORTER WRITINGS

1 CLANCY, JAMES HARVEY. "The Humourists: An Elizabethan Method of Characterization as Modified by Etherege and Congreve." Diss., Stanford University, pp. 91–249, passim.
Investigates the "influence of the concept of humours upon the comic characterization" of Etherege and Congreve. Includes references to all of Congreve's comedies.

2 DENT, ALAN. "John Gielgud: Actor." *Theatre Arts*, 31, no. 2 (February), pp. 27–29.
Praises Gielgud's interpretation of Valentine. Cover plate: Gielgud as Valentine. See 1943.B1; 1945.B3, B5; 1948.B1, B4.

3 KNIGHTS, L. C. "Restoration Comedy: The Reality and the Myth." In his *Explorations: Essays in Criticism Mainly on the Literature of the Seventeenth Century*. New York: George W. Stewart, pp. 149–68.
Reprint of 1937.B2.

4 MIGNON, ELISABETH. "Congreve." In her *Crabbed Age and Youth: the Old Men and Women in the Restoration Comedy of Manners*. Durham, N.C.: Duke University Press, pp. 94–131.
Congreve's comedies affirm that distinctions in his treatment of age and youth "are to be linked rather with his deeper and more balanced insight into character than with a real shift in attitude." See Ph.D. dissertation, 1943.B4.

5 SNUGGS, HENRY L. "The Comic Humours: A New Interpretation." *Publications of the Modern Language Association*, 42, no. 1, pt. 1 (March), pp. 114–22.
Traces the definition of humor in seventeenth-century drama and includes a discussion of Congreve's letter to John Dennis, "Concerning Humour in Comedy." Congreve "makes a clear-cut distinction between genuine humour and the comic humour of satirical drama..." Refers to *The Double Dealer*, *Love for Love*, and *The Way of the World*.

1947

6   WOOLF, VIRGINIA. "Congreve's Comedies." In her <u>The Moment and</u>
        <u>Other Essays</u>. London: Hogarth Press, pp. 30-38.
            Reprint of 1937.B6.

                                1948

A BOOKS

1   CONGREVE, WILLIAM. [Complete Plays]. In <u>William Congreve</u>.
        Edited by Alex. Charles Ewald. Mermaid Series. London:
        Ernest Benn, xli + 486 pp.
            Reprint of 1887.A1.

2   _____. <u>The Comedies</u>. Edited with an introduction by Norman
        Marshall. Chiltern Library. No. 17. London: John Lehmann,
        416 pp.
            The comedies demonstrate "exquisite perfection of...
        language, the richness of...characterisation, the sparkle
        of...wit, and...sheer exhilaration..." Also contains Hazlitt's
        "Lectures on the English Comic Writers" (1819.B1), Johnson's
        <u>Life</u> (1779.B1), Southerne's dedication to <u>The Old Bachelor</u>,
        and Congreve's "Concerning Humour in Comedy."

3   _____. <u>The Way of the World</u>. In <u>Understanding Drama: Twelve</u>
        <u>Plays</u>. Edited by Cleanth Brooks and Robert B. Heilman. New
        York: Henry Holt, pp. 389-452.
            Enlarged edition of 1945.A2; reprinted 1955.A5; 1958.A4;
        1960.A5; 1966.A9.

B SHORTER WRITINGS

1   BROWN, JOHN MASON. "Utopia of Gallantry." In his <u>Seeing More</u>
        <u>Things</u>. New York: McGraw-Hill, pp. 221-27.
            Reviews Gielgud's production of <u>Love for Love</u>, concluding
        that the disconcerting truth about the play is that it "seems
        as much of a bore as a delight." <u>See</u> 1943.B1; 1945.B3, B5;
        1947.B2; 1948.B4.

2   CHILD, HAROLD. "William Congreve." In <u>Essays and Reflections</u>.
        Edited with a memoir by S. C. Roberts. Cambridge: University
        Press, pp. 105-14.
            Congreve "saw strange beauties deep hidden under human
        affectations," but he had to "pull his hat over his brows and
        keep his vision and his thoughts to himself."

3 MERRIN, JAMES. "Theory of Comedy in the Restoration." Diss.,
   Chicago University, 172 pp., passim.
       Restoration criticism deals "much more specifically with
   problems of character portrayal, with kinds of characters,
   and with plot and incident than does subsequent criticism."
   Congreve's "contribution to comic theory is particularly
   interesting because of his undoubted superiority as a comic
   dramatist."

4 NATHAN, GEORGE JEAN. "Love for Love. May 26, 1947." In his
   The Theatre Book of the Year 1947-1948: A Record and an
   Interpretation. New York: Alfred A. Knopf, pp. 13-17.
       In reviewing Gielgud's production of Love for Love,
   Nathan believes the play, despite its emphasis on plot, to
   be a notable contribution to the "gallery of humorous char-
   acter." See 1943.B1; 1945.B3, B5; 1947.B2; 1948.B1.

5 SHERBURN, GEORGE. "Restoration Drama: II. Comedy." In The
   Restoration and Eighteenth Century (1660-1789). Book 3 of
   A Literary History of England. Edited by Albert C. Baugh.
   New York: Appleton-Century-Crofts, pp. 762-79.
       General and critical survey of Congreve's comedies.
   Revised edition by Donald Bond, 1967.B10.

6 SMITH, JOHN HARRINGTON. The Gay Couple in Restoration Comedy.
   Cambridge, Mass.: Harvard University Press, xi + 252 pp.,
   passim.
       Traces the rise, prosperity, and decline of the gay couple.
   Includes references to all of Congreve's comedies. See Ph.D.
   dissertation, 1946.B5.

7 _____. "Shadwell, the Ladies, and the Change in Comedy." Modern
   Philology, 46, no. 1 (August), pp. 22-23.
       Focuses upon the 1670s and 1680s. Shows that despite the
   endeavors of Southerne, Congreve, and Vanbrugh in the 1690s
   and the gallants in the audience, the "influence of the exemplary dramatists and the ladies progressively triumphs."
   Reprinted 1966.B28.

8 WOOLF, VIRGINIA. "Congreve's Comedies." In her The Moment and
   Other Essays. New York: Harcourt, Brace, pp. 31-42.
       Reprint of 1937.B6.

<u>1949</u>

A BOOKS

1 CONGREVE, WILLIAM. [Complete Plays]. In <u>William Congreve</u>.
   Edited by Alex. Charles Ewald. Mermaid Series. New York:
   A. A. Wyn, xli + 486 pp.
   Reprint of 1887.A1.

2 _____. <u>Comedies</u>. Edited by Bonamy Dobrée. World's Classics.
   No. 276. London and New York: Oxford University Press,
   xxviii + 441 pp.
   Reprint of 1925.A1.

3 _____. <u>Love for Love</u>. In <u>A Book of Dramas</u>. Edited and with an
   introduction by Bruce Carpenter. New York: Prentice-Hall,
   pp. xvii–xviii, 323–99.
   New edition of 1929.A5.

4 _____. <u>The Way of the World</u>. Edited with an introduction and
   explanatory notes by W. P. Barrett. Temple Dramatists.
   London: J. M. Dent, xii + 145 pp.
   Reprint of 1894.A1.

5 _____. <u>The Way of the World</u>. Edited by Robert Wieder. Rainbow
   Library. No. 20. Paris: Didier, 103 + 35 pp.
   Text in English; introduction, notes, and exercises in
   French. "<u>Le Train du Monde</u> est une fantaisie agréable...où
   l'intelligence et les défauts d'une époque s'expriment
   quasiment sans détours, avec leur brillant, leur faiblesses,
   leur charme à la fois décevant et irrésistible."

6 _____. <u>The Way of the World</u>. In <u>English Literature and Its</u>
   <u>Backgrounds</u>. Edited by Bernard D. N. Grebanier, et al.
   Vol. 1. New York: Dryden Press, pp. 726–60.
   Revised edition of 1939.A4.

B SHORTER WRITINGS

1 BOWERS, FREDSON. "The Cancel Leaf in Congreve's 'Double Dealer,'
   1694." <u>Papers of the Bibliographical Society of America</u>, 43
   (First Quarter), pp. 78–82.
   Explains the causes for the different states of the can-
   cellans leaf in the first edition of <u>The Double Dealer</u>.

2 HODGES, JOHN C. "Congreve's Letters." <u>The Times Literary</u>
   <u>Supplement</u> (9 April), p. 233.

Requests information about letters and documents in preparation for his edition of Congreve's correspondence
(1964.A3).

3 _____. "Congreve's Library." The Times Literary Supplement
(12 August), p. 521.
Seeks information in preparation for his work on Congreve's
library (1955.A7). See 1949.B4.

4 ISAACS, JOHN. "Congreve's Library." The Times Literary
Supplement (2 September), p. 569.
Reply to Hodges' letter (1949.B3), mentioning further
possible means by which books owned by Congreve may be traced.

5 KRUTCH, JOSEPH WOOD. Comedy and Conscience after the Restoration.
New York: Columbia University Press, xi + 300 pp., passim.
Reprint of 1924.B3 with two additions: index and bibliog-
raphy of relevant modern discussions prepared by G. S.
Alleman.

*6 MAGILL, LEWIS MALCOLM, JR. "Elements of Sentimentalism in
English Tragedy, 1680-1704." Diss., University of Illinois
at Urbana-Champaign, 278 pp.
Examines representative tragedies "to discover...elements
of sentimentalism which, when full-grown, give us the sentimental, middle-class tragedy of the eighteenth century."
Cited in Dissertation Abstracts, 10, no. 1, 1950, p. 89.

7 MUIR, KENNETH. "Leeds University and the Yorkshire Tradition:
II. William Congreve, Local Worthy." University of Leeds
Review, 1, no. 4 (1 December), pp. 274-82.
Through an analysis of The Way of the World, defends
Congreve against Knights's attack (1937.B2).

1950

A BOOKS

1 CONGREVE, WILLIAM. Love for Love. In The Development of English
Drama: An Anthology. Edited by Gerald Eades Bentley. New
York: Appleton-Century-Crofts, pp. 462-510.
Congreve masterfully fuses "his dual interests in dialogue
and character."

2 _____. The Way of the World. In The Book of the Play: An
Introduction to Drama. [Compiled by] Harold R. Walley. New
York: Charles Scribner's, pp. 257-61, [263]-308.

1950

> The question posed by the play is not "how virtuous or how rational the several characters are because of their code, but how felicitously they exemplify the principles which they profess."

3 _____. The Way of the World. In The Development of English Drama: An Anthology. Edited by Gerald Eades Bentley. New York: Appleton-Century-Crofts, pp. 511-54.
    "The ideas and the emotional effects are negligible[;] the polish of the dialogue and the exquisite calculation of the pose of the mannered characters" are Congreve's primary concerns.

4 _____. The Way of the World. In Four English Comedies of the 17th and 18th Centuries. Edited by J. M. Morrell. Baltimore: Penguin Books, pp. [131]-231.
    Reprinted 1951.A9; 1954.A1; 1959.A3; 1960.A3; 1962.A3; 1964.A5; 1965.A3; 1967.A6; 1969.A6; 1970.A5; 1971.A4; 1972.A5; 1974.A2; 1975.A1; 1976.A4; 1977.A2.

5 _____. The Way of the World. In Nine Great Plays from Aeschylus to Eliot. Edited by Leonard F. Dean. New York: Harcourt, Brace, pp. 274-354.
    The play reflects and criticizes the fashionable society of the Restoration, but the overtones of the bargaining scene make the play "perennially significant." Revised edition 1956.A2.

B SHORTER WRITINGS

1 DOBRÉE, BONAMY. "The Mourning Bride and Cato." In his Restoration Tragedy: 1660-1720. Oxford: Clarendon Press, pp. 167-78.
    Corrected edition of 1929.B5.

*2 FREEHAFER, JOHN H. "The Emergence of Sentimental Comedy, 1660-1707." Diss., University of Pennsylvania, 199 pp.
    Cited in Doctoral Dissertations Accepted by American Universities, 1949-1950, no. 17. New York: H. W. Wilson, 1950, p. 201.

3 FUJIMURA, THOMAS H. "The Comedy of Wit, 1660-1710." Diss., Columbia University, 314 pp.
    Restoration comedy is "witty, naturalist, and hedonic." Congreve is not a "cynical stylist, as conceived by the 'manners' school; for he expresses a sensible view of life, witty, common-sensical, and sober." See book, 1952.B1.

1951

4 GAGEN, JEAN ELIZABETH. "Foreshadowing of the New Woman in
   English Drama of the Seventeenth and Early Eighteenth
   Century." Diss., Columbia University, 311 pp.
       "The modern woman--or 'the new woman' who has achieved
   social, intellectual and spiritual equality with men--is
   frequently foreshadowed in English drama of the seventeenth
   and early eighteenth century." Includes references to
   Congreve's comedies. See book, 1954.B3.

5 ROBSON, W. W. "Hopkins and Congreve." The Times Literary
   Supplement (24 February), p. 121.
       Points out the similarity between the phrase "blue-bleak
   embers" in Hopkins's "The Windhover" and a reference in The
   Way of the World (V.i.).

                              1951

A BOOKS

1 AVERY, EMMETT L. Congreve's Plays on the Eighteenth-Century
   Stage. Modern Language Association of America Monograph
   Series, no. 18. New York: Modern Language Association of
   America, xi + 226 pp.
       Details the stage history of Congreve's plays and relates
   them to other eighteenth-century productions of late
   seventeenth-century comedies. See 1941.B1; also 1966.B10;
   1970.B17; 1972.B21; 1974.B14.

2 CONGREVE, WILLIAM. Comedies. Edited by Bonamy Dobrée. World's
   Classics. No. 276. London and New York: Oxford University
   Press, xxviii + 441 pp.
       Reprint of 1925.A1.

3 _____. "Character of Dryden." In Dryden: Poetry and Prose.
   Introduction and notes by David Nichol Smith. Oxford:
   Clarendon Press, pp. 1-3.
       Reprint of 1925.A3.

4 _____. Incognita. Introduction by Alan Pryce-Jones, engravings
   by Van Rossem. London: Folio Society, 71 pp.
       Although Incognita is and was meant to be nothing more than
   an amusing tale, in it is to be found a "confidential tone of
   voice allied to an exquisite precision of language."

5 _____. The Way of the World. Edited with an introduction and
   explanatory notes by W. P. Barrett. Temple Dramatists.
   London: J. M. Dent, xii + 145 pp.
       Reprint of 1894.A1.

                              111

1951

6   . The Way of the World. Edited by Henry Ten Eyck Perry.
    Crofts Classics. No. 551. New York: Appleton-Century-Crofts,
    pp. xviii + 105 pp.
        Explains the amatory and financial action of the play and
    discusses the language. "Congreve's greatest gift was his
    ability to find words in which different types of human
    beings could express their true natures amid the intricacies
    of civilized social intercourse."

7   . "Millamant and Mirabell" [from The Way of the World].
    In And So To The Playhouse. By Lynette Feasey. London:
    George G. Harrap, pp. 129-92.
        An abridged version of the play, with notes for its
    production.

8   . The Way of the World. In From Aeschylus to Turgenev.
    Vol. 1 of A Treasury of the Theatre. Revised edition for
    colleges, edited by John Gassner. New York: Simon and
    Schuster, pp. 430-62.
        Revised edition of 1935.A2. See 1940.A4.

9   . The Way of the World. In Four English Comedies of the
    17th and 18th Centuries. Edited by J. M. Morrell. Baltimore:
    Penguin Books, pp. [131]-231.
        Reprint of 1950.A4.

10   . The Way of the World. In From Beowulf to Sheridan.
    Vol. 1 of British Literature. Edited by Hazelton Spencer.
    Boston: D. C. Heath, pp. 631-71.
        The play is "a great comedy almost exclusively because its
    style is almost inhumanly brilliant."

11 LYNCH, KATHLEEN M. A Congreve Gallery. Cambridge, Mass.:
    Harvard University Press, xvi + 196 pp.
        Contemporary records used to "throw light from various
    angles on the personality, background, and times of William
    Congreve." Emphasis on the friends of Congreve's youth.
    Reprinted 1967.A9.

B SHORTER WRITINGS

1 BATESON, F. W. "Contributions to a Dictionary of Critical
    Terms: I. Comedy of Manners." Essays in Criticism, 1,
    no. 1 (January), pp. 89-93.
        Cites Congreve's view on comedy to define the eighteenth-
    century term genteel comedy.

2 DOBRÉE, BONAMY. "Congreve." In his <u>Restoration Comedy: 1660–1720</u>. London: Oxford University Press, pp. [121]–150. Reprint of 1924.B1.

*3 FELTHAM, FREDERIK G. "The Quality of the Wit in Comedies of Etherege, Wycherley, Congreve, and Shadwell." Diss., University of Chicago, 242 pp.
Cited in <u>Doctoral Dissertations Accepted by American Universities 1950–1951</u>, no. 18. New York: H. W. Wilson Company, 1951, p. 223.

4 LEECH, CLIFFORD. "Restoration Comedy: The Earlier Phase." <u>Essays in Criticism</u>, 1, no. 2 (April), pp. 165–84.
Refers to <u>Love for Love</u> and <u>The Way of the World</u> to illustrate continued use of conventions of plot and characterization found in earlier Restoration comedy.

<u>1952</u>

A BOOKS--NONE

B SHORTER WRITINGS

1 FUJIMURA, THOMAS H. <u>The Restoration Comedy of Wit</u>. Princeton: Princeton University Press, ix + 232 pp., passim.
Restoration comedy is a "witty presentation of a naturalistic outlook on life..." Congreve's work is the "culmination of the comedy of wit, but it is also transitional in nature, and points the way to the age of enlightenment." Reprinted 1968.B5; <u>see</u> Ph.D. dissertation, 1950.B3; section on <u>The Way of the World</u> reprinted 1966.B12.

2 KOZIOL, HERBERT. "Alexander Popes Sylphen und William Congreves 'Incognita.'" <u>Anglia</u>, 70: 433–35.
Cites several instances of the use of attendant spirits in literature, noticeably in <u>The Rape of the Lock</u> and <u>Incognita</u>.

3 KRONENBERGER, LOUIS. "Congreve." In his <u>The Thread of Laughter; Chapters on English Stage Comedy from Jonson to Maugham</u>. New York: Hill and Wang, pp. 117–45.
Although tarnished with a certain "shallow cynicism, a certain merely fashionable sophistication," Congreve does not just "mirror Restoration manners; he embodies the civilized point of view."

1952

*4 McCULLEY, CECIL MICHAEL. "A Study of Dramatic Comedy." Diss.,
      Columbia University, 348 pp.
          Investigates the "dramatic appeal of comedy in its various
      forms, with definition of the general concepts involved and
      intensive analysis of representative examples." Cited in
      Dissertation Abstracts, 12, no. 5, 1952, p. 614.

1953

A BOOKS

1 CONGREVE, WILLIAM. Love for Love. In Cavalcade of Comedy: 21
      Brilliant Comedies from Jonson and Wycherley to Thurber and
      Coward. Edited with introductions by Louis Kronenberger.
      New York: Simon and Schuster, pp. 156-92.
          "As acquiescent art, Love for Love stands halfway between
      the public's taste and the author's talent.... But the play,
      as art, is the supreme comedy of the Restoration."

2 ____. The Way of the World. In Cavalcade of Comedy: 21
      Brilliant Comedies from Jonson and Wycherley to Thurber and
      Coward. Edited with introductions by Louis Kronenberger.
      New York: Simon and Schuster, pp. 193-225.
          The play is not only "too witty for real life; it is
      probably too witty for the stage."

3 ____. The Way of the World. In Restoration Plays. With an
      introduction by Brice Harris. Modern Library of the World's
      Best Books. No. 287. New York: Modern Library, pp. vii-
      xviii, 515-95.
          "The brilliance and the cruelty of the play are over-
      whelming. But few readers will deny
      that [it] is the ultimate in the Restoration comedy of
      manners." Reprinted 1955.A4; 1966.A8.

4 ____. The Way of the World. In Three Restoration Comedies.
      Edited with introduction by Norman Marshall. London: Pan
      Books, pp. [7-8], [9]-86.
          It is the language "above all else which enchants the
      reader. It is deliberately and exquisitely artificial,
      subtle, rhythmic, beautifully balanced."

5 NOLAN, PAUL T. "William Congreve: His Artistic Milieu."
      Diss., Tulane University, 345 pp.
          Relates the works of Congreve to his "artistic environment,
      his education, his reading, his literary associations, his
      literary problems."

B SHORTER WRITINGS

*1 GOODMAN, OSCAR BERNARD. "English New Comedy." Diss., Columbia
University, 284 pp.
  Restoration comedy seen as part of the continuing tradition
of Greek new comedy. Cited in Dissertation Abstracts, 14,
no. 1, 1954, p. 110.

2 LYNCH, KATHLEEN M. "References to Congreve in the Evelyn MSS."
Philological Quarterly, 32, no. 3 (July), pp. 337-40.
  Two letters from Henrietta, Lady Godolphin to Lady Evelyn
refer to Congreve's efforts in behalf of and concern for
Charles Evelyn, Lady Godolphin's young protégé. Another
from Lord Godolphin to Charles shows the former's generosity
and forbearance as well as his esteem toward Congreve, revealing as it does that Congreve was then living with Henrietta
in Hampstead.

*3 SINGH, S. "A Study of the Critical Theory of the Restoration
Drama as Expressed in Dedications, Prefaces, Prologues,
Epilogues, and Other Dramatic Criticism of the Period."
Diss., University of London.
  Cited in McNamee, 1968.B10.

4 WEISS, SAMUEL ABBA. "Hobbism and Restoration Comedy." Diss.,
Columbia University, 240 pp., passim.
  Abstracts and analyzes "the psychological, ethical, and
critical principles related to Hobbesian doctrine that appear
in Restoration comedy and [contrasts] them with the antithet-
ical principles underlying sentimental comedy." Includes
references to Congreve's comedies.

1954

A BOOKS

1 CONGREVE, WILLIAM. The Way of the World. In Four English
Comedies of the 17th and 18th Centuries. Edited by J. M.
Morrell. Baltimore: Penguin Books, pp. [131]-231.
  Reprint of 1950.A4.

B SHORTER WRITINGS

1 COOKE, ARTHUR L. "Two Parallels Between Dryden's Wild Gallant
and Congreve's Love for Love." Notes and Queries, NS 1
(January), pp. 27-28.

1954

Two episodes in <u>Love for Love</u> (Foresight's conviction that
he is afflicted with a strange illness and the trick marriage
between Tattle and Mrs. Frail) closely resemble two incidents
in Dryden's play.

2 DOBRÉE, BONAMY. "<u>The Mourning Bride</u> and <u>Cato</u>." In his <u>Restora-</u>
   <u>tion Tragedy: 1660–1720</u>. Oxford: Clarendon Press,
   pp. 167–78.
   Reprint of 1950.B1.

3 GAGEN, JEAN. <u>The New Woman: Her Emergence in English Drama</u>
   <u>1600–1730</u>. New York: Twayne Publishers, 193 pp., passim.
   Traces the changing status of and attitudes to women.
   Discusses Lady Froth, Belinda, and Millamant as "The Lady
   Writer," "The Cultivated Lady," and "Ladies in Command,"
   respectively. <u>See</u> Ph.D. dissertation, 1950.B4.

4 HODGES, JOHN C. "The Library of William Congreve." <u>Bulletin of</u>
   <u>the New York Public Library</u>, 63, nos. 8–12 (August–December),
   pp. 367–85, 436–54, 478–88, 535–50, and 579–91.
   Includes plate of first page of Congreve's "Bibliotheca,"
   introduction to and a list and description of 461 works owned
   by Congreve. <u>See</u> 1955.A7; 1955.B5.

*5 HOWLING, ROBERT T. "Moral Aspects of Restoration Comedy."
    Diss., Pennsylvania State University, 199 pp.
    "Restoration comedy...is not as immoral as it has been
    considered to be and does contain aspects of morality."
    Cited in <u>Abstracts of Doctoral Dissertations Submitted to the</u>
    <u>Pennsylvania State University</u>, 17, 1954, p. 479.

6 McDOWELL, MARGARET BLAINE. "Moral Purpose in Restoration Comedy."
   Diss., University of Iowa, 438 pp.
   Includes an analysis of <u>The Way of the World</u>, demonstrating
   that a "serious satirical scrutiny" underlies the basic design
   of the plot, characterization, and dialogue.

<u>1955</u>

A BOOKS

1 CONGREVE, WILLIAM. <u>Ainsi va le monde</u>. Adaptée par Dominique
   Aury et Auguste Desclos. Le Monde Illustré/Supplément Théatral
   et Littéraire, no. 183. Paris: France Illustration, 31 pp.

2 _____. "Character of Dryden." In Dryden: Poetry and Prose.
Introduction and notes by David Nichol Smith. Oxford:
Clarendon Press, pp. 1-3.
Reprint of 1925.A3.

3 _____. The Way of the World. In College Survey of English
Literature. Edited by B. J. Whiting, et al. Vol. 1.
New York: Harcourt, Brace, 1955-57, pp. 739-73.
Reprint of 1942.A1.

4 _____. The Way of the World. In Restoration Plays. With an
introduction by Brice Harris. Modern Library of the World's
Best Books. No. 287. New York: Modern Library,
pp. vii-xviii, 515-95.
Reprint of 1953.A3.

5 _____. The Way of the World. In Understanding Drama: Twelve
Plays. Edited by Cleanth Brooks and Robert B. Heilman.
New York: Henry Holt, pp. 389-452.
Reprint of 1948.A3; see 1945.A2.

*6 FUCHS, ELINOR C. "The Moral and Aesthetic Achievement of William
Congreve." Archives of the Comm. on Hist. and Lit., Harvard
University. (Unpub.)
Cited in Holland, 1959.B5.

7 HODGES, JOHN C. The Library of William Congreve. New York:
New York Public Library, 116 pp.
Includes 659 books to which Congreve subscribed. All
items printed with spelling, capitalization, and punctuation
as in Congreve's forty-four-page manuscript booklist. See
1954.B4; 1955.B5.

B SHORTER WRITINGS

1 BERKELEY, DAVID S. "The Art of Whining Love." Studies in
Philology, 52, no. 3 (July), pp. 478-96.
Describes the Restoration equivalent of medieval amour
courtois--"whining" love. Refers to Act IV of The Double
Dealer, where "whining" is given as a stage direction.

2 _____. "Préciosité and the Restoration Comedy of Manners."
Huntington Library Quarterly, 18, no. 2 (February),
pp. 109-28.
Examines patterns of courtship in terms of préciosité,
referring to all four of Congreve's comedies.

1955

3 DOBRÉE, BONAMY. "Congreve." In his <u>Restoration Comedy: 1660-</u>
   <u>1720</u>. London: Oxford University Press, Geoffrey Cumberlege,
   pp. [121]-150.
       Reprint of 1924.B1.

4 GRIFFIN, ALICE. "An Experiment in Style." <u>Theatre Arts</u>,
   39, no. 10 (October), p. 12.
       Briefly explains the stylistic concept of a production of
   <u>The Way of the World</u> at Bennington College.

5 HODGES, JOHN C. "The Library of William Congreve." <u>Bulletin of</u>
   <u>the New York Public Library</u>, 59, nos. 1 and 2 (January and
   February), pp. 16-34, 82-97.
       Continuation of list of books owned by Congreve (<u>see</u>
   1954.B4). Includes 198 additional titles and an index of
   authors, editors, translators, composers, and anonymous
   titles as well as an index of places named in imprints.
   <u>See</u> 1955.A7.

6 MUDRICK, MARVIN. "Restoration Comedy and Later." In <u>English</u>
   <u>Stage Comedy</u>. Edited with an introduction by W. K.
   Wimsatt, Jr. New York: Columbia University Press,
   pp. 98-125.
       Includes a discussion of <u>The Way of the World</u>, concluding
   that Congreve polished the cultivated appearance of triviality
   into "an ironic gloss not quite dazzling enough to conceal the
   moral turbulence beneath."

7 VAN DER WEELE, STEVEN JOHN. "The Critical Reputation of
   Restoration Comedy in Modern Times." Diss., University of
   Wisconsin, 771 pp.
       Includes an examination of recent opinion about five major
   writers of Restoration comedy, according to which Congreve
   emerges as the greatest artist.

1956

A BOOKS

1 CONGREVE, WILLIAM. [Complete Plays]. In <u>William Congreve</u>.
   Edited by Alexander Charles Ewald. [Mermaid Dramabook.
   No. 2]. New York: Hill and Wang, 438 pp.
       New edition of 1887.A1.

2 _____. <u>The Way of the World</u>. In <u>Nine Great Plays from Aeschylus</u>
   <u>to Eliot</u>. Edited by Leonard F. Dean. New York: Harcourt
   Brace, pp. [317]-397.
       Revised edition of 1950.A5.

B SHORTER WRITINGS

1 BROSSMAN, S. W. "Dryden's Cassandra and Congreve's Zara."
   Notes and Queries, NS 3 (March), pp. 102-03.
   Notes resemblances in characterization, situations, and
   language between Dryden's Cleomenes, the Spartan Heroe (1692)
   and Congreve's The Mourning Bride (1697).

*2 DALLDORFF, HORST. "Die Welt der Restaurationkomoedie: Ein
   Querschnitt durch die Lustspiele Hauptsaechlich von Etherege,
   Wycherley, und Congreve zur Erfassung ihrer Stottlichen
   Wessenszeuge." Diss., Kiel.
   Cited in McNamee, 1968.B10.

*3 HOLLAND, NORMAN NORWOOD, JR. "A Critical Reading of the Comedies
   of Etherege, Wycherley, and Congreve." Diss., Harvard
   University.
   Cited in Comprehensive Dissertation Index 1861-1972.
   Vol. 35. Ann Arbor: Xerox University Microfilms, 1973,
   p. 30. See book, 1959.B5.

*4 KORNBLUTH, MARTIN LEONARD. "Friendship in Fashion: The Dramatic
   Treatment of Friendship in the Restoration and Eighteenth Cen-
   tury." Diss., Pennsylvania State University, 234 pp.
   Contains a discussion of the comedy of manners in which
   "friendship is a means to some other end, usually lust."
   Cited in Dissertation Abstracts, 17, no. 2, 1957, p. 361.

5 McCARTHY, MARY. "What a Piece of Work is Man!" In her Sights
   and Spectacles: 1937-1956. New York: Farrar, Straus and
   Cudahy, pp. 116-20.
   Referring to Gielgud's Love for Love, states that the
   peculiar quality of the play is that it is not comedy in the
   classic sense--it is a parody not of man's work, but of God's.

6 WAIN, JOHN. "Restoration Comedy and its Modern Critics."
   Essays in Criticism, 6, no. 4 (October), pp. 367-85.
   Although praises the plays for passages of broad comedy,
   questions the technical and moral confusion of the comedies,
   including Love for Love and The Way of the World. Concludes
   that Restoration comedies are "good documents rather than good
   plays." Reprinted 1957.B10.

1957

A BOOKS

1 CONGREVE, WILLIAM. <u>Comedies</u>. Edited by Bonamy Dobrée. World's
     Classics. No. 276. London and New York: Oxford University
     Press, xxviii + 441 pp.
        Reprint of 1925.A1.

*2 VAN VORIS, W. H. "William Congreve as a Dramatist." Diss.,
     Trinity College, Dublin.
        Cited in McNamee, 1968.B10; <u>see</u> book, 1965.A6.

B SHORTER WRITINGS

1 BATESON, F. W. "Second Thoughts: II. L. C. Knights and
     Restoration Comedy." <u>Essays in Criticism</u>, 7, no. 1 (January),
     pp. 56–67.
        Uses <u>Love for Love</u>, among other plays, to defend Restora-
     tion comedy against the attacks made by Knights (1937.B2)
     and Wain (1956.B6). Reprinted 1966.B1; 1972.B2.

2 COLLINS, P. A. W. "Restoration Comedy." In <u>From Dryden to
     Johnson</u>. Vol. 4 of <u>The Pelican Guide to English Literature</u>.
     Edited by Boris Ford. Baltimore: Penguin Books, pp. 156–72.
        Survey includes consideration of Congreve, who is seen as
     an "amusing but superficial observer of a superficial and
     restricted society."

3 EMPSON, WILLIAM. "Restoration Comedy Again: I." <u>Essays in
     Criticism</u>, 7, no. 3 (July), p. 318.
        Defends Mirabell against the contention that he is an
     "unbearable cad."

*4 HAZARD, BENJAMIN MUNROE. "The Theory of Comedy in the Restora-
     tion and Early Eighteenth Century." Diss., Northwestern
     University, 195 pp.
        Explores the different attitudes toward the purposes and
     methods of comedy, the decline of wit, and the ascent of
     humours comedy. Cited in <u>Dissertation Abstracts</u>, 18, no. 2,
     1958, p. 581.

5 HOLLAND, NORMAN N. "Restoration Comedy Again: II." <u>Essays in
     Criticism</u>, 7, no. 3 (July), pp. 319–22.
        <u>Love for Love</u> and <u>The Way of the World</u> show that Restora-
     tion comedy is "about" not sex, but the conflict between
     natural desires and social conventions. <u>See</u> 1959.B5.

*6 MINOR, CHARLES BYRON. "An Analytical Study of Grammatical Uses
      and Tendencies in some Restoration Playwrights of Comedies
      with Comparison to Present-Day Usages and Tendencies."
      Diss., University of Denver.
           Cited in <u>Comprehensive Dissertation Index 1861-1972</u>.
      Vol. 30. Ann Arbor: Xerox University Microfilms, 1973,
      p. 386.

 7 NOLAN, PAUL T. "Congreve's Last Works: The Artist in Escape."
      <u>Southwestern Louisiana Journal</u>, 1, no. 4 (October), pp. 244-70.
           Congreve, in the final period after <u>The Way of the World</u>,
      tried to make the relationship between life and art as slight
      as possible, which explains what is lacking in his later work
      and why it is inferior.

 8 OHARA, DAVID M. "The Restoration Comic Perspective: A Study
      of the Comedy of Manners." Diss., University of Pennsylvania,
      237 pp., passim.
           "The Restoration comedy of manners exhibits an expansive
      satiric scope, an unemotional objectivity, diverse dramatic
      moods, which regulate characterization and action into a truly
      comic theatrical form." <u>The Way of the World</u> attains "high-
      comedy effect" with its "astute commentary and tolerant
      humanity."

 9 UNDERWOOD, DALE. <u>Etherege and the Seventeenth-Century Comedy
      of Manners</u>. Yale Studies in Eng., no. 135. New Haven:
      Yale University Press, pp. 54, 75.
           Notes that the entire course of action between Millamant
      and Mirabell is an extended proviso and that the Machiavellian
      aspects of Etherege's Dorimant are similar to those of
      Congreve's Maskwell and Fainall.

10 WAIN, JOHN. "Restoration Comedy and its Modern Critics." In
      his <u>Preliminary Essays</u>. London: Macmillan; New York:
      St. Martin's Press, pp. 1-35.
           Reprint of 1956.B6.

<u>1958</u>

A BOOKS

 1 CONGREVE, WILLIAM. <u>The Way of the World</u>. Edited by Vincent F.
      Hopper and Gerald B. Lahey, with a note on the staging by
      George L. Hersey. Illustrations by Fritz Kredel. Great Neck,
      N. Y.: Barron's Educational Series, 195 pp.
           The principal theme deals with the "way in which the world
      behaves about money and love..."

1958

2 _____. The Way of the World. In La Commedia della Restaurazione.
Edited by Elio Chinol. Collono di Litterature Moderne III.
Napoli: Edizioni Scientifiche Italiane, pp. 46-64, [401]-534.
Text in English; introduction and footnotes in Italian.

3 _____. The Way of the World. In Four Great Comedies of the
Restoration and 18th Century. With an introduction by Brooks
Atkinson. New York: Bantam Books, pp. viii-ix, [89]-[165].
A "literary delight," The Way of the World is "artificial
rather than realistic comedy..." Reprinted 1959.A4; 1961.A3;
1962.A4; 1963.A4; 1966.A7; 1971.A5.

4 _____. The Way of the World. In Understanding Drama: Twelve
Plays. Edited by Cleanth Brooks and Robert B. Heilman.
New York: Henry Holt, pp. 389-452.
Reprint of 1948.A3; see 1945.A2.

5 MUESCHKE, PAUL and MIRIAM. A New View of Congreve's Way of the
World. Univ. of Michigan Contributions in Mod. Philol.,
no. 23. Ann Arbor: University of Michigan Press, 85 pp.
Detailed study of Congreve's last play to determine why
it "has survived, and deserves to survive, as the masterpiece
of Restoration comedy," and to show that Congreve's insight,
artistry, ingenuity, and wit establish the "eminence of The
Way of the World in the satiric tradition of Horace and Ben
Jonson."

B SHORTER WRITINGS

1 BERNBAUM, ERNEST. The Drama of Sensibility: A Sketch of the
History of English Sentimental Comedy and Domestic Tragedy
1696-1780. Gloucester, Mass.: Peter Smith, ix + 288 pp.,
passim.
Reprint of 1915.B1.

2 BROWN, T. J. "English Literary Autographs XXI: William
Congreve, 1670-1729." Book Collector, 6, no. 1 (Spring),
p. 61.
Copy of Congreve's New Year's letter to Edward Porter, a
likely date for it being 1 January, 1709.

3 CORDER, JIMMIE WAYNE. "The Restoration Way of the World: A
Study of Restoration Comedy." Diss., University of Oklahoma,
359 pp., passim.
Contains a study of Congreve's comedies, suggesting that
"the comic effect is the arousal of laughter by ridicule and
enlightenment by the spectacle of order being imposed upon
disorder."

4 DOBRÉE, BONAMY. "Congreve." In his <u>Restoration Comedy: 1660–</u>
   <u>1720</u>. London: Oxford University Press, pp. [121]–150.
   Reprint of 1924.B1.

5 EBBS, JOHN DALE. "The Principle of Poetic Justice Illustrated
   in Restoration Tragedy." Diss., University of North Carolina,
   218 pp.
      An examination of fourteen "representative" Restoration
   tragedies, including <u>The Mourning Bride</u>, demonstrates that
   they depict the principles of poetic justice. <u>See</u> book,
   1973.B5.

6 TURNER, DARWIN T. "The Servant in the Comedies of William
   Congreve." <u>College Language Association Journal</u>, 1, no. 2
   (March), pp. 68–74.
      The servants in the comedies do not remain a single type.
   They are "diversified, both in their personalities and in
   their roles."

7 VAN VORIS, WILLIAM. "Congreve's Gilded Carousel." <u>Educational</u>
   <u>Theatre Journal</u>, 10, no. 3 (October), pp. 211–17.
      The dramatic device in <u>The Way of the World</u> enables us to
   see Congreve's "posturing characters from several points of
   view as they circle before us," and the play becomes not a
   trivial symbol for an idle, aristocratic world but a reflec-
   tion of the "best ethical and political thought of the violent
   and fascinating" Whig aristocracy.

8 WILSON, JOHN HAROLD. <u>All the King's Ladies: Actresses of the</u>
   <u>Restoration</u>. Chicago: University of Chicago Press, pp. 21,
   93–96, 127.
      Refers to Congreve's relationship with Anne Bracegirdle.

1959

A BOOKS

1 CONGREVE, WILLIAM. <u>Comedies</u>. Edited with introduction and notes
   by Bonamy Dobrée. World's Classics. No. 276. London:
   Oxford University Press, xxviii + 441 pp.
   Reprint of 1925.A1.

2 _____. <u>The Way of the World</u>. With illustrations by T. M.
   Cleland and an introduction by Louis Kronenberger. New York:
   Heritage Press, xxiii + 108 pp.
      Congreve's fine perception makes <u>The Way of the World</u>
   superior to the "run of Restoration comedy," and his wit,

1959

tone, and prose make the play "supreme." Congreve "embodies the civilized point of view."

3 ____. *The Way of the World*. In Four English Comedies of the 17th and 18th Centuries. Edited by J. M. Morrell. Baltimore: Penguin Books, pp. [131]-231.
   Reprint of 1950.A4.

4 ____. *The Way of the World*. In Four Great Comedies of the Restoration and 18th Century. With an introduction by Brooks Atkinson. New York: Bantam Books, pp. viii-ix, [89]-[165].
   Reprint of 1958.A3.

5 ____. *The Way of the World*. In Plays of the Restoration and Eighteenth Century. Edited by Dougald Macmillan and Howard Mumford Jones. New York: Holt, Rinehart and Winston, pp. 400-44.
   Reprint of 1938.A3; see 1931.A3.

6 ____. *The Way of the World*. In Six Restoration Plays. Edited by John Harold Wilson. Riverside Editions. Boston: Houghton Mifflin Company, pp. 319-90.
   "Congreve's intellectual brilliance is never divorced from compassion."

B SHORTER WRITINGS

1 BERKELEY, DAVID S. The "Précieuse," or Distressed Heroine in Restoration Comedy. Oklahoma State Univ. Pub., 56, no. 19. Arts and Science Studies: Humanities Series, no. 6. Stillwater: Oklahoma State University, 21 pp.
   Refers to Lady Pliant in The Double Dealer as a parody of the distressed heroine.

2 CECIL, C. D. "Libertine and Précieux Elements in Restoration Comedy." Essays in Criticism, 9, no. 3 (July), pp. 239-53.
   Focuses upon the plays of Etherege, Wycherley, and Congreve in terms of values established by précieux attitudes.

3 DOBRÉE, BONAMY. "The Mourning Bride and Cato." In his Restora-tion Tragedy: 1660-1720. Oxford: Clarendon Press, pp. 167-78.
   Corrected edition; see 1929.B5.

4 HODGES, JOHN C. "Saint or Sinner: Some Congreve Letters and Documents." Tennessee Studies in Literature, 3: 3-15.

1960

Biographical sketch based on material to be included in a new edition of letters and documents pertaining to Congreve. See 1964.A3.

5   HOLLAND, NORMAN N. The First Modern Comedies: The Significance of Etherege, Wycherley, and Congreve. Cambridge, Mass.: Harvard University Press, pp. 131–98.
Examines the conflict and discrepancy between "manners" [i.e., social conventions] and antisocial "natural" desires. See Ph.D. dissertation, 1956.B3. See also 1957.B5. Chapter 14 reprinted 1966.B13.

6   LOFTIS, JOHN. Comedy and Society from Congreve to Fielding. Stanford, Calif. Stanford University Press, xiii + 154 pp., passim.
The comedy of this period reveals an "intense preoccupation with the social results of economic change..." Includes references to all of Congreve's comedies.

7   NOLAN, PAUL T. "The Way of the World: Congreve's Moment of Truth." Southern Speech Journal, 25, no. 2 (Winter), pp. 75–95.
"The Way of the World deals with a particular kind of artistic morality, the kind one sees when a man comes face-to-face with reality, when the matador stands face-to-face with the bull, 'the moment of truth' for both."

8   O'REGAN, M. J. "Two Notes on French Reminiscences in Restoration Comedy." Hermathena, 93 (May), pp. 63–70.
Argues that "Congreve knew Corneille's Le Baron d'Albrikac and remembered it when he wrote The Way of the World." See 1938.B3; 1946.B6.

1960

A BOOKS

1   CONGREVE, WILLIAM. Amour pour Amour. Texte français de Guy Dumur. Répertoire pour un théâtre populaire, no. 22. Paris: L'Arche, 92 pp.

2   _____. Love for Love. In Twelve Famous Plays of the Restoration and Eighteenth Century. Introduction by Cecil A. Moore. New York: Modern Library, pp. vii–xxiii, [255]–342.
Reprint of 1933.A1.

1960

3 _____. The Way of the World. In Four English Comedies of the
  17th and 18th Centuries. Edited by J. M. Morrell. Baltimore:
  Penguin Books, pp. [131]-231.
    Reprint of 1950.A4.

4 _____. The Way of the World. In Twelve Famous Plays of the
  Restoration and Eighteenth Century. Introduction by Cecil A.
  Moore. New York: Modern Library, pp. [419]-497.
    Reprint of 1933.A3.

5 _____. The Way of the World. In Understanding Drama: Twelve
  Plays. Edited by Cleanth Brooks and Robert B. Heilman. New
  York: Holt, Rinehart and Winston, pp. 389-452.
    Reprint of 1948.A3; see 1945.A2.

B SHORTER WRITINGS

1 AVERY, EMMETT L., ed. The London Stage, Part 2: 1700-1729.
  2 vols. Carbondale: Southern Illinois University Press.
  Vol. 1: clxxviii + 460 + clxxix-ccxii pp., passim; vol. 2:
  xiv + 461-1044 + xv-xliii pp., passim.
    "A Calendar of Plays, Entertainments and Afterpieces
  Together with Casts, Box-Receipts and Contemporary Comment
  Compiled from the Playbills, Newspapers and Theatrical Diaries
  of the Period." References to Congreve's works. See 1968.B2.

*2 BARRON, LEON OSER. "The Quest for the Good Society: Friends
  and Families in Restoration Comedy." Diss., Harvard University.
    Cited in Comprehensive Dissertation Index 1861-1972.
  Vol. 30. Ann Arbor: Xerox University Microfilms, 1973,
  p. 386.

3 BARTEL, ROLAND. "Suicide in Eighteenth-Century England: The
  Myth of a Reputation." Huntington Library Quarterly, 23,
  no. 2 (February), pp. 145-58.
    Quotes Congreve on the tendency of the English to commit
  suicide.

*4 CHELLIS, BARBARA A. "Sex or Sentiment: a Study in the Period
  between 1696 and 1707." Diss., Brandeis University.
    Cited in Comprehensive Dissertation Index 1861-1972.
  Vol. 33. Ann Arbor: Xerox University Microfilms, 1973,
  p. 777.

5 MONK, SAMUEL H. "A Note in Montague Summers's Edition of The
  Way of the World, Corrected." Notes and Queries, NS 7, no. 1
  (February), p. 70.

The comparison between Sir Wilfull Witwoud and the monster in The Tempest alludes not to Sycorax but more appropriately to Caliban.

6 NOYES, ROBERT GALE. "Congreve and His Comedies in the Eighteenth-Century Novel." Philological Quarterly, 39, no. 4 (October), pp. 464-80.

Based on an examination of almost 750 novels published between 1740 and 1780, this essay explores the treatment of Congreve's relationship with Henrietta, Lady Godolphin by several prose writers and their attitudes toward Congreve's plays.

7 SHARP, WILLIAM L. "A Play: Scenario or Poem." Tulane Drama Review, 5, no. 2 (December), pp. 73-84.

The language of The Old Bachelor and The Double Dealer disproves the contention that a play in prose "comes close to being a mere scenario, dependent for its success upon the mechanical aids of the theatre."

8 TAVE, STUART M. The Amiable Humorist: A Study in the Comic Theory and Criticism of the Eighteenth and Early Nineteenth Centuries. Chicago: University of Chicago Press, xi + 304 pp., passim.

"...certain conventions of comic theory and criticism were so altered as to produce a new group of conventions...called amiable humor." Cites Congreve's works.

1961

A BOOKS

1 CONGREVE, WILLIAM. (Complete Plays). In William Congreve. Edited by Alexander Charles Ewald. [Mermaid Dramabook]. London: Ernest Benn Ltd; New York: Hill and Wang, 438 pp.

Reset edition of 1956.A1; see 1887.A1.

2 _____. The Way of the World. Testo, introduzione, e note a cura di Nicoletta Neri. Bari: Adriatica, 168 pp.

3 _____. The Way of the World. In Four Great Comedies of the Restoration and Eighteenth Century. With an introduction by Brooks Atkinson. New York: Bantam Books, pp. viii-ix, [89]-[165].

Reprint of 1958.A3.

1961

B SHORTER WRITINGS

1 HOWARTH, R. G. "Congreve and Ann Bracegirdle." English Studies
  in Africa, 4, no. 2 (September), pp. 159-61.
    Disagrees that Ann Bracegirdle and Henrietta, the young
  Duchess of Marlborough, were Congreve's mistresses.

2 HOY, CYRUS. "The Effect of the Restoration on Drama."
  Tennessee Studies in Literature, 6: 85-91.
    Restoration drama is the "final working out of tendencies
  present in English drama for at least a half century prior to
  1660." Cites The Mourning Bride and The Way of the World.

3 KRUTCH, JOSEPH WOOD. Comedy and Conscience After the Restoration.
  New York: Columbia University Press, xi + 300 pp., passim.
    Reprint of 1924.B3 with two additions, an index and a
  bibliography of relevant modern discussion prepared by
  G. S. Alleman.

4 PORTE, MICHAEL SHELDON. "The Servant in Restoration Comedy."
  Diss., Northwestern University, 204 pp., passim.
    Discusses the sociological position and literary treatment
  of the domestic servant in the Restoration, showing "that the
  stereotype is an oversimplification of conditions in real
  life and in the plays." Includes the comedies of Congreve.

5 SCOUTEN, ARTHUR H., ed. The London Stage, Part 3: 1729-1747.
  2 vols. Carbondale: Southern Illinois University Press.
  Vol. 1: clxxxviii + 596 + clxxxix-ccxxxiii pp., passim;
  vol. 2: xiv + 597-1315 + xv-lii pp., passim.
    See 1960.B1; 1968.B13.

6 SHARMA, R. C. "Conventions of Speech in the Restoration Comedy
  of Manners." Indian Journal of English Studies, 2, no. 1
  (December), pp. 23-38.
    The comic dramatists added to the "simplicity and precision
  of English prose" the "feminine qualities of wit, grace, elegance, and even a vigour of a kind, and thus helped to make
  it a fit tool for the use of the 'civilized' eighteenth century." Includes Congreve's four comedies.

*7 TATUM, NANCY R. "Attitudes Toward the Country in the Restoration
  Comedy, 1660-1728." Diss., Bryn Mawr, 134 pp.
    "The charges leveled at the country in Restoration comedy
  are related to its unchanged pattern of life and its isola-
  tion.... The virtues of the old-fashioned are thrust aside
  in the town's endless pursuit of fashion and variety." Cited
  in Dissertation Abstracts, 21, no. 11, 1961, p. 3452.

1962

A BOOKS

1 CONGREVE, WILLIAM. <u>Incognita</u>. In <u>Shorter Novels: Seventeenth Century</u>. Edited by Philip Henderson. Everyman's Library. No. 841. London: J. M. Dent; New York: E. P. Dutton, pp. [237]-303.
    Reprint of 1930.A3.

2 _____. <u>Światowe sposoby</u> [The Way of the World]. In <u>Angielska Komedia Restauracji</u>. Introduction by Grzegorz Sinko, pp. [385]-559.
    Text, footnotes, and introduction to political and theatrical background, in Polish.

3 _____. <u>The Way of the World</u>. In <u>Four English Comedies of the 17th and 18th Centuries</u>. Edited by J. M. Morrell. Baltimore: Penguin Books, pp. [131]-231.
    Reprint of 1950.A4.

4 _____. <u>The Way of the World</u>. In <u>Four Great Comedies of the Restoration and Eighteenth Century</u>. With an introduction by Brooks Atkinson. New York: Bantam Books, pp. viii-ix, [89]-[165].
    <u>See</u> 1958.A3.

5 _____. <u>The Way of the World</u>. In <u>The Genius of the Later English Theater</u>. Edited with an introduction by Sylvan Barnet, Morton Berman, and William Burto. Mentor Book. New York: New American Library, pp. 21-27, [29]-113.
    Because <u>The Way of the World</u> is a comedy, we "regard the persons...aesthetically as well as morally, and do not judge them exactly as we would the happenings if they took place outside the theater."

6 _____. <u>The Way of the World</u>. In <u>Introduction to Drama</u>. Edited by Robert C. Roby and Barry Ulanov. New York: McGraw-Hill, pp. 327-76.
    Includes critical excerpts from Gosse, Taylor, Kronenberger, the Mueschkes, Holland, and Palmer.

7 _____. <u>The Way of the World</u>. In <u>The Norton Anthology of English Literature</u>. General editor M. H. Abrams. Vol. 1. New York: W. W. Norton, pp. 1239-1307.
    Not simply a "frivolous examination of manners in the beau monde," the play is "informed with a moral insight into the nature of illicit and married love, and though it is no sermon,

1962

it seriously examines sexual morality." Revised edition
1968.A3; third edition 1974.A4.

8 _____. The Way of the World. In Plays of the Restoration and
Eighteenth Century. Edited by Dougald MacMillan and Howard
Mumford Jones. New York: Holt, Rinehart and Winston,
pp. 400–44.
  Reprint of 1938.A3; see 1931.A3.

9 _____. The Way of the World. In Restoration Plays. Introduction
by Edmund Gosse Everyman Paperback. New York: Dutton,
pp. xiii–xiv, [163]–235.
  Reprint of 1932.A1; see 1912.A2.

10 _____. The Way of the World. In William Congreve. With a
detailed study and text by G. S. Banhatti. Masters of Eng.
Lit. Series, no. 4. Allahabad: Kitab Mahal PVT. Ltd.,
[viii] + 192 pp.
  Introduction to social and literary background of the
period and the play; concludes by giving earlier estimates
of the play, which is considered to be a masterpiece of the
comedy of manners.

11 GOSSE, ANTHONY CABOT. "Dramatic Theory and Practice in the
Comedies of William Congreve." Diss., Columbia University,
334 pp.
  "Congreve's growing technical skill was matched by a
development in the meaningful structure of his action."

B SHORTER WRITINGS

1 BEVAN, ALLAN R. "Restoration Comedy Once Again." Dalhousie
Review, 42, no. 2 (Summer), pp. 248–53.
  Reviews recent books by Holland (1959.B5) and Loftis
(1959.B6).

2 CORRIGAN, BEATRICE. "Congreve's Mourning Bride and Coltellini's
Almeria." Istituto Universitario Orientale (Napoli). Annali
Sezione Romanza, 4, no. 2 (July), pp. 145–66.
  Traces the background of Coltellini's adaptation of The
Mourning Bride into an opera, examines the problems encoun-
tered in transposing the play into a suitable libretto, and
details its first performance in 1761 at Livorno.

3 DOBRÉE, BONAMY. "Congreve." In his Restoration Comedy: 1660–
1720. London: Oxford University Press, pp. [121]–150.
  Reprint of 1924.B1.

4 FUJIKI, HAKUHO. "The Use of Conjunctions in Congreve's Works."
   Anglica (Anglica Society of Kansai University, Osaka), 5, no.
   no. 1 (November), pp. 63-97.
      Classifies eight kinds of conjunctions from the five plays
   and Squire Trelooby. In Japanese, with a summary in English.

*5 GIBB, CARSON. "Figurative Structure in Restoration Comedy."
    Diss., University of Pennsylvania, 342 pp.
       The imagery and the figurative structure "compel one to
    see that love, lust, ambition, avarice, belligerence, and wit
    can be reduced to two motives: love of pleasure and love of
    power." Includes The Way of the World. Cited in Dissertation
    Abstracts, 23, no. 12, 1963, pp. 4683-84.

6 KNIGHT, G. WILSON. "Restoration." In his The Golden Labyrinth:
   A Study of British Drama. New York: W. W. Norton,
   pp. 130-70, passim.
      Congreve is included in this critical survey of Restoration
   drama.

7 LEECH, CLIFFORD. "Congreve and the Century's End." Philological
   Quarterly, 41, no. 1 (January), pp. 275-93.
      A study of the four comedies leads to the conclusion that
   "Congreve brings the diverse and often conflicting elements
   of Restoration comedy into a unity....into clear focus" and
   "for a brief moment, into a larger world." Reprinted
   1966.B17; 1970.B12.

8 NOLAN, PAUL T. "Congreve's Lovers: Art and the Critic." Drama
   Survey, 1, no. 3 (February), pp. 330-39.
      The Way of the World possesses "the morality of an ethical,
   but worldly, statesman, not of a saintly martyr."

*9 NORELL, LEMUEL N. "The Cuckold in Restoration Comedy." Diss.,
    Florida State University, 163 pp.
       "As the butt of the comedy, the cuckold represents points
    of view at variance both with other stage characters and with
    the audience.... Because all that is subject to ridicule has
    been attributed to him, the cuckold may indeed be called the
    scapegoat of Restoration comedy." Cited in Dissertation
    Abstracts, 23, no. 10, 1963, p. 3889.

*10 ROTHSTEIN, ERIC. "Unrhymed Tragedy, 1660-1702." Diss.,
     Princeton University, 238 pp.
        Discusses unrhymed tragedy of this period in practical and
     theoretical terms and the interrelationships between content
     and style. Cited in Dissertation Abstracts, 23, no. 5, 1962,
     p. 1689. See book, 1967.B8.

1962

11 STONE, GEORGE WINCHESTER, JR., ed. The London Stage, Part 4:
    1747-1776. 3 vols. Carbondale: Southern Illinois University
    Press. Vol. 1: ccxii + 492 + ccxiii-cclxxviii pp., passim;
    vol. 2: xvi + 493-1266 + xvii-lxvi pp., passim; vol. 3: xvi +
    1267-1994 + xvii-lxv pp., passim.
        See 1960.B1.

                              1963

A BOOKS

1 CONGREVE, WILLIAM. (Complete Plays). In William Congreve.
    Edited by Alexander Charles Ewald. New York: Hill and Wang,
    438 pp.
        Reprint of 1956.A1; see 1887.A1.

2 _____. Comedies. Edited by Bonamy Dobrée. World's Classics.
    No. 276. London and New York: Oxford University Press,
    xxviii + 441 pp.
        Reprint of 1925.A1.

3 _____. "Concerning Humour in Comedy." In English Literary
    Criticism: Restoration and 18th Century. Edited by Samuel
    Hynes. New York: Appleton-Century-Crofts, pp. 86-95.
        With notes and bibliography.

4 _____. The Way of the World. In Four Great Comedies of the
    Restoration and Eighteenth Century. With an introduction by
    Brooks Atkinson. New York: Bantam Books, pp. viii-ix,
    [89]-[165].
        Reprint of 1958.A3.

5 _____. The Way of the World. In World Drama from Aeschylus to
    Turgenev. Vol. 1 of A Treasury of the Theatre. Revised
    edition by John Gassner. New York: Simon and Schuster,
    pp. 430-62.
        Revised edition of 1935.A2. See 1940.A4.

6 DOBRÉE, BONAMY. William Congreve. Writers and Their Work,
    no. 164. London: Longmans Green, 35 pp.
        Biographical and critical, emphasizing the relationship be-
    tween the Restoration comedy of manners and Congreve's plays.

7 TAYLOR, D. CRANE. William Congreve. New York: Russell and
    Russell, xi + 252 pp.
        Reprint of 1931.A4.

B SHORTER WRITINGS

1   ANON. "An Early Theatre Ticket." Theatre Notebook, 18, no. 2
        (Winter), p. 42.
            Notes (with plate) on London theater ticket for a perform-
        ance in 1717 of The Old Bachelor.

2   DOBRÉE, BONAMY. "The Mourning Bride and Cato." In his Restora-
        tion Tragedy: 1660-1720. Oxford: Clarendon Press,
        pp. 167-78.
            Reprint of 1959.B3; see 1929.B5.

*3   GERMER, ERICH. "Sentimentale Zeuge in den Lustspielgestalten
        Ethereges, Wycherleys, Congreves, Vanbrughs und Farquhars."
        Diss., Muenster.
            Cited in McNamee, 1968.B10.

4   GOSSE, ANTHONY. "The Omitted Scene in Congreve's Love for Love."
        Modern Philology, 61, no. 1 (August), pp. 40-42.
            Argues that the eleventh scene of Act III was the one
        omitted in the initial production of the play.

5   LINCOLN, STODDARD. "Eccles and Congreve: Music and Drama on the
        Restoration Stage." Theatre Notebook, 18, no. 1 (Autumn),
        pp. 7-18.
            Congreve's lyrics can be more fully appreciated when
        placed within the context of Eccles' music. References to
        The Way of the World, The Judgment of Paris, Semele, and
        "Ode for St. Cecilia's Day."

6   _____. "The First Setting of Congreve's 'Semele.'" Music and
        Letters, 44, no. 2 (April), pp. 103-17.
            Although mainly concerned with the musical aspects of
        Semele, this study touches upon the collaboration of Congreve
        and Eccles. Congreve's metrical distinction between recita-
        tive and aria and his skillfully arranged "human and penetrat-
        ing situations" greatly contribute to the richness of the
        musical composition.

7   PAYNE, RHODA. "Stage Direction during the Restoration." Theatre
        Annual, 20: 41-62.
            Congreve instructed Betterton and Barry when they took part
        in his comedies.

8   SIMON, IRÈNE. "Restoration Comedy and the Critics." Revue des
        Langues Vivants, 29 (Spring), pp. 397-430.
            Reviews the major criticism from Collier to Holland. Dis-
        agrees with some of Holland's ideas about The Way of the World,

1963

arguing that the play deals with the "relationship between art and nature...or...passional nature [and] civilized nature.... As such it reflects a central concern of the age."

9 SINGH, SARUP. The Theory of Drama in the Restoration Period. Calcutta: Orient Longmans, xv + 299 pp., passim.
   Analyzes the "critical theory of the Restoration drama as expressed in its Dedications, Prefaces, Prologues and Epilogues." Cites those from Congreve's plays.

10 TIEDJE, EGON. Die Tradition Ben Jonsons in der Restaurationskomödie. Britannica et Americana, Band 11. Hamburg: Cram, de Gruyter, 168 pp., passim.
   Traces the influence of Jonson on Restoration comedy, including Congreve's four comedies.

1964

A BOOKS

1 CONGREVE, WILLIAM. The Complete Works. Edited by Montague Summers. 4 vols. New York: Russell & Russell.
   Reissue of the Nonesuch edition of 1923.A1.

2 ____. "Concerning Humour in Comedy." In Theories of Comedy. Edited by Paul Lauter. New York: Doubleday, pp. 206–14.

3 ____. Letters & Documents. Collected and edited by John C. Hodges. New York: Harcourt, Brace, and World, xxii + 295 pp.
   Contains ninety-three additional items to the sixty-four letters collected by Summers and Dobrée. All 157 items are now dated and edited; footnotes indicate location of manuscript (if extant), first printed source (if any), and one or more later editions. Also included are fifteen notes and receipts signed by Congreve, sixteen verse letters by or to Congreve, and over five items about Congreve. Collection separated into four divisions: personal, business, literary, and events following Congreve's death (an appendix).

4 ____. Love for Love. In The Play's the Thing: An Anthology of Dramatic Types. Edited by Fred B. Millet and Gerald Eades Bentley. New York: Appleton-Century-Crofts, pp. 247–87.
   Reprint of 1936.A1.

5 _____. The Way of the World. In Four English Comedies of the 17th and 18th Centuries. Edited by J. M. Morrell. Baltimore: Penguin Books, pp. [131]-231.
  Reprint of 1950.A4.

6 _____. The Way of the World. In Four Great Restoration Plays. Edited and with an introduction by Louis B. Wright and Virginia A. LaMar. New York: Washington Square Press, pp. xxvii-xxix, [251]-369.
  Introduction gives historical background to the period.

7 _____. The Way of the World. In Plays of the Restoration and Eighteenth Century. Edited by Dougald MacMillan and Howard Mumford Jones. New York: Holt, Rinehart and Winston, pp. 400-44.
  Reprint of 1938.A3; see 1931.A3.

8 _____. The Way of the World. In Three Restoration Comedies. Edited by George G. Falle. London: Macmillan; New York: St. Martin's Press, pp. 11-20, [145]-251.
  Central to the action is the contrast between appearance and reality, but the success of the play depends upon the range of its poetic expression.

9 SCHMID, D. William Congreve, sein Leben und seine Lustspiele. New York and London: Johnson Reprint Corporation, viii + 179 pp.
  Reprint of 1897.A2.

B SHORTER WRITINGS

1 BARNARD, JOHN. "Did Congreve Write A Satyr Against Love?" Bulletin of the New York Public Library, 68, no. 5 (May), pp. 308-22.
  External evidence and the lack of any firm internal evidence contradict the ascription of this poem to Congreve. Includes a full collation of the text from Narcissus Luttrell's copy.

2 BLISTEIN, ELMER M. Comedy in Action. Durham, N. C.: Duke University Press, pp. 78-109, passim.
  The proposal scene in The Way of the World "comes as close to romantic drama as is possible in this brilliantly cold comedy of manners."

3 CHAPPLE, J. A. V. "Manuscript Texts of Poems by the Earl of Dorset and William Congreve." Notes and Queries, NS 11, no. 1 (March), pp. 97-100.

1964

Textual comparison between various editions of Congreve's "Imitation of Horace" (Book II, Ode 14), suggesting that its appearance in a seventeenth-century manuscript book of Charles Cotton's poetry reminds us that Congreve's earliest writings were composed at Ilam.

4 GAGEN, JEAN. "Congreve's Mirabell and the Ideal of the Gentleman." Publications of the Modern Language Association, 79, no. 4 (September), pp. 422-27.
   "To read into the play any moral condemnation of Mirabell or any blanket condemnation of adultery is to misread Congreve and to fail to understand the ideal of the gentleman which Mirabell exemplifies."

5 GRAY, CHARLES HAROLD. Theatrical Criticism in London to 1795. New York: Benjamin Blom, vii + 333 pp., passim.
   Reprint of 1931.B2.

*6 HAYMAN, JOHN GRIFFITHS. "Raillery during the Restoration Period and Early Eighteenth Century." Diss., Northwestern University, 209 pp.
   Study undertaken to "demonstrate the prevalence of both affable and satiric raillery; to determine the influence which social uses of raillery had on raillery as a type of literary satire; and to mark any changes in the concept and use of raillery within the period under discussion." Cited in Dissertation Abstracts, 25, no. 7, 1965, pp. 4146-47.

7 HOY, CYRUS. "The Pleasures and the Perils of Deception." In his The Hyacinth Room: An Investigation into the Nature of Comedy, Tragedy, and Tragi-comedy. New York: Alfred A. Knopf, pp. 119-85, passim.
   Traces the theme of deception in Congreve's comedies.

8 KNIGHTS, L. C. "Restoration Comedy: The Reality and the Myth." In his Explorations: Essays in Criticism Mainly on the Literature of the Seventeenth Century. Middlesex: Penguin Books, pp. 139-57.
   Reprint of 1937.B2.

9 LOVE, H. H. "Satire in the Drama of the Restoration." Diss., Pembroke College, Cambridge.
   Cited in McNamee, 1969.B6.

10 LYONS, CHARLES R. "Congreve's Miracle of Love." Criticism, 6, no. 4 (Fall), pp. 331-48.
   Neither "insouciant" nor "morally ambiguous," Love for Love celebrates "the rationality of an appropriate and real

exchange of love" and "affirms the value of an honest and faithful union in marriage."

11 McDONALD, CHARLES O. "Restoration Comedy as Drama of Satire: An Investigation into Seventeenth Century Aesthetics." <u>Studies in Philology</u>, 61, no. 3 (July), pp. 522–44.
     Claims "Restoration comedy to be the most complexly and consciously moral comedy...avoiding the sentimental conception of the 'hero'...and basing its humorous effects on the Hobbesian idea of laughter..." References to Congreve.

12 McMANAWAY, JAMES G. "Unrecorded Performances in London about 1700." <u>Theatre Notebook</u>, 19, no. 2 (Winter), pp. 68–70.
     Refers to the performance of <u>Love for Love</u> on 25 December, 1700, not recorded in <u>The London Stage</u>, and to the possibility that Thomas Doggett may have taken liberties with several of Ben's lines.

13 PRICE, MARTIN. "Orders and Forms." In his <u>To The Palace of Wisdom: Studies in Order and Energy from Dryden to Blake</u>. Garden City, N. Y.: Doubleday, pp. 241–45.
     "Flexibility...marks the central figures of Congreve's The Way of the World."

14 WILCOX, JOHN. <u>The Relation of Molière to Restoration Comedy</u>. New York: Benjamin Blom, xi + 240 pp.
     Reprint of 1938.B4.

15 WILKINSON, D. R. M. <u>The Comedy of Habit: An Essay on the Use of Courtesy Literature in a Study of Restoration Comic Drama</u>. Leidse Germanistische en Anglistische Reeks van de Rijksuniversiteit te Leiden, Deel 1V. Leiden: Universitaire Pers, xii + 188 pp., passim.
     Restoration comic wit "is the product of habit rather than an expression of creative art..." Cites all of Congreve's comedies.

<u>1965</u>

A BOOKS

1 CONGREVE, WILLIAM. [<u>Love for Love</u>]. Moscow, 145 pp. Russian translation. Cited in <u>BM</u> (1971.B5), vol. 5, col. 1017.

2 _____. <u>The Way of the World</u>. Edited by Kathleen M. Lynch. Regents Restoration Drama Series. Lincoln: University of Nebraska Press, xxii + 136 pp.

1965

    Congreve explores the vagaries of the limited world of an
    artificial society in "matchless prose, with never a false
    note to mar the interpretation."

3 _____. The Way of the World. In Four English Comedies of the
    17th and 18th Centuries. Edited by J. M. Morrell. Baltimore:
    Penguin Books, pp. [131]-231.
        Reprint of 1950.A4.

4 _____. The Way of the World. In Great Plays, Sophocles to
    Brecht. Edited by Morton W. Bloomfield and Robert C. Elliott.
    New York: Holt, Rinehart and Winston, pp. [185]-247.
        The play is, above all, about "style in its most inclusive
    sense..." Revised edition 1975.A2.

5 DeMENT, JOSEPH WILLIS, JR. "The Ironic Image: Metaphoric
    Structure and Texture in the Comedies of William Congreve."
    Diss., Indiana University, 304 pp.
        Congreve's comedies illustrate "the ironic juxtaposition
    of a society whose Christian, honest-man ethics were a mere
    facade, and the Machiavellian, expedient ethic which operates
    beneath that facade."

6 VAN VORIS, W. H. The Cultivated Stance: The Designs of
    Congreve's Plays. Dublin: Dolmen Press; London: Oxford
    University Press, 186 pp.
        Because all is subject to time in the natural world, and
    if art gives the illusion of permanence, why not make an art
    of oneself; why not "cultivate some role of one's own making
    that prolongs what is desirable and assures some measure of
    grace?" Such an attempt to adopt a cultivated stance shapes
    the dramatic form of the plays. See Ph.D. dissertation,
    1957.A2.

B SHORTER WRITINGS

1 BRIDGES-ADAMS, W. "Period, Style and Scale." Drama, no. 77
    (Summer), pp. 28-31.
        Restoration comedies claim "our attention both in their
    own right and as an indispensable commentary on their own
    time." Includes The Way of the World.

2 HARRIS, BERNARD. "The Dialect of those Fanatic Times." In
    Restoration Theatre. Edited by John Russell Brown and
    Bernard Harris. Stratford-upon-Avon Studies, no. 6.
    London: Edward Arnold; New York: St. Martin's Press,
    pp. 10-40.

The language of Restoration comedy had "for its object
not so much clarity of analysis as substantial human mimicry."
Includes references to Congreve's comedies.

3 HUNT, HUGH. "Restoration Acting." In <u>Restoration Theatre</u>.
   Edited by John Russell Brown and Bernard Harris. Stratford-
   upon-Avon Studies, no. 6. London: Edward Arnold; New York:
   St. Martin's Press, pp. 178-92.
   "Congreve is the most realistic of the comic playwrights
   of his period..."

*4 JORDAN, ROBERT JOHN. "The Libertine Gentleman in Restoration
   Comedy." Diss., King's College, London.
   Cited in McNamee, 1969.B6.

5 MUIR, KENNETH. "The Comedies of William Congreve." In <u>Restora-
   tion Theatre</u>. Edited by John Russell Brown and Bernard Harris.
   Stratford-upon-Avon Studies, no. 6. London: Edward Arnold;
   New York: St. Martin's Press, pp. 220-37.
   Between Shakespeare and Shaw, Congreve remains the best
   writer of comedy. The world of the comedies is not narrow,
   the central characters are not heartless, and the satire
   implies that an ideal marriage is based on reason and respect.
   <u>See</u> 1970.B13.

*6 POTTER, L. D. "The Fop and Related Figures in Drama from Jonson
   to Cibber." Diss., Girton College, Cambridge.
   Cited in McNamee, 1969.B6.

7 SHARMA, R. C. <u>Themes and Conventions in the Comedy of Manners</u>.
   New York: Asia Publishing House, xv + 354 pp., passim.
   Numerous references to Congreve's comedies.

8 SHARROCK, ROGER. "Modes of Satire." In <u>Restoration Theatre</u>.
   Edited by John Russell Brown and Bernard Harris. Stratford-
   upon-Avon Studies, no. 6. London: Edward Arnold; New York:
   St. Martin's Press, pp. 108-32.
   "...much of the liveliness of Restoration satire comes from
   its defiant assertion of the new mode of the life of the
   town." Cites <u>The Double Dealer</u>.

9 SUCKLING, NORMAN. "Molière and English Restoration Comedy."
   In <u>Restoration Theatre</u>. Edited by John Russell Brown and
   Bernard Harris. Stratford-upon-Avon Studies, no. 6. London:
   Edward Arnold; New York: St. Martin's Press, pp. 92-107.
   English writers had few illustions as to what <u>was</u>, Molière
   a stronger conviction...of what <u>should be</u>." References to
   Congreve.

1965

10 TAYLOR, CHARLENE MAE. "Aspects of Social Criticism in Restoration Comedy." Diss., University of Illinois at Urbana-
Champaign, 263 pp.
     Examines the satiric use of the figure of the social
climber in plays written between 1660 and 1706. Chapter IV
includes Congreve.

11 THORNDIKE, ASHLEY H. <u>Tragedy</u>. New York: Cooper Square Publishers, pp. 3, 273-77, passim.
     Reprint of 1908.B1.

12 VAN LENNEP, WILLIAM, ed. <u>The London Stage, Part I: 1660-1700</u>.
Critical introduction by Emmett L. Avery and Arthur H.
Scouten. Carbondale: Southern Illinois University Press,
clxxvi + 532 + clxxvii-ccxcii pp., passim.
     <u>See</u> 1960.B1; 1968.B1.

13 WILSON, JOHN HAROLD. "The Comedy of Wit." In his <u>A Preface
to Restoration Drama</u>. Boston: Houghton Mifflin, pp. 177-86.
     In <u>The Way of the World</u>, "Congreve contemplates the ways of
his world judiciously, meting out rewards and punishments
according to the deserts of his characters, but he expects
us to be tolerant of their faults and amused, as he is, by
their foibles."

1966

A BOOKS

1 CONGREVE, WILLIAM. (Complete Plays). In <u>William Congreve</u>.
Edited by Alexander Charles Ewald. New York: Hill and Wang,
438 pp.
     Reprint of 1956.A1; <u>see</u> 1887.A1.

2 _____. <u>Comedies</u>. Edited by Bonamy Dobrée. World's Classics.
No. 276. London and New York: Oxford University Press,
xxviii + 441 pp.
     Reprint of 1925.A1.

3 _____. <u>Incognita and The Way of the World</u>. Edited by A. Norman
Jeffares. Arnold's English Texts. London: Edward Arnold,
192 pp.
     The situations in <u>Incognita</u> are made for the stage, and the
work manifests an intellect able to present the events with
"elegance and ease."

While the essence of The Way of the World is its use of language, the play also probes into the "possibilities of deeper, more lasting and more complementary relationships between men and women." American edition 1970.A2.

4   _____. Love for Love. Edited by Emmett L. Avery. Regents Restoration Drama Series. Lincoln: University of Nebraska Press, xvii + 147 pp.
A "highly readable play" and a "fine stage vehicle," Love for Love presents in a "broad perspective many facets of human nature"; and Congreve "brings to comic justice those who deviate foolishly from the standard of good sense and genuine passion." British edition 1967.A3.

5   _____. The Way of the World. Introduction by Gerald Weales. Chandler Editions in Drama. San Francisco: Chandler Publishing Company, xvii + 85 pp.
Congreve, a "good-mannered satirist," knew how to "manipulate a conventional hero-villain plot to give an audience a standard reaction and at the same time to suggest that admirers of his play were a special breed of men."

6   _____. The Way of the World [Iv.i.]. In The Drama Bedside Book. [Compiled by] H. F. Rubinstein and J. C. Trewin. New York: Atheneum, pp. [158]-163.

7   _____. The Way of the World. In Four Great Comedies of the Restoration and Eighteenth Century. With an introduction by Brooks Atkinson. New York: Bantam Books, pp. vii-ix, [89]-[165].
Reprint of 1958.A3.

8   _____. The Way of the World. In Restoration Plays. With an introduction by Brice Harris. Modern Library of the World's Best Books. No. 287. New York: Modern Library, pp. vii-xviii, 515-95.
Reprint of 1953.A3.

9   _____. The Way of the World. In Understanding Drama: Twelve Plays. Edited by Cleanth Brooks and Robert B. Heilman. New York: Holt, Rinehart and Winston, pp. 389-452.
Reprint of 1948.A3; see 1945.A2.

10   KLAUS, CARL HANNA. "The Scenic Art of William Congreve: An Approach to Restoration Comedy." Diss., Cornell University, 366 pp.
The substance, construction, and disposition of scenes are part of a highly articulated sequential process that

indirectly defines the meaning of the comedies: "the way of
the world at its best is altogether too similar to the way of
the world at its worst."

B SHORTER WRITINGS

1 BATESON, F. W. "L. C. Knights and Restoration Comedy." In
   Restoration Drama: Modern Essays in Criticism. Edited by
   John Loftis. New York: Oxford University Press, pp. 22-31.
       Reprint of 1957.B1.

2 British Museum General Catalogue of Printed Books. Photolitho-
   graphic edition to 1955. Vol. 42. London: Trustees of the
   British Museum, cols. 977-91.

3 CECIL, C. D. "Delicate and Indelicate Puns in Restoration
   Comedy." Modern Language Review, 61, no. 4 (October),
   pp. 572-78.
       Includes Congreve's use of puns.

4 ____. "'Une espèce d'éloquence abrégée': The Idealized Speech
   of Restoration Comedy." Etudes Anglaises, 19, no. 1
   (Janvier-Mars), pp. 15-25.
       Examines the refinement of English prose style, including
   that to be found in Congreve's plays.

5 ____. "Raillery in Restoration Comedy." Huntington Library
   Quarterly, 29, no. 2 (February), pp. 147-59.
       Uses Congreve's comedies to demonstrate that raillery is
   the "Augustan mode for clarifying the tenets and refining the
   values of conversational man."

6 CUNNINGHAM, JOHN E. "Congreve." In his Restoration Drama.
   London: Evans, pp. 111-31.
       Historical and critical survey. Leads to the conclusion
   that Congreve was "the perfect expression of his age."

7 DOBRÉE, BONAMY. "Congreve." In his Restoration Comedy: 1660-
   1720. London: Oxford University Press, pp. [121]-150.
       Reprint of 1924.B1.

8 ____. "Congreve." In Restoration Drama: Modern Essays in
   Criticism. Edited by John Loftis. New York: Oxford University Press, pp. 97-121.
       Reprint of 1924.B1.

9 _____. "The Mourning Bride and Cato." In his Restoration
   Tragedy: 1660-1720. Oxford: Clarendon Press, pp. 167-78.
   Reprint of 1959.B3; see 1929.B5.

10 DOWNER, ALAN S. "Mr. Congreve Comes to Judgement." Humanities
   Association Bulletin, 17, no. 2 (Autumn), pp. 5-12.
       Examines Macready's London revival in 1842 of Love for
   Love, the New York revivals in 1852 and 1854, and their
   reception by the press. See 1951.A1; 1970.B17; 1972.B21;
   1974.B14.

11 ELWIN, MALCOLM. "Congreve." In his The Playgoer's Handbook to
   Restoration Drama. New York: Kennikat Press, pp. 164-79.
   Reprint of 1928.B2.

12 FUJIMURA, THOMAS H. "Congreve's Last Play." In Restoration
   Dramatists: A Collection of Critical Essays. Edited by
   Earl Miner. Twentieth Century Views. Englewood Cliffs,
   N. J.: Prentice-Hall, pp. 165-74.
       Reprint of the closing section of Chapter 7, "William
   Congreve," from his The Restoration Comedy of Wit (1952.B1).
   The Way of the World is not "as good a comedy of wit as The
   Man of Mode or Love for Love" because it "lacks not only a
   strong naturalistic substratum but sceptical and sexual wit,
   comic wit that is easily grasped, and a consistent attitude
   toward life."

13 HOLLAND, NORMAN N. "Love for Love." In Restoration Dramatists:
   A Collection of Critical Essays. Edited by Earl Miner.
   Twentieth Century Views. Englewood Cliffs, N. J.: Prentice-
   Hall, pp. 151-64.
       Reprint of Chapter 14 from his The First Modern Comedies
   (1959.B5). Love for Love deals with "three different kinds
   of knowledge, three different ways of life...presocial, social,
   suprasocial."

14 HOY, CYRUS. "Renaissance and Restoration Dramatic Plotting."
   Renaissance Drama, 9: 247-64.
       The structural principle of The Mourning Bride is similar
   to such heroic plays as The Indian Queen and Aureng-Zebe,
   the mainspring of whose action arises from frustrated passion.

15 KNIGHTS, L. C. "Restoration Comedy: The Reality and the Myth."
   In Restoration Drama: Modern Essays in Criticism. Edited
   by John Loftis. New York: Oxford University Press, pp. 3-31.
   Reprint of 1937.B2.

1966

16 LANGHANS, EDWARD A. "Restoration Manuscript Notes in Seventeenth
    Century Plays." Restoration and 18th Century Theatre Research,
    5, no. 1 (May), pp. 30–39.
        Contains references to the Folger copy of The Mourning
    Bride and the Newberry Library copy of The Old Bachelor.

17 LEECH, CLIFFORD. "Congreve and the Century's End." In
    Restoration Drama: Modern Essays in Criticism. Edited by
    John Loftis. New York: Oxford University Press, pp. 122–43.
    Reprint of 1962.B7.

18 LEGOUIS, P. et al. "Les voies de la critique récente: Comment
    elle étudie la comédie de la restauration." Etudes Anglaises,
    19, no. 4 (Octobre–Décembre), pp. 412–23.
        Reviews recent criticism on Restoration comedy, including
    works that deal with Congreve. Concludes that much of recent
    criticism follows traditional methods.

19 LOFTIS, JOHN, ed. Restoration Drama: Modern Essays in Criticism.
    New York: Oxford University Press, xi + 371 pp.
        Introduction covers essays in anthology. See 1966.B1, B8,
    B15, B17, B24, B28.

*20 McLAUGHLIN, JOHN JOSEPH. "Cruelty in the Comic: A Study of
    Aggression in Drama." Diss., University of California, Los
    Angeles, 321 pp.
        Includes a discussion of sexual aggression in The Way of
    the World. Cited in Dissertation Abstracts, 27, no. 8A,
    1967, pp. 2503A–04A.

21 MILBURN, D. JUDSON. The Age of Wit, 1650–1750. London:
    Collier–Macmillan; New York: Macmillan, 348 pp., passim.
        Quotes from Congreve to define wit.

22 MINER, EARL, ed. Restoration Dramatists: A Collection of
    Critical Essays. Twentieth Century Views. Englewood Cliffs,
    N. J.: Prentice–Hall, ix + 179 pp.
        Introduces essays in anthology and suggests "fruitful
    approaches" to Restoration drama. See 1966.B12, B13.

23 MOHANTY, HARENDRA PRASAD. "Restoration Comedy: A Revaluation."
    Literary Criterion, 7, no. 2 (Summer), pp. 21–27.
        Restoration comedy is "verbal" rather than "intellectual."
    Passages from The Way of the World demonstrate that its prose,
    lacking the "weight and 'tough reasonableness' that one en-
    counters in Donne," does not "illuminate, irradiate the emo-
    tional content of experience."

24 MONTGOMERY, GUY. "The Challenge of Restoration Comedy." In
    Restoration Drama: Modern Essays in Criticism. Edited by
    John Loftis. New York: Oxford University Press, pp. 32–43.
        Reprint of 1929.B8.

*25 RIDDELL, JAMES ALLEN. "The Evolution of the Humours Character
    in Seventeenth-Century English Comedy." Diss., University
    of Southern California, 256 pp.
        Part II includes the comedies of Congreve. Cited in
    Dissertation Abstracts, 27, no. 4A, 1966, pp. 1037A–38A.

26 ROSE ANTHONY, SISTER. The Jeremy Collier Stage Controversy:
    1698–1726. New York: Benjamin Blom, xv + 328 pp., passim.
        Reprint of 1937.B3.

27 SCOUTEN, A. H. "Notes toward a History of Restoration Comedy."
    Philological Quarterly, 45, no. 1 (January), pp. 62–70.
        "Scrutiny of a chronological list of Restoration stage
    productions shows (1) that there were two clearly distinct
    and separate periods in which the comedy of manners appeared,
    (2) ...[there were] several other types of drama besides this
    new genre... and (3) ...the comedy of manners was by no means
    the first new type of drama to appear upon the restoration of
    Charles II." Study contains references to The Double Dealer
    and The Way of the World.

28 SMITH, JOHN HARRINGTON. "Shadwell, the Ladies, and the Change
    in Comedy." In Restoration Drama: Modern Essays in Criti-
    cism. Edited by John Loftis. New York: Oxford University
    Press, pp. 236–52.
        Reprint of 1948.B7.

29 STRATMAN, CARL J., comp. and ed. Bibliography of English
    Printed Tragedy 1565–1900. Carbondale and Edwardsville:
    Southern Illinois University Press; London and Amsterdam:
    Feffer and Simons, pp. 125–31, 712–61, passim.
        Lists both individual editions of The Mourning Bride and
    those that appear in collections and anthologies, and names
    libraries that possess copies of specific editions.

30 TRAUGOTT, JOHN. "The Rake's Progress from Court to Comedy:
    A Study in Comic Form." Studies in English Literature, 6,
    no. 3 (Summer), pp. 381–407.
        Congreve perfected the "natural form of the comedy of the
    rake" in The Way of the World.

31 WHITMAN, ROBERT F. The Play-Reader's Handbook. [Indianapolis]:
    Bobbs-Merrill, pp. 167–77.

1967

"...the friction between personal desires and social pressure
supplies the central conflict" in The Way of the World.

1967

A BOOKS

1 CONGREVE, WILLIAM. The Complete Plays. Edited by Herbert Davis.
   Curtain Playwrights. Chicago and London: University of
   Chicago Press, vii + 503 pp.
      Introductory notes to each play, footnotes and textual
   notes.

2 _____. Liebe für Liebe. Deutsche Bühenfassung von Robert
   Gillner mit einem Nachwort von Ivan Nagel. Stuttgart:
   Reclam, 102 pp.

3 _____. Love for Love. Edited by Emmett L. Avery. Regents
   Restoration Drama Series. London: Edward Arnold, xvii +
   147 pp.
      Reprint of American edition, 1966.A4.

4 _____. Love for Love. Edited by A. Norman Jeffares.
   Macmillan's English Classics, New Series. London: Macmillan;
   New York: St. Martin's Press, xxi + 144 pp.
      Although it lacks some of the literary brilliance and the
   satiric subtlety of The Way of the World, Love for Love is
   dramatically effective because of its more straightforward
   and comprehensible plot.

5 _____. The Way of the World. Edited with an introduction and
   explanatory notes by W. P. Barrett. Temple Dramatists.
   London: J. M. Dent, xii + 145 pp.
      Reprint of 1894.A1.

6 _____. The Way of the World. In Four English Comedies of the
   17th and 18th Centuries. Edited by J. M. Morrell. Baltimore:
   Penguin Books, pp. [131]–231.
      Reprint of 1950.A4.

7 _____. The Way of the World [Excerpt from the proviso scene].
   In To 1900. Vol. 1 of Theatre. Edited by Moira Kerr and
   John Bennett. Vancouver: Copp Clark, pp. 315–18.

8 _____. The Way of the World. In World Drama from Aeschylus to
   Ostrovsky. Vol. 1 of A Treasury of the Theatre. Revised

and expanded edition, edited by John Gassner. New York:
Simon and Schuster, pp. 430-62.
Revised edition of 1935.A2. See 1940.A4.

9 LYNCH, KATHLEEN M. A Congreve Gallery. New York: Octagon
Books, xvi + 196 pp.
Reprint of 1951.A11.

*10 SCHOPPER, GUENTER. "Aufbau und Sprache von Congreves Incognita."
Diss., University of Mainz.
Cited in McNamee, 1969.B6.

B SHORTER WRITINGS

1 AVERY, EMMETT L. "Rhetorical Patterns in Restoration Prologues
and Epilogues." In Essays in American and English Literature
Presented to Bruce Robert McElderry, Jr. Edited by Max
Schultz, et al. Athens: Ohio University Press, pp. 221-37.
Includes the prologues to The Old Bachelor and The Double
Dealer.

2 BARTLETT, LAURENCE. "Congreve." Plays and Players, 14, no. 5
(February), p. 74.
Response correcting a claim made in an earlier issue that
Congreve was Irish.

3 BIRDSALL, VIRGINIA OGDEN. "The English Comic Spirit on the
Restoration Stage." Diss., Brown University, 328 pp.
The "heroes and heroines of Etherege, Wycherley, and
Congreve must, if they are to be properly understood, be
approached as the genuinely comic and wholly English figures
that they are." Congreve's heroes and heroines, "having become like their creator noticeably more philosophical, issue
the challenge that is the most difficult of all, involving as
it does first the acceptance of man's slightly ridiculous
natural state and then the creation from that raw material
of a transcendant poetic world." See book, 1970.B2.

4 DOBRÉE, BONAMY. "William Congreve: A Conversation between
Jonathan Swift and John Gay, at the house of the Duke of
Queensbury near London. June, 1720." and "Young Voltaire:
A Conversation between William Congreve and Alexander Pope.
Twickenham. September, 1726." In his As Their Friends Saw
Them: Biographical Conversations. Freeport, N. Y.: Books
for Libraries Press, pp. 63-72, 73-92.
Reprint of 1933.B1; see 1926.B1 and 1929.B6.

1967

5 _____. "William Congreve: I. His Life.... II. His Work."
In his *Variety of Ways: Discussions on Six Authors*. Freeport,
N. Y.: Books for Libraries Press, pp. 46-85.
Reprint of 1932.B2.

*6 LOTT, JAMES DAVID. "Restoration Comedy: The Critical View,
1913-1965." Diss., University of Wisconsin, 446 pp.
A summary of the various critical approaches to Restoration comedy, covering relevant criticism on Congreve. Cited
in *Dissertation Abstracts*, 28, no. 7A, 1968, p. 2688A.

7 MAUROCORDATO, ALEXANDRE. *Ainsi va le monde: étude sur la
structure d'une "comedy of manners."* Archives des Lettres
Modernes. No. 76. Paris, 54 pp.
Detailed structural analysis of *The Way of the World*.

8 ROTHSTEIN, ERIC. *Restoration Tragedy: Form and the Process of
Change*. Madison and Milwaukee: University of Wisconsin
Press, xiii + 194 pp., passim.
Includes references to the use of language in *Love for
Love* and *The Mourning Bride*. See Ph.D. dissertation, 1962.B10.

9 SCHIRMANN, JEFIM. "The First Hebrew Translation from English
Literature: Congreve's *Mourning Bride*." In *Scripta
Hierosolymitana*, 19. Studies in Drama. Edited by Arieh
Sachs. Jerusalem: Magnes Press, Hebrew University, pp. 3-15.
Discusses the 1768 Hebrew translation, possibly by Abraham
Tang, which is the "first attempt to present an English work
in Hebrew garb." Appendix contains translation of part of
I.ii.

10 SHERBURN, GEORGE and DONALD F. BOND. "Restoration Drama:
II. Comedy." In *The Restoration and Eighteenth Century
(1660-1789)*. Vol. 3 of *A Literary History of England*.
Edited by Albert C. Baugh. New York: Appleton-Century-
Crofts, pp. 762-79.
Revised edition of 1948.B5, by Donald Bond.

11 SILVETTE, HERBERT. *The Doctor on the Stage: Medicine and
Medical Men in Seventeenth-Century England*. Edited by
Francelia Butler. Knoxville: University of Tennessee Press,
ix + 291 pp., passim.
Includes numerous references to Congreve's plays.

12 WALKLEY, A. B. "Way of the World." In his *Drama and Life*.
Freeport, N. Y.: Books for Libraries Press, pp. 304-08.
Reprint of 1907.B2.

13 WEALES, GERALD. "The Shadow on Congreve's Surface." <u>Educational</u>
      <u>Theatre Journal</u>, 19, no. 1 (March), pp. 30-32.
        Suggests that Vainlove's fastidious attitude toward women
      may indicate sexual abnormality.

<u>1968</u>

A BOOKS

1 CONGREVE, WILLIAM. <u>Love for Love</u>. In <u>Baroque and Restoration</u>
      <u>Theatre</u>. Vol. 4 of <u>Masterworks of World Drama</u>. Compiled by
      Anthony Caputi. Boston: D. C. Heath, pp. 337-411.
        Although no innovator, Congreve "took the comedy of
      manners...and used its conventions to achieve a superb
      richness of texture."

2 _____. <u>Love for Love</u>. In <u>Three Restoration Comedies</u>. Edited
      with an introduction by Gámini Salgádo. Middlesex: Penguin
      Books, pp. 36-39, [259]-365.
        "Implicit in the title...are the various forms of 'love
      (in exchange) for money' which are displayed throughout the
      action." Reprinted 1973.A3; 1976.A2.

3 _____. <u>The Way of the World</u>. In <u>The Norton Anthology of English</u>
      <u>Literature</u>. General editor M. H. Abrams. Vol. 1. New York:
      W. W. Norton, pp. 1417-85.
        Revised edition of 1962.A7.

4 _____. <u>The Way of the World</u>. In <u>Restoration Drama</u>. Edited and
      with an introduction by Eugene Waith. Preface by John
      Gassner. Toronto, [etc.]: Bantam Books, pp. ix-xxiii,
      [513]-607.
        For all his benevolence, Congreve holds all his characters
      at a distance. "The skeptical wit of Restoration comedy
      remains in control."

5 KAUFMAN, ANTHONY DAVID. "Characterization and Style in the
      Comedies of William Congreve." Diss., Yale University,
      168 pp.
        Congreve's style exists not only for the sake of wit, but
      to define the plays' comic values.

1968

B SHORTER WRITINGS

1 AVERY, EMMETT L. and ARTHUR H. SCOUTEN. The London Stage
   1660-1700: A Critical Introduction. Carbondale: Southern
   Illinois University Press, clxxxvii pp.
       Reprint of critical introduction from 1965.B12.

2 AVERY, EMMETT L. The London Stage 1700-1729: A Critical Introduction. Carbondale: Southern Illinois University Press,
   cxcii pp.
       Reprint of critical introduction from 1960.B1.

3 BACH, BERT C. "Congreve's Gulliver; The Character of Vainlove
   in The Old Bachelor." Ball State University Forum, 9, no. 2
   (Spring), pp. 70-75.
       The characterization of Vainlove deviates from the stereo-
   typed gallant because of the originality in the method by
   which it is presented and developed. Is it not possible,
   then, that "Vainlove's vanity, like that of Lemuel Gulliver,
   so clouds his vision that he both mistakes and underrates the
   potential of mankind, thus isolating himself from it?"

4 British Museum General Catalogue of Printed Books: Ten-Year
   Supplement 1956-1965. Vol. 10. London: Trustees of the
   British Museum, cols. 384-87.

5 FUJIMURA, THOMAS H. The Restoration Comedy of Wit. New York:
   Barnes and Noble, ix + 232 pp.
       Reprint of 1952.B1.

6 GOSSE, ANTHONY. "Plot and Character in Congreve's Double-Dealer."
   Modern Language Quarterly, 29, no. 1 (March), pp. 274-88.
       Although Maskwell and Lady Touchwood may be villainous,
   they are also comical characters. Congreve subordinates
   villainy to comic action by creating five plot strands from
   three types of characters, separating the plots, and deempha-
   sizing the villains. The play therefore may be seen not
   necessarily as a comical melodrama, but as an "ironic dark-
   comedy," deriving its strength from the unified tone.

7 HAYMAN, JOHN. "Raillery in Restoration Satire." Huntington
   Library Quarterly, 31, no. 2 (February), pp. 107-22.
       Discusses the effect of social manners upon the concept
   of satire. Contains references to The Old Bachelor, The
   Double Dealer, and "Doris."

8 HOGAN, CHARLES BEECHER, ed. The London Stage Stage, Part 5:
   1776-1800. 3 vols. Carbondale: Southern Illinois University

1968

Press. Vol. 1: ccxviii + 632 + ccxix-cclxxxix pp., passim;
vol. 2: xvi + 633-1472 + xvii-cxviii pp., passim; vol. 3:
xvi + 1473-2298 + xvii-cxvii pp., passim.
See 1960.B1.

9 HOGAN, CHARLES BEECHER. The London Stage 1776-1800: A Critical
   Introduction. Carbondale: Southern Illinois University Press,
   ccxxiv pp.
   Reprint of critical introduction from 1968.B8.

10 McNAMEE, LAWRENCE F., [comp]. Dissertations in English and
    American Literature. Theses Accepted by American, British
    and German Universities 1865-1964. New York and London:
    R. R. Bowker, pp. 509-12, 515.
    Entries for Restoration drama and Congreve.

11 NETTLETON, GEORGE HENRY. "Congreve, Vanbrugh, and Farquhar."
    In his English Drama of the Restoration and Eighteenth Century
    (1642-1780). New York: Cooper Square Publishers, pp. 120-40.
    Reprint of 1932.B5.

12 SCHNEIDER, BEN R. "The Coquette-Prude as an Actress's Line in
    Restoration Comedy during the Time of Mrs. Oldfield." Theatre
    Notebook, 22, no. 4 (Summer), pp. 143-56.
    Discusses and documents roles performed by eighteen actres-
    ses in eighty-three plays to show "that some actresses avoided
    the coquette-prude type as decisively as others sought it."
    Includes Congreve's comedies.

13 SCOUTEN, ARTHUR H. The London Stage 1729-1747: A Critical
    Introduction. Carbondale: Southern Illinois University
    Press, cci pp.
    Reprint of critical introduction from 1961.B5.

14 SHARP, WILLIAM L. "Restoration Comedy: An Approach to Modern
    Production." Drama Survey, 7, nos. 1 and 2 (Winter),
    pp. 69-86.
    Modern productions of Restoration comedy, if they are to be
    successful, must stress the "realistic picture of the diffi-
    culties the sexes have in living with each other." Includes
    Love for Love and The Way of the World.

15 SHIPLEY, JOHN B. "The Authorship of The Cornish Squire."
    Philological Quarterly, 47, no. 2 (April), pp. 145-56.
    Asserts that the play represents basically Squire Trelooby,
    the Walsh-Congreve-Vanbrugh adaptation of Molière's Monsieur
    de Pourceaugnac. See 1928.B3; 1970.B8.

1968

16 SIMON, IRÈNE. "Early Theories of Prose Fiction: Congreve and
      Fielding." In Imagined Worlds: Essays on Some English Novels
      and Novelists in Honour of John Butt. Edited by Maynard Mack
      and Ian Gregor. London: Methuen, pp. 19–35.
         "Congreve's Preface to Incognita...foreshadows Fielding's
      classic Preface." Concludes that "Congreve's characters wear
      masks or other men's clothes as at a masquerade; Fielding's
      only wear the masks of their vanities and hypocrisies, or of
      their simplicity, as men do in life."

17 WAGONER, MARY. "The Gambling Analogy in The Way of the World."
      Tennessee Studies in Literature, 13: 75–80.
         Congreve uses the analogy to "establish both social judg-
      ment and situation."

18 WILLIAMS, AUBREY. "Congreve's Incognita and the Contrivances of
      Providence." In Imagined Worlds: Essays on Some English
      Novels and Novelists in Honour of John Butt. Edited by
      Maynard Mack and Ian Gregor. London: Methuen, pp. 3–18.
         The design and theme of Incognita reveal the shaping hand
      of Providence, foreshadowing a similar pattern and theme found
      in the plays.

19 _____. "Poetical Justice, the Contrivances of Providence, and
      the Works of William Congreve." Journal of English Literary
      History, 35, no. 4 (December), pp. 540–65.
         Congreve's major works conform to the "Christian vision of
      human experience which still prevailed at the end of the
      17th century..."

20 WILSON, JOHN HAROLD. The Influence of Beaumont and Fletcher on
      Restoration Drama. Columbus: Ohio State University Press,
      pp. 21–100, passim.
         Reprint of 1928.B8.

1969

A BOOKS

1 CONGREVE, WILLIAM. "Concerning Humour in Comedy." In The Idea
      of Comedy: Essays in Prose and Verse, Ben Jonson to George
      Meredith. Edited by W. K. Wimsatt. Englewood Cliffs, N. J.:
      Prentice-Hall, pp. 71–86.

2 _____. Love for Love. Menston: Scolar Press, 92 pp.
         Facsimile reprint of the first edition of 1695.

3 _____. Love for Love. Edited by M. M. Kelsall. London:
       Ernest Benn, xxiii + 130 pp.
           Congreve's art is a "deliberate flirtation with experience,
       and its triumph is to tantalise with the appearance of life
       while denying the substance." American editions 1970.A3;
       1976.A1.

4 _____. The Way of the World. Menston: Scolar Press, 91 pp.
       Facsimile reprint of the first edition of 1700.

5 _____. The Way of the World. In British Dramatists from Dryden
       to Sheridan. Edited by George H. Nettleton, Arthur E. Case,
       and George Winchester Stone. Boston: Houghton Mifflin,
       pp. [307]-[347].
           Congreve's development of the stock figures from caricature,
       his "thematic contention that unchecked folly degenerates into
       vice, and his attack on the marriage of convenience, all sup-
       port the view that he intended to write serious social criti-
       cism." Revised edition of 1939.A3.

6 _____. The Way of the World. In Four English Comedies of the
       17th and 18th Centuries. Edited by J. M. Morrell. Baltimore:
       Penguin Books, pp. [131]-231.
           Reprint of 1950.A4.

7 DAVIS, JOHN BENJAMIN. "A Stylistic Analysis of the Comedies of
       William Congreve." Diss., Northwestern University, 224 pp.
           The structural and linguistic elements of Congreve's style
       are analyzed and differentiated from those of Etherege and
       Wycherley.

8 MANN, DAVID DOUGLAS. "A Concordance to the Complete Plays of
       William Congreve." 7 vols. Diss., Indiana University,
       3977 pp.
           Computer concordance to The Complete Plays of William
       Congreve (1967.A1). See book, 1973.A7.

9 SEID, KENNETH ARTHUR. "William Congreve and the Language of
       Restoration Comedy." Diss., University of California,
       Los Angeles, 263 pp.
           Aspects of Congreve's style related to a Restoration mode
       of perceiving.

B SHORTER WRITINGS

1 AGATE, JAMES. "'The Way of the World' by William Congreve.
       Lyric Theatre, Hammersmith." In his The Contemporary

1969

Theatre, 1924. With an introduction by Noel Coward. New
York and London: Benjamin Blom, pp. 81-85.
Reissue of 1925.B1.

2 ARMSTRONG, CECIL FERARD. "William Congreve." In his Shakespeare
to Shaw: Studies in the Life's Work of Six Dramatists of the
English Stage. New York: AMS Press, pp. 128-46.
Reprint of 1913.B1.

3 DOBRÉE, BONAMY. William Congreve: A Conversation between
Jonathan Swift and John Gay, at the house of the Duke of
Queensbury near London. June, 1730. Folcroft, Pa.:
Folcroft Press, 24 pp.
Reprint of 1929.B6.

*4 KOONCE, HOWARD LEE. "Comic Values and Comic Form: The Restora-
tion Comedy of Manners in its Tradition." Diss., University
of Maryland, 188 pp.
Restoration comedy is part of a "comic tradition dating
back through Roman comedy to Greek New Comedy, a tradition
that embraces many of the comedies of seventeenth-century
Italy." Includes a discussion of The Way of the World.
Cited in Dissertation Abstracts International, 30, no. 11A,
1970, p. 4990A.

5 KRONENBERGER, LOUIS. "The Way of the World." In his The
Polished Surface: Essays in the Literature of Worldliness.
New York: Knopf, pp. 55-72.
Representing less a period than a tradition, Congreve
not only reflects Restoration manners but embodies the
civilized point of view. Yet The Way of the World unexpectedly
suggests "the lees beneath the froth and the tarnish that
diminishes the glitter."

6 McNAMEE, LAWRENCE F., [comp]. Dissertations in English and
American Literature. Theses Accepted by American, British
and German Universities. Supplement One: 1964-1968. London
and New York: R. R. Bowker, pp. 204-06.
Entries for Restoration drama and Congreve.

7 MUECKE, D. C. The Compass of Irony. London: Methuen; New York:
Barnes and Noble, p. 72.
Cites Foible's remark to Lady Wishfor't (III.i.) as an
example of impersonal irony.

8 NOVAK, MAXIMILLIAN E. "The Artist and the Clergyman: Congreve,
Collier and the World of the Play." College English, 30,
no. 7 (April), pp. 555-61.

There could be "no real interchange between Congreve and Collier on [the] crucial issue of the relationship between the real world and the world of the play" because they responded according to type, as artist and as clergyman.

9 _____. "Congreve's 'Incognita' and the Art of the Novella." <u>Criticism</u>, 11, no. 4 (Fall), pp. 329–42.
Congreve belongs to the tradition of those who "conceived of fiction in terms of the reality of art rather than the reality of life," and he attempts "to give the novella the kind of structure associated with dramatic plotting and form..."

10 RICHETTI, JOHN J. <u>Popular Fiction before Richardson: Narrative Patterns, 1700–1739</u>. Oxford: Clarendon Press, pp. 174–77.
Cites the preface to <u>Incognita</u> within the context of the decline of the romance and the rise of the novella.

*11 RUBIN, BARBARA L. "The Dream of Self-Fulfillment in Restoration Comedy: A Study in Two Parts: The Heroic Pattern in Aristophanic and Roman Comedy and Its Design and Decadence in English Comedy from 1660 to 1700." Diss., University of Rochester, 326 pp.
In the plays of the 1690s (including Congreve's), "'the pleasure principle' by which the early heroes governed their lives yields to a 'reality principle' which transforms the actions of the comedies." Cited in <u>Dissertation Abstracts International</u>, 30, no. 12A, 1970, pp. 5419A–20A.

*12 STALLING, DONALD LANGHORNE. "From Dryden to Lillo: The Course of English Tragedy 1660–1731." Diss., University of Texas, Austin, 165 pp.
Suggests that neoclassical doctrines forced tragic drama "into a mold too narrow and too shallow for the scope and the profundity which have characterized enduring tragedy." Cited in <u>Dissertation Abstracts International</u>, 30, no. 7A, 1970, p. 2981A.

*13 STEPHENSON, PETER STANSFIELD. "Three Playwright-Novelists: The Contribution of Dramatic Techniques to Restoration and Early Eighteenth-Century Prose Fiction." Diss., University of California, Davis, 261 pp.
"Detailed analyses of the plays and novels of Mrs. Aphra Behn, William Congreve and Mrs. Mary Davys show how their experience with drama, particularly comedy, led to improved characterization and increased realistic detail in their novels." Cited in <u>Dissertation Abstracts International</u>, 30, no. 9A, 1970, p. 3920A.

1969

14 STRATMAN, CARL J., ed. <u>Restoration and 18th Century Theatre</u>
    <u>Research Bibliography 1961-1968</u>. Compiled by Edmund A.
    Napieralski and Jean E. Westbrook. Troy, N. Y.: Whitston,
    pp. 33-39.
        Thirty-seven annotated entries include both criticism and
    editions of Congreve's work.

15 SUTHERLAND, JAMES. <u>English Literature of the Late Seventeenth</u>
    <u>Century</u>. <u>Oxford History of English Literature</u>. Edited by
    Bonamy Dobrée and Norman Davis. Oxford: Clarendon Press,
    pp. 146-50, 219.
        Surveys Congreve's career.

<u>1970</u>

A BOOKS

1 BARTLETT, LAURENCE. "The Development of Congreve the Dramatist
   in Relation to Restoration and Eighteenth-Century Comedy."
   Diss., Michigan State University, 197 pp.
       "Congreve's comedies gain in interest and meaning if they
   are related to both Restoration and eighteenth-century comedy,
   and...Congreve's development as a dramatist may be explained
   with reference to the plays' changing relationship to the two
   comic traditions."

2 CONGREVE, WILLIAM. <u>Incognita and The Way of the World</u>. Edited
   by A. Norman Jeffares. Columbia: University of South Carolina
   Press, 192 pp.
       American edition of 1966.A3.

3 _____. <u>Love for Love</u>. Edited by M. M. Kelsall. Mermaid Dramabook. No. 1117. New York: Hill and Wang, xxiii + 130 pp.
       American edition of 1969.A3.

4 _____. <u>The Way of the World</u> [the proviso scene]. In <u>50 Great</u>
   <u>Scenes for Student Actors</u>. Compiled by Lewy Olfson. New
   York: Bantam Books, pp. 18-23.
       The scene is used as the "prototype for the highest
   Restoration style."

5 _____. <u>The Way of the World</u>. In <u>Four English Comedies of the</u>
   <u>17th and 18th Centuries</u>. Edited by J. M. Morrell. Baltimore:
   Penguin Books, pp. [131]-231.
       Reprint of 1950.A4.

6 LYLES, ALBERT M., and JOHN DOBSON, comp. <u>The John C. Hodges</u>
<u>Collection of William Congreve in the University of Tennessee</u>
<u>Library: A Bibliographical Catalog</u>. Univ. of Tenn. Libraries
Occasional Publication, no. 1 (Spring). Knoxville: University of Tennessee Libraries, xiv + 135 pp.
     Describes and collates 128 Congreve items, 120 published
before 1800 and eight additional Congreveana. Also includes
two appendices: eighty-seven ornaments used by Tonson in his
editions of Congreve, and twenty-one titles in the Hodges
Collection that duplicate items in Congreve's library.

7 McCLELLAND, CHARLES BLAKE. "A Critical Edition of William
Congreve's <u>Love for Love</u>." Diss., University of Tennessee,
563 pp.
     "The study consists of a critical introduction, a textual
introduction, a text of the play, exhaustive collations of
other editions, and a detailed commentary or set of explanatory
notes."

B SHORTER WRITINGS

*1 BELANGER, TERRY. "Booksellers' Sales of Copyright: Aspects of
the London Book Trade, 1718-1768." Diss., Columbia University,
305 pp.
     Concerns the 1767 sale of the Tonson copyrights of the
works of various authors, including those by Congreve. Cited
in <u>Dissertation Abstracts International</u>, 32, no. 1A, 1971,
p. 379A.

2 BIRDSALL, VIRGINIA OGDEN. <u>Wild Civility: The English Comic</u>
<u>Spirit on the Restoration Stage</u>. Bloomington: Indiana
University Press, pp. 178-248.
     Detailed study of eleven Restoration comedies, including
Congreve's, with the focus upon the rake-hero. <u>See</u> Ph.D.
dissertation, 1967.B3.

*3 BODE, ROBERT F. "A Study of the Development of the Theme of Love
and Duty in English Comedy from Charles I to George I."
Diss., University of South Carolina, 149 pp.
     Traces the transformation of the theme of love and honor
into that of love and duty in the comedies of Davenant, Dryden,
Etherege, Wycherley, Congreve, and Steele. Cited in <u>Disserta-</u>
<u>tion Abstracts International</u>, 31, no. 10A, 1971, p. 5351A.

*4 CARROLL, JOHN ELLISON. "Masking and Disguise in the Plays of
Etherege, Wycherley, and Congreve." Diss., University of
New Mexico, 261 pp.

1970

The mask "provides the plays with spectacle and serves
numerous other dramaturgic functions--structural, thematic,
symbolic, and satiric.... Disguises and masking make possible
a surprising double denouement in Congreve's The Old Batchelor.
Congreve's later comedies find him experimenting further with
the value of disguise in providing a twist to the traditional
method of plot resolution via undisguising." Cited in Dissertation Abstracts International, 31, no. 10A, 1971,
pp. 5353A-54A.

5 DOBRÉE, BONAMY. "Congreve." In his Restoration Comedy: 1660-
1720. [London, New York]: Oxford University Press,
pp. [121]-150.
    Facsimile reprint of the first edition of 1924.B1.

6 DONALDSON, IAN. "'Dear Liberty': The Way of the World." In
his The World Upside-Down: Comedy from Jonson to Fielding.
Oxford: Clarendon Press, pp. 119-58.
    The Way of the World "remains a comedy which, in its very
intricacy and accomplishment, continues to reveal to us the
difficulty of those technical problems which every writer of
comedy must face."

7 ELLEHAUGE, MARTIN. English Restoration Drama: Its Relation to
Past English and Past and Contemporary French Drama. From
Jonson via Molière to Congreve. [Folcroft, Pa.]: Folcroft
Press, pp. 185-310, passim.
    Reprint of 1933.B2.

8 HARLEY, GRAHAM D. "Squire Trelooby and The Cornish Squire:
A Reconsideration." Philological Quarterly, 49, no. 4
(October), pp. 520-29.
    Questions James Ralph's claim that his play The Cornish
Squire was substantially Squire Trelooby, the acted but un-
published translation by Congreve, Vanbrugh, and Walsh of
Molière's farce Monsieur de Pourceaugnac. See 1928.B3 and
1968.B15.

9 HOFFMAN, ARTHUR W. "Congreve's Love for Love, II, i, 171-259."
The Explicator, 28, no. 9 (May), item 72.
    Contends that Sir Sampson's Latin tag, sapiens dominabitur
astris, means not "a wise man will be ruled by the stars,"
but more appropriately, "a wise man will rule the stars."

10 KAUL, A. N. "The Inverted Abstractions of Restoration Comedy."
In his The Action of English Comedy: Studies in the Encounter
of Abstraction and Experience from Shakespeare to Shaw. New
Haven, Conn.: Yale University Press, pp. 90-130.

An "insufferably dull play," The Way of the World neither judges nor tests but only exemplifies the values of the period.

11 KREUTZ, IRVING. "Who's Holding the Mirror?" Comparative Drama, 4, no. 2 (Summer), pp. 79–88.
     The "comedy of manners presents the world not as it is but as it appears to be." Refers to Love for Love and The Way of the World.

12 LEECH, CLIFFORD. "Congreve and the Century's End." In his The Dramatist's Experience: With Other Essays in Literary Theory. London: Chatto and Windus; New York: Barnes and Noble, pp. 172–96.
     Reprint of 1962.B7.

13 MUIR, KENNETH. "William Congreve." In his The Comedy of Manners. London: Hutchinson, pp. 96–125.
     Praises Congreve for his mastery of dialogue and method of characterization. See 1965.B5.

14 National Union Catalog: Pre-1956 Imprints. Vol. 119. London: Mansell, pp. 581–96.

15 National Union Catalog: 1956 through 1967. Vol. 25. Totowa, N. J.: Rowman and Littlefield, p. 215.

16 NOVAK, MAXIMIL[L]IAN E. "Congreve's The Old Bachelor: From Formula to Art." Essays in Criticism, 20, no. 2 (April), pp. 182–99.
     The originality of Congreve already manifests itself in his first play: in the plots, in the swiftly flowing wit, in the creation of character through dialogue, and in the particular adaptation of religious imagery to love.

17 OLSHEN, B. N. "Early Nineteenth-Century Revisions of Love for Love." Theatre Notebook, 24, no. 4 (Summer), pp. 164–75.
     Deals with revisions and lists performances of Love for Love between 1800 and 1828. The revisions "serve as indices of the changing taste, manners, and morals of the age..." Includes two engravings of nineteenth-century performances of Love for Love: plate 2, Sailor Ben; plate 3, II. i. See 1951.A1; 1966.B10; 1972.B21; 1974.B14.

*18 PERSSON, AGNES VALKAY. "Comic Character in Restoration Drama." Diss., University of Colorado, 292 pp., passim.
     A study of comic characters in terms of their various degrees and kinds of ignorance. Includes The Double Dealer, Love for Love, and The Way of the World. Cited in

1970

> *Dissertation Abstracts International*, 31, no. 7A, 1971,
> p. 3517A. <u>See</u> book, 1975.B11.

19 ROGERS, J. P. W. "Congreve's First Biographer: The Identity of
      'Charles Wilson.'" <u>Modern Language Quarterly</u>, 31, no. 3
      (September), pp. 330–44.
        Questions whether "Charles Wilson," the author of <u>Memoirs</u>
      <u>of the Life, Writings, and Amours of William Congreve Esq.</u>,
      (published not in 1730--the date usually given--but on
      11 August 1729), should still be identified as John Oldmixon.
      Suggests that Edmund Curll, the publisher of the work, could
      be a likely candidate. <u>See</u> 1730.A5.

20 SHAFER, YVONNE BONSALL. "The Proviso Scene in Restoration
      Comedy." <u>Restoration and 18th Century Theatre Research</u>, 9,
      no. 1 (May), pp. 1–10.
        Traces the use of the proviso scene in several Restoration
      comedies, including <u>The Way of the World</u>, where it is "a
      serious attempt to form a union which would last, and...allow
      liberty to both parties without leading to a corruption of
      their relationship."

21 SHAW, SHARON KAEHELE. "The Burying of the Living in Restoration
      and Eighteenth Century Comedy." <u>Ball State University Forum</u>,
      11, no. 4 (Autumn), pp. 74–79.
        While using marriage or the courting relationship as a
      focal point, neither Restoration nor sentimental comedy
      "makes any attempt to see the relationship as having emotional
      potential..." Affirms that in <u>The Way of the World</u>, "whatever
      insights Congreve may have into marriage, they are not the
      stuff of comedy."

<u>1971</u>

A BOOKS

1 CONGREVE, WILLIAM. [Criticism]. In <u>Dryden: The Critical</u>
     <u>Heritage</u>. Edited by James and Helen Kinsley. New York:
     Barnes and Noble, pp. 203–06, 263–66.
        Contains Congreve's poem to Dryden's translation of <u>Persius</u>
     and extracts from Congreve's epistle dedicatory addressed to
     the Duke of Newcastle, as well as Southerne's "To Mr. Congreve"
     and Higgons's "To Mr. Congreve on...<u>The Old Batchelor</u>."

2 _____. <u>Incognita</u>. Menston: Scolar Press, 128 pp.
       Facsimile reprint of the 1692 edition.

3 _____. The Way of the World. Edited by Brian Gibbons. New
   Mermaids. London: Ernest Benn, xxxv + 116 pp.
      "If Congreve succeeds in The Way of the World in modifying
   the art of comedy to make its morality more inclusive and
   reconciliatory, less ideal and remote, he remains faithful to
   the spirit of romantic comedy, in its central affirmation of
   the power of love..." Reprinted 1976.A3.

4 _____. The Way of the World. In Four English Comedies of the
   17th and 18th Centuries. Edited by J. M. Morrell. Baltimore:
   Penguin Books, pp. [131]-231.
      Reprint of 1950.A4.

5 _____. The Way of the World. In Four Great Comedies of the
   Restoration and 18th Century. With an introduction by Brooks
   Atkinson. New York: Bantam Books, pp. viii-ix, [89]-[165].
      Reprint of 1958.A3.

6 CORMAN, BRIAN. "William Congreve and the Development of Comic
   Form." Diss., University of Chicago, 278 pp.
      Studies Congreve's artistic development. The Old Bachelor
   resembles a "typical Restoration comedy," The Double Dealer
   looks back to Jonson and is to be regarded as a "punitive
   comedy," Love for Love looks forward to eighteenth-century
   sentimental comedy, and The Way of the World is "unmatched
   both in quality and form by any Restoration or eighteenth-
   century comedy."

7 NOVAK, MAXIMILLIAN E. William Congreve. Twayne's English
   Authors. New York: Twayne, 197 pp.
      Treats Congreve's works and specifically the plays in terms
   of "English art and society after the Glorious Revolution of
   1688."

8 WILLIAMS, AUBREY and MAXIMILLIAN E. NOVAK. Congreve Consider'd.
   Foreword by H. T. Swedenberg. Clark Library Seminar,
   5 December 1970. Los Angeles: William Andrews Clark
   Memorial Library, iv + 55 pp.
      Foreword reminds us of the occasion of the seminar, the
   three-hundredth anniversary of Congreve's birth, and intro-
   duces papers by Williams and Novak. See 1971.B13 and B20.

B SHORTER WRITINGS

1 ARCHER, STANLEY L. "The Epistle Dedicatory in Restoration
   Drama." Restoration and 18th Century Theatre Research, 10,
   no. 1 (May), pp. 8-13.

1971

The epistle dedicatory is examined as a literary genre and
as a source of information regarding literary patronage. Includes several by Congreve.

2 BARNARD, JOHN. "Drama from the Restoration till 1710." In
   English Drama to 1710. Edited by Christopher Ricks. Sphere
   History of Literature in the English Language. No. 3.
   London: Sphere, pp. 375-407.
       Includes a critical survey of Congreve's plays.

3 BARTLETT, LAURENCE. "Bibliography for William Congreve and
   Restoration Comedy." Restoration and 18th Century Theatre
   Research, 10, no. 2 (November), pp. 41-43.
       Nonannotated bibliography supplementing items found in
   Restoration and Eighteenth-Century Theatre Research: A
   Bibliographical Guide, 1900-1968. See 1971.B16.

4 BENTLEY, THOMAS ROY. "Money: God and King, Economic Aspects of
   Restoration Comedy." Diss., Memorial University of Newfound-
   land, 436 pp., passim.
       "The new comedies produced...between 1660 and 1700 depict
   a society in which money is the measure of all values,...the
   catalytic force in all actions,...[and] both god and king."
   Includes all of Congreve's comedies.

5 British Museum General Catalogue of Printed Books. Five-Year
   Supplement 1966-1970. Vol. 5. London: Trustees of the
   British Museum, cols. 1016-18.

6 CARPER, THOMAS R. "Congreve's Popular Tragedy." Thoth, 12,
   no. 1 (Fall), pp. 3-10.
       Congreve's contemporaries approved of The Mourning Bride
   because its "somber light...helped illuminate the dark side"
   of their world.

7 HUGHES, LEO. The Drama's Patrons: A Study of the Eighteenth-
   Century London Audience. Austin and London: University of
   Texas Press, ix + 209 pp., passim.
       Contains several references to the reception given in the
   eighteenth century to Congreve's plays.

8 HUME, ROBERT D. "A Revival of The Way of the World in December
   1701 or January 1702." Theatre Notebook, 26, no. 1 (Autumn),
   pp. 30-36.
       Evidence suggests that The Way of the World was not
   immediately dropped from the repertory but was performed in
   1701 or 1702, several years before the date recorded by
   Emmett L. Avery.

9   HURLEY, PAUL J.   "Law and the Dramatic Rhetoric of <u>The Way of
     the World</u>."   <u>South Atlantic Quarterly</u>, 70, no. 2 (Spring),
     pp. 191-202.
          Congreve uses the "rhetoric of law...to suggest that true
     comedy is entirely compatible with serious art."

10 LYONS, CHARLES R.   "Disguise, Identity, and Personal Value in
     <u>The Way of the World</u>."   <u>Educational Theatre Journal</u>, 23,
     no. 3 (October), pp. 258-68.
          Analyzes "Congreve's use of the traditional comic image
     of disguise in the subtle and revealing forms of artifice" in
     a play that "explores the problem of value in a world dedicated
     to appearance..."

11 McCOLLOM, WILLIAM G.   <u>The Divine Average: A View of Comedy</u>.
     Cleveland: Case Western Reserve University Press, pp. 108-14.
          Examines the function of language in <u>Love for Love</u> and
     <u>The Way of the World</u>.

*12 MYERS, CHARLES ROBERT.   "Game-Structure in Selected Plays."
     Diss., University of Iowa, 296 pp.
          Includes a structural analysis of <u>The Way of the World</u>,
     arguing that it is "formally responsive to a 'game-structure'"
     and that this structure molds the material of the play into
     its peculiar form.   Cited in <u>Dissertation Abstracts Inter-
     national</u>, 32, no. 3A, 1971, pp. 1676A-77A.

13 NOVAK, MAXIMILLIAN E.   "Love, Scandal, and the Moral Milieu of
     Congreve's Comedies."   In his <u>Congreve Consider'd</u>.   Los
     Angeles: William Andrews Clark Memorial Library, pp. 23-50.
          The only hope for happiness in a corrupt world is the
     private love between men and women of sensibility and genuine
     wit.   <u>See</u> 1971.A8.

14 ROPER, ALAN.   "The Beaux' Stratagem: Image and Action."   In
     <u>Seventeenth-Century Imagery: Essays on Uses of Figurative
     Language from Donne to Farquhar</u>.   Edited by Earl Miner.
     Berkeley and Los Angeles: University of California Press,
     pp. 169-97.
          Includes comments on Congreve's style.

15 SCHNEIDER, BEN ROSS, JR.   <u>The Ethos of Restoration Comedy</u>.
     Urbana, Chicago, and London: University of Illinois Press,
     ix + 203 pp., passim.
          Describes and documents the moral characteristics of 1127
     characters from eighty-three plays most frequently performed
     between 1660 and 1730.   Includes the four comedies by Congreve.

1971

16 STRATMAN, CARL J., DAVID G. SPENCER, and MARY ELIZABETH DEVINE,
    eds. <u>Restoration and Eighteenth-Century Theatre Research:</u>
    <u>A Bibliographical Guide. 1900-1968</u>. Carbondale and
    Edwardsville: Southern Illinois University Press; London
    and Amsterdam: Feffer, pp. 139-58.
        One hundred and seventy-four annotated entries for
    Congreve.

17 SULLIVAN, WILLIAM ARNETT, JR. "Fielding's Dramatic Comedies:
    The Influence of Congreve and Molière." Diss., Louisiana
    State University and Agricultural and Mechanical College,
    224 pp., passim.
        "Fielding draws heavily upon the thought and embodiment"
    of Congreve's comedies. Both writers "depict ideal worlds,
    in which the evil that exists is always subdued by prevalent
    virtue." Both "write drama in the tradition of Ben Jonson's
    comedy of behavior," but behavior "portraying vice and folly
    is presented more for diversion than for instruction..."

18 TEYSSANDIER, H. "Congreve's <u>Way of the World</u>: Decorum and
    Morality." <u>English Studies</u>, 52, no. 2 (April), pp. 124-31.
        Although <u>The Way of the World</u> may disregard conventional
    moral standards, it has its own intrinsic "social and moral
    code to which everything is referred, and according to which
    certain things should be done and others should not."

19 WALSH, BETSY. "Sunlight of the Mind...?" <u>Barat Review</u>, 6,
    no. 2, pp. 51-61.
        Compares and contrasts Congreve's <u>The Way of the World</u>
    with Meredith's <u>The Egoist</u> by examining "the idea of comedy
    present to each author, his application of the theory in his
    own work, and then how each relates to the other."

20 WILLIAMS, AUBREY. "The 'Just Decrees of Heav'n' and Congreve's
    <u>Mourning Bride</u>." In his <u>Congreve Consider'd</u>. Los Angeles:
    William Andrews Clark Memorial Library, pp. 1-22.
        The concept of poetic justice in <u>The Mourning Bride</u>
    dramatizes a providentially ordered universe. Congreve's
    view of life was therefore neither Epicurean nor naturalistic,
    but essentially Christian. <u>See</u> 1971.A8.

21 ZEIDBERG, DAVID S. "Fainall and Marwood: Vicious Characters
    and Limits of Comedy." <u>Thoth</u>, 12, no. 1 (Fall), pp. 33-38.
        Questions whether the comic structure can endure the kind
    of suffering caused and felt by Fainall and Marwood.

1972

A BOOKS

1 CONGREVE, WILLIAM. <u>Amendments of Mr. Collier's False and Imper-
fect Citations</u>. Preface by Arthur Freeman. New York:
Garland, 6 + 109 + (43-44) pp.
Reprint of the 1698 edition.

2 _____. <u>The Old Bachelor</u>. Menston: Scolar Press, 56 pp.
Facsimile reprint of the 1693 first edition.

3 _____. <u>The Way of the World</u>. Edited by John Barnard.
Fountainwell Drama Texts. No. 17. Edinburgh: Oliver and
Boyd, 127 pp.
"Judgment, analysis, antithesis--these qualities dominate
in a comedy concerned with the necessary decorum and artifices
through which individual feeling must fulfil itself within a
society where love easily founders on cold financial
calculation."

4 _____. <u>The Way of the World</u>. In <u>The Forms of Drama</u>. Edited
and with introduction by Robert W. Corrigan. Headnotes by
Glenn M. Loney. Boston: Houghton Mifflin, pp. 439-505.
The play is the "finest of the period and the genre." The
asides of the young couple establish "what is to be accepted
as a truly realistic, sensible approach to living in an
artificial world."

5 _____. <u>The Way of the World</u>. In <u>Four English Comedies of the
17th and 18th Centuries</u>. Edited by J. M. Morrell. Baltimore:
Penguin Books, pp. [131]-231.
Reprint of 1950.A4.

6 GOSSE, EDMUND. <u>Life of William Congreve</u>. Port Washington,
N. Y.: Kennikat Press, 192 + ix pp.
Reprint of 1888.A3.

7 MORRIS, BRIAN, ed. <u>William Congreve</u>. Mermaid Critical
Commentaries. London: Benn; Totowa, N. J.: Rowman and
Littlefield, xvi + 176 pp.
Critical introduction covers recent studies on Congreve and
the nine essays included in this anthology, concluding with a
discussion on the relevance of Congreve. <u>See</u> 1972.B1, B6,
B7, B10, B15, B18, B19, B22, B25.

8 NICKLES, MARY A. "The Women in Congreve's Comedies: Characters
and Caricatures." Diss., New York University, 397 pp.

Through the characterizations of Araminta, Cynthia, Angelica, and Millamant, which inform the comedies with a "moral ideal...Congreve pierces...the crust of the superficial Restoration world and arrives at the core of what is permanent in the minds and passions of women."

B SHORTER WRITINGS

1 BARNARD, JOHN. "Passion, 'Poetical Justice,' and Dramatic Law in The Double-Dealer and The Way of the World. In William Congreve. Edited by Brian Morris. Mermaid Critical Commentaries. London: Benn; Totowa, N. J.: Rowman and Littlefield, pp. 93-112.
    Explores "the interplay between Congreve's use of the... neoclassical theory of dramatic structure, his appeal to classical precedent, and his attempt to achieve a seriousness differing in kind from that of other Restoration comedies."

2 BATESON, F. W. "Second Thoughts: L. C. Knights and Restoration Comedy." In his Essays in Critical Dissent. Totowa, N. J.: Rowman and Littlefield, pp. 117-27.
    Reprint, with minor revisions, of 1957.B1.

3 BEAR, ANDREW. "Restoration Comedy and the Provok'd Critic." In Restoration Literature: Critical Approaches. Edited by Harold Love. London: Methuen; New York: Barnes and Noble, pp. 1-26.
    Explores the reasons why Restoration comedy, including that by Congreve, has been attacked.

4 DEITZ, JONATHAN ERIC. "The Designs of Plot: The New Direction in Plot Resolution of Late Restoration Satiric Comedy." Diss., University of Pennsylvania, 242 pp., passim.
    Moving away from the thoroughly ironic plot structure utilized by Dryden, Etherege, and Wycherley and avoiding the sentimental direction followed by Cibber, Congreve's comedies (as well as Vanbrugh's and Farquhar's) manifest a satiric structure.

5 EDGAR, IRVING I. "Restoration Comedy and William Congreve." In his Essays in English Literature and History. New York: Philosophical Library, pp. 52-70.
    With the exception of the excellent wit and marked refinement in language, the comedies of Congreve "are no different than those of his predecessors."

6   EVANS, GARETH LLOYD. "Congreve's Sense of Theatre." In <u>William
    Congreve</u>. Edited by Brian Morris. Mermaid Critical Commen-
    taries. London: Benn; Totowa, N. J.: Rowman and Littlefield,
    pp. 155-69.
        Discusses the art and craft of stage communication in
    Congreve's comedies.

7   FOAKES, R. A. "Wit and Convention in Congreve's Comedies." In
    <u>William Congreve</u>. Edited by Brian Morris. Mermaid Critical
    Commentaries. London: Benn; Totowa, N. J.: Rowman and
    Littlefield, pp. 55-71.
        The comedies exploit the full seriousness of "wit" and
    redefine it in relation to convention.

8   FOSS, MICHAEL. "Politics and the State." In his <u>The Age of
    Patronage: The Arts in England, 1660-1750</u>. Ithaca, N. Y.:
    Cornell University Press, pp. 138-61.
        Mentions Congreve's political affiliations.

9   FOX, JAMES HARVEY. "The Actor-Audience Relationship in Restora-
    tion Comedy, with Particular Reference to the Aside." Diss.,
    University of Michigan, 213 pp.
        A study of the aside as a "special form of communication
    which heightens, refines, and manipulates the response of the
    Restoration audience in an essentially paradoxical manner."
    Examines the asides in several plays, including <u>The Way of
    the World</u>.

10 GIBBONS, BRIAN. "Congreve's <u>The Old Batchelour</u> and Jonsonian
    Comedy." In <u>William Congreve</u>. Edited by Brian Morris.
    Mermaid Critical Commentaries. London: Benn; Totowa, N. J.:
    Rowman and Littlefield, pp. 1-20.
        Although Congreve was "clearly uneasy with the dark and
    cruel element in Jonson's art," the design and comic mood
    of Congreve's first comedy manifest a careful observance of
    Jonsonian precepts.

11 HAWKINS, HARRIETT. <u>Likenesses of Truth in Elizabethan and
    Restoration Drama</u>. Oxford: Clarendon Press, pp. 98-114,
    115-38.
        "'Diversity of signification': religious imagery in
    Restoration comedy and secular reality in <u>Love for Love</u>."
    "'Offending against decorums': the reflection of social
    experience in <u>The Way of the World</u>."

12 JARVIS, F. P. "The Philosophical Assumptions of Congreve's
    <u>Love for Love</u>." <u>Texas Studies in Literature and Language</u>,
    14, no. 3 (Fall), pp. 423-34.

1972

      Greatly influenced by Locke's <u>An Essay Concerning Human</u>
<u>Understanding</u>, <u>Love for Love</u> "is a sophisticated and somewhat
skeptical statement of the limitations of human reason."

13 JORDAN, ROBERT. "The Extravagant Rake in Restoration Comedy."
    In <u>Restoration Literature: Critical Approaches</u>. Edited by
    Harold Love. London: Methuen; New York: Barnes and Noble,
    pp. 69-90.
        Refers to the gap between surface and real emotions in
    <u>The Way of the World</u>.

14 KAUFMAN, ANTHONY. "A Possible Allusion to the Death of Mountford
    in Congreve's 'The Old Bachelor.'" <u>Notes and Queries</u>, NS 19,
    no. 12 (December), pp. 463-64.
        The characterization of Wittoll and Bluffe, and especially
    Bellmour's biting reference to the latter, may have reminded
    the audience of the alleged murderers of the actor-playwright
    William Mountford.

15 KELSALL, MALCOLM. "Those Dying Generations." In <u>William Congreve</u>.
    Edited by Brian Morris. Mermaid Critical Commentaries.
    London: Benn; Totowa, N. J.: Rowman and Littlefield,
    pp. 113-30.
        Examines, with an emphasis upon the "old" characters, the
    relationship between beauty and power in the comedies.

16 LOFTIS, JOHN. "The Limits of Historical Veracity in Neoclassical
    Drama." In <u>England in the Restoration and Early Eighteenth</u>
    <u>Century: Essays on Culture and Society</u>. Edited by H. T.
    Swedenberg, Jr. Berkeley: University of California Press,
    pp. 27-50.
        Considers the innovative qualities of <u>The Way of the World</u>.

17 LOVE, HAROLD, ed. <u>Restoration Literature: Critical Approaches</u>.
    London: Methuen; New York: Barnes and Noble, xii + 322 pp.
        Includes two essays on the Restoration (1972.B3, B13) and
    one on Restoration tragedy (1972.B23).

18 MUIR, KENNETH. "Congreve on the Modern Stage." In <u>William</u>
    <u>Congreve</u>. Edited by Brian Morris. Mermaid Critical Commen-
    taries. London: Benn; Totowa, N. J.: Rowman and Littlefield,
    pp. 131-54.
        Recalls some twentieth-century productions of the comedies,
    including several cast lists, and proves that Congreve is
    still a "living dramatist."

19 MYERS, WILLIAM. "Plot and Meaning in Congreve's Comedies." In
    <u>William Congreve</u>. Edited by Brian Morris. Mermaid Critical

Commentaries. London: Benn; Totowa, N. J.: Rowman and
Littlefield, pp. 73-92.

The comedies record Congreve's "struggle to reconcile the
contradictions in his literary and ideological inheritance."

*20 NICKSON, RICHARD. "William Congreve: Tragedian." [Paper],
Northeast Modern Language Association.

Summarizes eighteenth-century responses to The Mourning
Bride and then affirms that Congreve's prosody is "destitute."
Cited in Scriblerian, 5, no. 1 (Autumn), p. 53.

*21 OLSHEN, BARRY NEIL. "The Reception of Restoration Comedy of
Manners in Nineteenth-Century England: An Account of
Wycherley, Congreve, Vanbrugh, and Farquhar on the Stage
and in the Study." Diss., University of Toronto.

Includes a detailed analysis of textual alterations,
remarks on individual productions, and chronological list
of London performances. Cited in Dissertation Abstracts
International, 34, no. 8A, 1974, pp. 5374A-75A. See 1951.A1;
1966.B10; 1970.B17; 1974.B14.

22 PARFITT, GEORGE. "The Case Against Congreve." In William
Congreve. Edited by Brian Morris. Mermaid Critical Commentaries. London: Benn; Totowa, N. J.: Rowman and Littlefield,
pp. 21-38.

Examines characterization, style, and the world of the
comedies, concluding that "Congreve's limitation is...that
his own vision is neither large enough nor sufficiently clear
to be really satisfying."

23 PARSONS, PHILIP. "Restoration Tragedy as Total Theatre." In
Restoration Literature: Critical Approaches. Edited by
Harold Love. London: Methuen; New York: Barnes and Noble,
pp. 27-68.

Refers to the visual, verbal, and musical interplay in
The Mourning Bride.

24 RODWAY, ALLAN. "Restoration Comedy Re-examined." Renaissance
and Modern Studies, 16: 37-60.

Restoration comedy "made a real attempt to explore the
possibilities of a different life-style and to test seriously,
though not earnestly, the validity of some of the traditional
assumptions about sexual morality in a society where arranged,
monetary marriage was the norm." Includes a discussion of
The Way of the World.

25 ROBERTS, PHILIP. "Mirabell and Restoration Comedy." In William
Congreve. Edited by Brian Morris. Mermaid Critical
Commentaries.

1972

London: Benn; Totowa, N. J.: Rowman and Littlefield,
pp. 39–53.
The Way of the World criticizes the priorities of earlier
Restoration comedy and "explodes the artifices of...'the
comic dance.'"

26 SNIDER, ROSE. "William Congreve." In her Satire in the Comedies
of Congreve, Sheridan, Wilde, and Coward. New York: Phaeton
Press, pp. 1–40.
Reprint of 1937.B4.

27 STEPHENSON, PETER S. "Congreve's 'Incognita': The Popular
Spanish Novela Form Burlesqued." Studies in Short Fiction,
9, no. 4 (Fall), pp. 333–42.
Incognita derives its comedy from a combination of the
Spanish novela and Restoration stage comedy.

*28 WARD, JOHN CHAPMAN. "The Tradition of the Hypocrite in
Eighteenth-Century English Literature." Diss., University
of Virginia, 136 pp.
"The figure of the hypocrite as it appears in critical
or didactic comedy of the eighteenth century is remarkably
consistently portrayed throughout the century." Contains a
discussion of Congreve's The Double Dealer. Cited in Dissertation Abstracts International, 34, no. 8A, 1974, p. 5128A.

29 WILLIAMS, AUBREY. "The 'Utmost Tryal' of Virtue and Congreve's
Love for Love." Tennessee Studies in Literature, 17: 1–18.
The play presents us "with a very witty dramatization of
some basic Christian truths and paradoxes."

30 YAMADA, TOSHIAKI. ["Love for Love: A World of Opposing Values"].
Studies in the Humanities (Osaka City University), 23: 838–47.
The play depicts a world of contradictory values: love
and money. Printed in Japanese.

31 ZIMANSKY, CURT A. "Editing Restoration Comedy: Vanbrugh and
Others." In Editing Seventeenth Century Prose. Edited by
D. I. B. Smith. Conference on Editorial Problems Series.
Toronto: Hakkert, pp. 95–122.
Discusses editorial problems in preparing modern editions
of Restoration comedies. References to Love for Love and
The Way of the World.

1973

A BOOKS

1 CONGREVE, WILLIAM. The Double Dealer. London: Scolar Press,
   80 pp.
       Facsimile reprint of the 1694 first edition.

2 _____. "Epistle Dedicatory to Thomas Pelham-Holles, Duke of
   Newcastle" [extract]. In Critics on Dryden. Edited by Robert
   McHenry and David Lougee. Readings in Literary Criticism.
   No. 15. London: Allen and Unwin; Miami: Miami University
   Press, pp. 1-3.

3 _____. Love for Love. In Three Restoration Comedies. Edited
   with an introduction by Gámini Salgádo. Middlesex: Penguin
   Books, pp. 36-39, [259]-365.
       Reprint of 1968.A2.

4 _____. The Way of the World. In The Oxford Anthology of
   English Literature. Vol. 1: The Middle Ages through the
   Eighteenth Century. The Restoration and the Eighteenth
   Century, edited by Martin Price. New York: Oxford Univer-
   sity Press, pp. 1669-733.
       To master the way of the world requires a "vigilance that
   Congreve never underestimates, even as he refuses to allow
   that it need cost us our hearts."

5 _____. The Way of the World. In Restoration and Eighteenth-
   Century Comedy. Edited by Scott McMillin. Norton Critical
   Edition. New York: W. W. Norton, pp. 153-217.
       Also contains selected criticism on Restoration comedy,
   including Holland's chapter on The Way of the World from The
   First Modern Comedies (1959.B5) and Price's "Form and Wit in
   The Way of the World" from To The Palace of Wisdom (1964.B13).

*6 GOSSE, EDMUND W. Life of William Congreve. [Folcroft, Pa.]:
   Folcroft Library Editions.
       Reprint of 1888.A3. Cited in Cumulative Book Index, 1974,
   p. 436.

7 MANN, DAVID, ed. A Concordance to the Plays of William Congreve.
   Ithaca and London: Cornell University Press, xxi + 888 pp.
       Based on Herbert Davis' The Complete Plays of William
   Congreve (1967.A1). See Ph.D. dissertation, 1969.A8.

1973

B SHORTER WRITINGS

1 CAMPBELL, HILBERT H. "James Thomson and David Mallet: 'A Poem to the Memory of Mr. Congreve,' 1729." <u>Notes and Queries</u>, NS 20, no. 11 (November), p. 415.
Should accept McKillop's evidence (1939.B4) that David Mallet, and not James Thomson, as some critics affirm, is the author of the poem. <u>See</u> 1729.B1; 1930.B3; 1939.B4.

2 CARLOCK, JOHN BRUCE, JR. "Military Influences on Theme, Plot, and Style in English Comic Drama from the Glorious Revolution to the Death of Queen Anne." Diss., University of South Carolina, pp. 116-23, 135-43, 232-37.
Includes references to Captain Bluffe and Sailor Ben and explains the initial stage failure of <u>The Way of the World</u>.

3 DOBRÉE, BONAMY. <u>William Congreve: A Conversation between Jonathan Swift and John Gay, at the house of the Duke of Queensbury near London. June, 1730</u>. [Folcroft, Pa.]: Folcroft Library Editions, 24 pp.
Reprint of 1929.B6.

4 _____. "William Congreve: I. His Life.... II. His Work." In <u>Variety of Ways: Discussions on Six Authors</u>. [Folcroft, Pa.]: Folcroft Library Editions, pp. 46-85.
Reprint of 1932.B2.

5 EBBS, JOHN DALE. <u>The Principle of Poetic Justice Illustrated in Restoration Tragedy</u>. Salzburg Studies in English Literature: Poetic Drama, no. 4. Salzburg: Institut für englische Sprache und Literatur, pp. 153-58.
Congreve's depiction of poetic justice in <u>The Mourning Bride</u> contributed to the play's favorable acceptance. <u>See</u> Ph.D. dissertation, 1958.B5.

6 FERRELL, DAVID MICHAEL. "The Structural Functions of Rake Characters in Restoration Comedy." Diss., University of Missouri, 193 pp., passim.
Analyzes the character of the rake in selected comedies by Etherege, Wycherley, and Congreve. Discusses Bellmour as a "mature rake" and Valentine and Mirabell as "metamorphic rakes."

7 HUME, ROBERT D. "Theory of Comedy in the Restoration." <u>Modern Philology</u>, 70, no. 4 (May), pp. 302-18.
Explores the diversity in the aims and methods of Restoration comedy. Includes references to Congreve.

8 KAUFMAN, ANTHONY. "Language and Character in Congreve's The
   Way of the World." Texas Studies in Literature and Language,
   15, no. 3 (Fall), pp. 411–27.
      "The ways in which the characters of the play speak
   individuate their personalities quite clearly, create dramatic
   conflict, and establish a moral perspective within the play."

9 _____. "'A Libertine Woman of Condition': Congreve's 'Doris.'"
   Yearbook of English Studies, 3: 120–23.
      A detailed analysis of the poem that places it between the
   "Cavalier-Libertine tradition of earlier times and Swift's
   harsher poems."

10 LANGHANS, EDWARD A. "Players and Playhouses, 1695–1710 and Their
   Effect on English Comedy." The Theatre Annual, 29: 28–39.
      Refers to Betterton's production of Love for Love at the
   opening of the theater in Lincoln's Inn Fields and to the
   continuing popularity of Congreve's plays in the eighteenth
   century.

11 LEWIS, MINEKO S. "Humor Characterization in Restoration Comedy
   1600–1700." Diss., University of Tennessee, 217 pp., passim.
      "...as a literary technique humor characterization extended
   beyond the generic limits of the so-called Restoration comedy
   of humors. A common tradition which demonstrably affects the
   spectator's response to the plays binds the comedies of
   Shadwell, Dryden, and Wycherley with those of Etherege and
   Congreve."

12 LIGHTFOOT, JOHN EWELL, JR. "The Treatment of Women in Restoration Comedy of Manners." Diss., Texas Tech University,
   206 pp., passim.
      Etherege, Wycherley, and Congreve were "willing to grant
   women more intellectual and social freedom than was available
   to the sex at large in England from 1660 to 1700." Contains
   a study of Love for Love and The Way of the World.

13 LOVE, HAROLD. "Dryden, Durfey, and the Standard of Comedy."
   Studies in English Literature, 13, no. 3 (Summer), pp. 422–36.
      The relevance of several works, including Congreve's The
   Old Bachelor and The Double Dealer, to Dryden's "mature theory
   of comedy."

14 National Union Catalog 1968–1972. Vol. 20. Ann Arbor: J. W.
   Edwards, p. 435.

15 ROPER, ALAN. "Language and Action in The Way of the World, Love's
   Last Shift, and The Relapse." Journal of English Literary
   History, 40, no. 1 (Spring), pp. 44–69.

1973

> Congreve's play is superior to both Cibber's and Vanbrugh's
> because it achieves an integrity which is "moral in its mature
> sense of life...psychological in its truth to life, and...
> aesthetic in its concordance of language and action."

16 SCHULZ, DIETER. "'A Novel,' 'Romance,' and Popular Fiction in
the First Half of the Eighteenth Century." Studies in
Philology, 70, no. 1 (January), pp. 77-91.
    Discusses the significance of Congreve's distinction between
the novel and the romance to later theories concerning prose
fiction.

17 WERTIME, STEVEN FREDERICK. "An Approach to Drama: A Theory of
Drama with Discussions of Congreve's Love for Love, Shaw's
Major Barbara, Shakespeare's King Lear, and Beckett's Waiting
for Godot." Diss., University of Chicago, pp. 60-96.
    Love for Love "subsumes the best of Restoration comedy,
rejects the masquerade of wit and intrigue, and looks forward
to the later dramatic comedy of Vanbrugh and Farquhar (but
without their occasional sentimentality), and to the fictional
comedies of Fielding."

<u>1974</u>

A BOOKS

1 CONGREVE, WILLIAM. Love for Love. In Restoration Comedy.
Edited by A. Norman Jeffares. Vol. 3. London: Folio Press;
Totowa, N. J.: Rowman and Littlefield, pp. [223]-334.
    "Beneath the persiflage...we can experience the author's
disquiet about conventional views of life."

2 _____. The Way of the World. In Four English Comedies of the
17th and 18th Centuries. Edited by J. M. Morrell. Baltimore:
Penguin Books, pp. [131]-231.
    Reprint of 1950.A4.

3 _____. The Way of the World. In Masterpeices of the Drama.
Edited by Alexander W. Allison, Arthur J. Carr, and Arthur M.
Eastman. New York: Macmillan, pp. 359-403.
    The conclusion to the play is a "testament to the hopeful
and fearful human need to establish a fostering and enduring
love."

4 _____. The Way of the World. In The Norton Anthology of English
Literature. General editor M. H. Abrams. Vol. 1. New York:
W. W. Norton, pp. 1786-854.
    Third edition of 1962.A7.

5 _____. The Way of the World. In Restoration Comedy. Edited by
A. Norman Jeffares. Vol. 4. London: Folio Press; Totowa,
N. J.: Rowman and Littlefield, pp. [101]-202.
The play "probably represents the highest achievement of
the comedy of manners."

6 _____. The Way of the World. In Restoration Plays. Introduc-
tion by Sir Edmund Gosse. Everyman's Library. London: Dent;
New York: Dutton, pp. xiii-xiv, [163]-235.
Reprint of 1932.A1; see 1912.A2.

7 LOVE, HAROLD. Congreve. Plays and Playwrights Series. Oxford:
Basil Blackwell, vii + 131 pp.
The comedies of Congreve show the authentic dramatic
individuality of the characters, who in their relationship
to each other reflect the "ambiguities, indeterminacies and
conflicting perspectives" of real life. American edition
1975.A3.

B SHORTER WRITINGS

1 BRUCE, DONALD. Topics of Restoration Comedy. London: Victor
Gollancz; New York: St. Martin's Press, 189 pp., passim.
Restoration comedy is viewed as a "debating comedy, and
as morally purposeful within its debates." Incorporates all
of Congreve's comedies.

2 BUCKROYD, PETER. "British Printed Tragedy, 1695-1740." Diss.,
McMaster University, 355 pp., passim.
Provides a survey of research in this field, an analysis
of recurring patterns, a study of the settings and adaptations,
and an examination of the tragedies by Nicholas Rowe and
George Lillo. Includes numerous references to The Mourning
Bride.

3 CORMAN, BRIAN. "'The Mixed Way of Comedy': Congreve's The
Double-Dealer." Modern Philology, 71, no. 4 (May), pp. 356-65.
The play fulfills Dryden's specification for the "mixed
way of comedy": "that which is neither all wit, nor all
humour, but the result of both." The Double Dealer, therefore,
is the first significant step toward "the final transcendence
of Restoration comedy in The Way of the World."

4 EHRENPREIS, IRVIN. Literary Meaning and Augustan Value.
Charlottesville: University Press of Virginia, pp. 21-25.
Rejects the idea that Congreve's plays reflect the workings
of Divine Providence.

1974

5 ELLEHAUGE, MARTIN. <u>English Restoration Drama</u>. Folcroft, Pa.:
     Folcroft Library Editions, pp. 185-310, passim.
        Reprint of 1933.B2.

6 FLATTERY, BRUCE. "Renaissance and Restoration Perspectives on
     the Experience of Comedy." Diss., University of Toronto,
     pp. 201-77, passim.
        Probes "the nature, and to some degree the causes, of
     those differences which lurk beneath the surface of generic
     convention," concluding that as the seventeenth century drew
     to its close, the circle of comedy became smaller. Section
     on Restoration comedy, which includes references to Congreve's
     plays, deals with various aspects of wit and with that kind of
     understanding associated with love, friendship, and the inter-
     mediate ground of family relationships.

7 FUJIMURA, THOMAS H. "The Personal Element in Dryden's Poetry."
     <u>Publications of the Modern Language Association</u>, 89, no. 5
     (October), pp. 1007-23.
        Includes a discussion of Dryden's poem "To My Dear Friend,
     Mr. Congreve."

8 HANSON, JOHN H. "The Language of Eros in Restoration Comedy."
     Diss., State University of New York, Buffalo, 181 pp., passim.
        The comedies of Etherege, Wycherley, and Congreve are, "at
     their most profound level, dramatisations of a collective
     psychological experience of society and ideology" in late
     seventeenth-century England. Deals with paternity and prop-
     erty in Congreve's comedies.

9 HARTMAN, JAY HARRY. "A Stylistic Study of the Comedies of
     Etherege, Wycherley, and Congreve." Diss., Lehigh University,
     395 pp., passim.
        Suggests which "characteristics of Wycherley may have come
     from Etherege, and which...of Congreve may have come from both
     his predecessors."

10 LYLES, ALBERT M. "Lowndes' Editions of Congreve." <u>Restoration</u>
      <u>and 18th Century Theatre Research</u>, 13, no. 2 (November), p. 58.
         Supplements Rogal's list (1974.B16) of Congreve's works
      from entries in the John C. Hodges collection (1970.A6).

11 McNAMEE, LAWRENCE F. <u>Dissertations in English and American</u>
      <u>Literature</u>. Theses Accepted by American, British and German
      Universities. Supplement Two: 1969-1973. New York and
      London: R. R. Bowker, pp. 290-93.
         Entries on Restoration drama and Congreve.

12 MARINO, MARY ELEANOR GRAY. "William Congreve and Oscar Wilde:
    A Comparative Study of Their Social Comedy." Diss., Purdue
    University, 173 pp., passim.
        Parallels occur in structure, character, theme, and symbol,
    but the fundamental difference arises from the facts that
    "fewer of Wilde's characters are reintegrated into the new
    society at the conclusion of the plays, that his characters
    already belong to that paternal group to which Congreve's
    aspire, and that his characters are more interested in and
    able to express their individuality throughout the play..."

13 MINER, EARL. The Restoration Mode from Milton Dryden. Princeton,
    N. J.: Princeton University Press, pp. 535-39.
        Discusses Dryden's poem "To My Dear Friend, Mr. Congreve."

14 OLSHEN, BARRY N. "John Hollingshead and the Restoration Comedy
    of Manners." Nineteenth Century Theatre Research, 2, no. 1
    (Spring), pp. 1-10.
        Unfavorable theatrical conditions in the middle of the
    nineteenth century rendered the genre of Restoration comedy
    virtually extinct on the London stage. Refers to the single
    evening performance of Love for Love on 27 June, 1848, and to
    the bowdlerized version of 1871. See 1951.A1; 1966.B10;
    1970.B17; 1972.B21.

15 POPSON, JOSEPH JOHN, III. "The Collier Controversy: A Critical
    Basis for Understanding Drama of the Restoration Period."
    Diss., University of Florida, 170 pp., passim.
        Defenders of the stage against Collier's attacks recognized
    "that there were abuses of the drama, but they also saw therein
    a moral value which they maintained was a necessary part of
    its artistic value." Emphasizes those defences by Dryden,
    Congreve, Vanbrugh, D'Urfey, Dennis, Settle, Drake, Oldmixon,
    and Filmer.

16 ROGAL, SAMUEL J. "Thomas Lowndes' 1777 Listing of Dramatic Works
    Works." Restoration and 18th Century Theatre Research, 13,
    no. 1 (May), pp. 53-58.
        Includes various editions of Congreve's plays. See
    1974.B10.

17 ROSENBALM, JOHN OLMSTED. "The Restoration Players: Their Per-
    formances and Personalities." Diss., North Texas State Uni-
    versity, 288 pp., passim.
        Examines the influence of actors and actresses upon the
    direction of Restoration drama and includes the suggestion
    that "Anne Bracegirdle's talent and beauty...contributed
    substantially to the creation of the character of Millimant
    [sic] in The Way of the World."

1975

1975

A BOOKS

1 CONGREVE, WILLIAM. The Way of the World. In Four English
   Comedies of the 17th and 18th Centuries. Edited by J. M.
   Morrell. Baltimore: Penguin Books, pp. [131]-231.
   Reprint of 1950.A4.

2 _____. The Way of the World. In Great Plays: Sophocles to
   Albee. Edited by Morton W. Bloomfield and Robert C. Elliott.
   New York: Holt, Rinehart and Winston, pp. [185]-247.
   Revised edition of 1965.A4.

3 LOVE, HAROLD. Congreve. Plays and Playwrights Series. Totowa,
   N. J.: Rowman and Littlefield, vii + 131 pp.
   American edition of 1974.A7.

B SHORTER WRITINGS

1 BARNARD, JOHN. "Etherege, Shadwell, Wycherley, Congreve,
   Vanbrugh, and Farquhar." In English Drama (Excluding
   Shakespeare): Select Bibliographical Guides. Edited by
   Stanley Wells. [London]: Oxford University Press, pp. 173-80,
   183-86.
   Includes works on the Restoration theater, editions of and
   critical commentaries and studies on Congreve's plays.

2 BRATTON, CLINTON WOODROW. "The Use of Marriage in the Comedies
   of Etherege, Wycherley, Dryden and Congreve." Diss., University of Colorado, 174 pp.
   Congreve, like Wycherley, expresses libertinism as total
   self-interest. In Congreve's plays, however, "it is neither
   the hero nor the heroine who is the libertine, but the villain..." He must be "defeated, and excluded from the society
   of the play, before the marriage of the hero and the heroine
   can take place."

3 CORMAN, BRIAN. "The Way of the World and Morally Serious Comedy."
   University of Toronto Quarterly, 44, no. 3 (Spring),
   pp. 199-212.
   The "moral seriousness depends upon a realistic presenta-
   tion of alternatives to the happiness of Mirabell and
   Millamant."

4 DEITZ, JONATHAN E. "Congreve's Better Way to Run the World."
   Papers on Language & Literature, 11, no. 4 (Fall), pp. 367-79.

The Way of the World provides "an open, positive statement not merely by the example of a virtuous character or set of characters, but through instances of an exemplary movement by which characters may reach and use virtue within their flawed society."

5 EAVES, T. C. DUNCAN and BEN D. KIMPEL. "The Text of Congreve's Love for Love." The Library, 30, no. 4 (December), pp. 334-36.
    Differences exist between the first printed edition and the acting version in regard to several "objectionable" lines (later altered as a result of an indictment) spoken by Ben and Sir Sampson Legend.

6 FRUSHELL, RICHARD C. "Congreve's Plays and The Rape of the Lock." American Notes and Queries, 13, no. 8 (April), pp. 114-15.
    Similarities in diction between Congreve's plays and The Rape of the Lock indicate that Pope may have just reread Congreve's plays when he expanded his two-canto version after 1712.

7 GRATZ, DAVID KENNETH. "Emotion, Modes of Expression and Effects on Plot, in Selected Comedies: 1670-1780." Diss., Syracuse University, 265 pp.
    "When the expression of a positive emotion becomes necessary or important, as in The Way of the World, such expression is often indirect--through metaphor or displacement to other emotions."

8 McDONALD, MARGARET LAMB. "The Independent Woman in the Restoration Comedy of Manners." Diss., University of Colorado, 262 pp., passim.
    Surveys the independent woman in comedy from Shakespeare to Steele, with emphasis upon the Restoration period. Views Angelica and Millamant (among others) as ideal comic heroines because they "balance fancy and judgment, handle the play of ideas as well as a play on words, and manage to cope with the repressive limitations of their respective societies."

9 MANN, DAVID D. "Congreve's Revisions of The Mourning Bride." Papers of the Bibliographical Society of America, 69, no. 4 (Fourth Quarter), pp. 526-46.
    A comparison between the first quarto edition of the play (1697) and that prepared for the Works (1710) tells us something about Congreve's poetic practice and gives us a "definite view of the moral stance that is behind it."

1975

10 MARSHALL, GEOFFREY. "Comedy and Tragedy, the Sentimental, and a
    Critical Crux." In his Restoration Serious Drama. Norman:
    University of Oklahoma Press, pp. 161-210, passim.
        Cites The Way of the World to demonstrate similarities in
    style, structure, theme, and characterization between Restora-
    tion comedy and tragedy.

11 PERSSON, AGNES V. Comic Character in Restoration Drama. De
    Proprietatibus Litterarum Series Practica. No. 99. The
    Hague: B. V. Mouton, 151 pp., passim.
        See Ph.D. dissertation, 1970.B18.

12 RODWAY, ALLAN. "Etherege, Wycherley, Congreve, Farquhar."
    In his English Comedy: Its Role and Nature from Chaucer to
    the Present Day. London: Chatto & Windus, pp. 124-43.
        Congreve "carries further than Etherege the concern of the
    Comedy of Manners with behavioural psychology...while also
    extending the range of Wycherley's social criticism."

13 ROOT, ROBERT LATHROP, JR. "The Problematics of Marriage:
    English Comedy 1688-1710." Diss., University of Iowa,
    301 pp.
        The Way of the World expresses "a concern with marriage
    fraud which finds its basis in the plays of Southerne and
    Vanbrugh, and which is expressed less powerfully in
    [Congreve's] earlier plays..."

14 TREADWELL, J. M. "Congreve Bereaved." American Notes and
    Queries, 13, no. 5 (January), pp. 67-68.
        Registers of the parish of St. Clement Danes confirm
    Hodges's gloss that Congreve, in his letter to Joseph Keally
    (dated 12 May, 1708), does in fact refer to the death of his
    father. Another entry, referring to the burial of a "Mary
    Congrave," may indicate that this is Congreve's mother and
    that Congreve arranged for her to be buried with her husband.

15 _____. "Congreve, Tonson, and Rowe's 'Reconcilement.'" Notes
    and Queries, NS 6, 22 (June), pp. 265-69.
        The fact that Congreve actually lodged with Tonson helps
    to explain the significance of Rowe's poem.

16 TULLY, VELMA ANITA. "Innocence and Experience as Structural
    Comic Values in Selected Plays of the Restoration and
    Eighteenth Century." Diss., University of Arkansas, 251 pp.,
    passim.
        Studies several plays, including Love for Love and The Way
    of the World, that either "implicitly or explicitly dramatize
    the comic valuations assigned by their authors to innocence

and experience." Also explicates "the manner in which the elements of comedy...combine to determine a variety of forms which are too different from each other to be subsumed accurately under the terms 'comedy of manners' and 'sentimental comedy.'"

17 WILLIAMS, AUBREY. "No Cloistered Virtue: Or, Playwright versus Priest in 1698." Publications of the Modern Language Association, 90, no. 2 (March), pp. 234-46.
The basis of the conflict arises from the Aristotelian view of Congreve and the Platonic view held by Collier.

1976

A BOOKS

1 CONGREVE, WILLIAM. Love for Love. Edited by Malcolm Kelsall. New Mermaids. New York: W. W. Norton, xxiii + 130 pp. American edition of 1969.A3.

2 _____. Love for Love. In Three Restoration Comedies. Edited with an introduction by Gámini Salgádo. Middlesex: Penguin Books, pp. 36-39, [259]-365. Reprint of 1968.A2.

3 _____. The Way of the World. Edited by Brian Gibbons. New Mermaids. New York: W. W. Norton, xxxv + 116 pp. Reprint of 1971.A3.

4 _____. The Way of the World. In Four English Comedies of the 17th and 18th Centuries. Edited by J. M. Morrell. Baltimore: Penguin Books, pp. [131]-231. Reprint of 1950.A4.

5 DROUGGE, HELGA. The Significance of Congreve's Incognita. Diss., University of Uppsala. Acta Universitatis Upsaliensis. Studia Anglistica Upsaliensia 28. Uppsala: Almqvist and Wiksell International.
Defines the "special quality" of the work and shows it to be a "single artistic whole...a significant prologue to Congreve's plays."

B SHORTER WRITINGS

1 BARKER, NICHOLAS. "Congreve and control of the printed text." The Times Literary Supplement (24 September), p. 1221.

1976

Reviews D. F. McKenzie's Sandars Lectures on "The London
Book Trade in the Later Seventeenth Century." Many influences
without and within the book trade converged as Congreve first
wrote and then prepared his plays for press.

2 BERTELSEN, LANCE. "The Canonical Hours." American Notes and
Queries, 15, no. 3 (November), pp. 35-36.
The confusion about the actual period of the canonical
hours arises from an amendment to the canons of the Church
of England in 1887. In the original 62nd Canon, written in
1604, the time given is noon. Applies this to a reference in
The Way of the World.

3 DOBRÉE, BONAMY. William Congreve: A Conversation between
Jonathan Swift and John Gay, at the house of the Duke of
Queensbury near London. June, 1730. Norwood, Pa.: Norwood
Editions, 24 pp.
Reprint of 1929.B6.

4 ____. "William Congreve: I. His Life.... II. His Work."
In his Variety of Ways: Discussions on Six Authors. Norwood,
Pa.: Norwood Editions, pp. 46-85.
Reprint of 1932.B2.

5 HUME, ROBERT D. The Development of English Drama in the Late
Seventeenth Century. Oxford: Clarendon Press, xv + 525 pp.,
passim.
The drama in this period was extremely varied and complex
because different types changed and interacted on an "almost
season-by-season basis." Includes all of Congreve's plays.

6 KENNY, SHIRLEY STRUM. "Perennial Favorites: Congreve, Vanbrugh,
Cibber, Farquhar, and Steele." Modern Philology (Supplement
to Honor Arthur Friedman), 73, no. 4, pt. 2 (May), pp. S4-S11.
Traces the popularity of the plays and concludes that their
omnipresence on stage and bookstall "made them so much a part
of the cultural milieu that they became embedded in the memo-
ries of educated men. Their energy, vitality, and good humour
became inextricable elements of the eighteenth-century context."

7 LINK, FREDERICK M. English Drama, 1660-1800. A Guide to Infor--
mation Sources. Vol. 9. American Literature, English Literature, and World Literature in English Information Guide Series.
Detroit, Michigan: Gale Research, pp. 124-29.
Select critical bibliography includes collected and individual works by Congreve, biographies, and criticism.

1977

8   NOVAK, MAXIMILLIAN E.   "Congreve as the Eighteenth Century's
    Archetypal Libertine."   Restoration and 18th Century Theatre
    Research, 15, no. 2 (November), pp. 35-39, 60.
        "To a truly sentimental age, Congreve was anything but a
    man of sentiment.   To an age which examined plays carefully
    for immorality, Congreve was a wit and libertine."

9   ROSOWSKI, SUSAN J.   "Thematic Development in the Comedies of
    William Congreve: The Individual in Society."   Studies in
    English Literature, 16, no. 3 (Summer), pp. 387-406.
        In the first play, Congreve examines society itself; in the
    second, the effect of society on the individual; in the third,
    individual responsibility; and in the last, "the ideal recon-
    ciliation of these elements--individually defined in a social
    context and expressed through manipulation of Restoration
    dramatic convention."

10 SCOUTEN, ARTHUR H.   "William Congreve."   In 1660-1750.   Vol. 5
    of The Revels History of Drama in English.   London: Methuen,
    pp. 214-220.
        "In The Way of the World, William Congreve achieved his
    most perfectly wrought drama.   It lacks the boisterous, if
    imitative vitality of The Old Bachelor, the harsh satire of
    The Double Dealer, the blithe high spirits of Love for Love.
    But [in The Way of the World, Congreve created] a work which
    was both serious and dazzlingly witty."

11 WESTCOTT, I. M.   "The role of the Narrator in Congreve's
    Incognita."   Trivium, 11 (May), pp. 40-48.
        "It is the role of the narrator to hold a delicate artistic
    balance between a commitment to romance, to love and friend-
    ship, and an objective response to human foibles and fantasies,
    so that the reader shares the narrator's regard for his friends
    and his good-natured amusement at their conduct in unusual
    circumstances.   The narrator's presence is essential to the
    success of the novel."

1977

A BOOKS

1   CONGREVE, WILLIAM.   Love for Love.   In Drama through Performance.
    [Edited by] Mark S. Auburn and Katherine H. Burkman.   Boston:
    Houghton Mifflin, pp. 319-408.
        Although of her world, Angelica is better than it, and she
    has "first to use her wit and then to wager love for love."
    Also includes analysis of action and suggestions for
    performance.

1977

2 _____. The Way of the World. In Four English Comedies of the
17th and 18th Centuries. Edited by J. M. Morrell. Baltimore:
Penguin Books, pp. [131]-231.
Reprint of 1950.A4.

B SHORTER WRITINGS

1 HINNANT, CHARLES H. "Wit, Propriety, and Style in The Way of
The World." Studies in English Literature, 17, no. 3
(Summer), pp. 373-86.
Argues that "Dryden's formulation of wit gives the ideal
audience of The Way of the World a standard indispensable for
the proper response not only to these improprieties [caused
by the pretensions of ordinary mortals] but also to the successful exchanges in the play."

2 HUME, ROBERT D. "Marital Discord in English Comedy from Dryden
to Fielding." Modern Philology, 74, no. 3 (February),
pp. 248-72.
In The Way of the World, Congreve "sees all the follies
and imperfections clearly but tolerates what he knows cannot
be changed, albeit with an underlying sense of sadness..."
Refers also to the optimism in Congreve's use of the romance
conventions in Love for Love.

3 _____. "The Myth of the Rake in 'Restoration' Comedy." Studies
in the Literary Imagination, 10, no. 1 (Spring), pp. 25-55.
After examining the so-called rakes in Restoration comedy,
concludes that it gives "precious little support to libertinism." "The harshness of the seventies libertine is never
present in a Congreve protagonist."

4 KENNY, SHIRLEY STRUM. "Humane Comedy." Modern Philology, 75,
no. 1 (August), pp. 29-43.
Different from the comedy of manners and sentimental
comedy, humane comedy is a distinct mode. It manifests good
nature and possesses its own style and shape. Includes The
Double Dealer, Love for Love, and The Way of the World.

5 McCOMB, JOHN KING. "Congreve's The Old Batchelour: A Satiric
Anatomy." Studies in English Literature, 17, no. 3 (Summer),
pp. 361-72.
Congreve "presents the stock characters of Restoration
comedy...as stages in a single life's progress." Consequently,
"Congreve's originality lies ultimately in his employment of
the materials of Restoration comedy for the purposes of
Augustan satire."

6   WAITH, EUGENE M.. "Aristophanes, Plautus, Terence, and the
    Refinement of English Comedy." <u>Studies in the Literary
    Imagination</u>, 10, no. 1 (Spring), pp. 91-108.
        Cites Congreve's views on Terence to show that the latter,
    rather than Plautus or Aristophanes, appealed to a more
    educated audience.

7   WILLIAMS, AUBREY. "Of 'One <u>Faith</u>': Authors and Auditors in the
    Restoration Theatre." <u>Studies in the Literary Imagination</u>,
    10, no. 1 (Spring), pp. 57-76.
        Both author and auditor shared a view that "fallen human
    nature is forgivable and redeemable..." Includes a justifica-
    tion as to why Mirabell deserves to be rewarded--because of
    his "sincere remorse" and "hearty contrition."

Index

Included in the index are the titles of articles, books in which chapters on or references to Congreve appear, and names of authors. Editions (single and in collections) and criticism of Congreve's works may be found under "Congreve" and the appropriate title. Not included are the names of editors and their anthologies, titles of journals, and entries containing reprinted secondary material.

"Aristophanes, Plautus, Terence, and the Refinement of English Comedy," 1977.B6

Armstrong, Cecil Ferard, 1913.B1

"The Art of Whining Love," 1955.B1

"'Artificial' Comedy," 1928.B4, B6, B7, B9

"The Artist and the Clergyman: Congreve, Collier and the World of the Play," 1969.B8

Arundell, Dennis, 1925.B4

As Their Friends Saw Them: Biographical Conversations, 1933.B1

Ashby, Stanley Royal, 1927.B1

Aspects and Impressions, 1922.B1

"Aspects of Social Criticism in Restoration Comedy," 1965.B10

"Attitudes of Some Restoration Dramatists Toward Farce," 1940.B5

"Attitudes Toward the Country in the Restoration Comedy, 1660-1728," 1961.B7

"Aufbau und Sprache von Congreves Incognita," 1967.A10

"The Authorship of 'A Poem to the Memory of Mr. Congreve,'" 1939.B4

"The authorship of 'A soldier and a sailor,'" 1935.B5

"The Authorship of Squire Trelooby," 1928.B3

"The Authorship of The Cornish Squire," 1968.B15

Avery, Emmett L., 1941.B1; 1942.B3; 1945.B2; 1951.A1; 1960.B1; 1966.A4; 1967.B1; 1968.B1, B2

Bach, Bert C., 1968.B3

Baker, David Erskine, 1812.B1

Ball, F. Elrington, 1921.B1

"The Ballad in Congreve's Love for Love," 1933.B3

Banhatti, G. S., 1962.A10

Barker, Nicholas, 1976.B1

Barnard, John, 1964.B1; 1971.B2; 1972.A3, B1; 1975.B1

Barrett, W. P., 1894.A1

Barron, Leon Oser, 1960.B2

Bartel, Roland, 1960.B3

Bartlett, Laurence, 1967.B2; 1970.A1; 1971.B3

Bateson, F. W., 1930.A1; 1951.B1; 1957.B1

Bear, Andrew, 1972.B3

"The Beau Monde at the Restoration," 1934.B3

"The Beaux' Stratagem: Image and Action," 1971.B14

Belanger, Terry, 1970.B1

Beljame, Alexandre, 1881.B1

Bennewitz, Alexander, 1890.A1, A2

Bentley, Thomas Roy, 1971.B4

Bergson's Theory of the Comic in the Light of English Comedy, 1920.B1

Berkeley, David S., 1955.B1, B2; 1959.B1

Berkeley, George-Monck, 1789.A1

Bernbaum, Ernest, 1915.B1

Bertelsen, Lance, 1976.B2

Bevan, Allan R., 1962.B1

Bhushan, V. N., 1944.B1

Haggard, Stephen, 1946.B4
Hanson, John H., 1974.B8
Haraszti, Zoltán, 1934.B1
Harley, Graham D., 1970.B8
Harris, Bernard, 1965.B2
Hartman, Jay Harry, 1974.B9
The Hawk Over Heron, 1944.B1
Hawkins, Harriett, 1972.B11
Hayman, John, 1968.B7
Hayman, John Griffiths, 1964.B6
"The Haymarket and the New: London Flocks to Repertory," 1945.B5
Hazard, Benjamin Munroe, 1957.B4
Hazlitt, William, 1818.B1; 1819.B1
Heldt, W., 1923.B3
Henderson, Philip, 1930.A3
Henley, W. E., 1890.B1
"Heroes and Heroines in English Comedy, 1660-1750," 1946.B5
Heuss, Alfred, 1913.B3
"High Comedy in Terms of Restoration Practice," 1929.B3
Hinnant, Charles H., 1977.B1
Histoire de la Comédie Anglaise (1672-1707), 1878.B1
A History of English Dramatic Literature to the death of Queen Anne,
    1875.B1
History of English Humour, 1878.B2
A History of English Literature, 1927.B2
A History of Restoration Drama 1660-1700, 1923.B6
"Hobbism and Restoration Comedy," 1953.B4
Hodges, John C., 1928.B3; 1929.B7; 1933.B3; 1935.B2; 1936.B1-B3;
    1939.B1; 1941.A2; 1943.B2; 1949.B2, B3; 1954.B4; 1955.A7, B5;
    1959.B4; 1964.A3
Hoffman, Arthur W., 1970.B9
Hogan, Charles Beecher, 1968.B8, B9
Holland, Norman N., 1956.B3; 1957.B5; 1959.B5
Homer. See Congreve, William.
"Hopkins and Congreve," 1950.B5
Horne, Mark Daniel, 1940.B4
Houghton, Walter E., Jr., 1943.B3
Howarth, R. G., 1936.B4; 1946.B2; 1961.B1
Howling, Robert T., 1954.B5
Hoy, Cyrus, 1961.B2; 1964.B7; 1966.B14
Hughes, Leo, 1940.B5; 1971.B7
"Humane Comedy," 1977.B4
Hume, Robert D., 1971.B8; 1973.B7; 1976.B5; 1977.B2, B3
"Humor Characterization in Restoration Comedy, 1600-1700," 1973.B11
"The Humourists: An Elizabethan Method of Characterization as
    Modified by Etherege and Congreve," 1947.B1
Hunt, Hugh, 1965.B3
Hunt, Leigh, 1840.A1, B1
Hurley, Paul J., 1971.B9
Hutton, Laurence, 1885.B1

The Hyacinth Room: An Investigation into the Nature of Comedy, Tragedy, and Tragi-comedy, 1964.B7

"The Idea of Comedy--II. Comedy of Manners. High Comedy, or Comedy of Character," 1914.B1
Imagined Worlds: Essays on Some English Novels and Novelists in Honour of John Butt, 1968.B16, B18
"The Independent Woman in the Restoration Comedy of Manners," 1975.B8
"The Influence of Beaumont and Fletcher on Restoration Drama," 1927.B5
The Influence of Beaumont and Fletcher on Restoration Drama, 1928.B8
The Influence of Molière on Restoration Comedy, 1910.B2
"Innocence and Experience as Structural Comic Values in Selected Plays of the Restoration and Eighteenth Century," 1975.B16
An Introduction to Dramatic Theory, 1923.B7
"The Ironic Image: Metaphoric Structure and Texture in the Comedies of William Congreve," 1965.A5
Isaacs, J., 1927.B3; 1939.B2; 1949.B4

Jackson, Alfred, 1932.B4
Jaggard, Wm., 1929.B3
"James Thomson and David Mallet: 'A Poem to the Memory of Mr. Congreve,' 1729," 1973.B1
Jarvis, F. P., 1972.B12
Jeffares, A. Norman, 1966.A3; 1967.A4
J[ennings], R[ichard], 1925.B6
The Jeremy Collier Stage Controversy: 1698-1726, 1937.B3
The John C. Hodges Collection of William Congreve in the University of Tennessee Library: A Bibliographical Catalog, 1970.A6
"John Gielgud: Actor," 1947.B2
"John Hollingshead and the Restoration Comedy of Manners," 1974.B14
Johnson, Frank L., 1935.B3
Johnson, Samuel, 1781.B1
Jordan, Robert John, 1965.B4; 1972.B13
"The 'Just Decrees of Heav'n' and Congreve's Mourning Bride," 1971.B20
Juvenal. See Congreve, William.
"The Juvenalian and Persian Element in English Literature from the Restoration to Dr. Johnson," 1932.B3

Kames, Lord (Henry Home), 1762.B1
Kaufman, Anthony David, 1968.A5; 1972.B14; 1973.B8, B9
Kaul, A. N., 1970.B10
Kelsall, M. M., 1969.A3; 1972.B15
Kenny, Shirley Strum, 1976.B6; 1977.B4
Kerby, William Moseley, 1907.B1
Kimpel, Ben D., 1975.B5
"The Kit-Kat Club and the Theatres," 1931.B1
Klaus, Carl Hanna, 1966.A10
Knight, G. Wilson, 1962.B6
Knights, L. C., 1937.B2

Koonce, Howard Lee, 1969.B4
Kornbluth, Martin Leonard, 1956.B4
Koziol, Herbert, 1952.B2
Kreutz, Irving, 1970.B11
Krohne, Wilhelm, 1924.A5
Kronenberger, Louis, 1952.B3; 1969.B5
Krutch, Joseph Wood, 1924.B3; 1927.A1

"L. C. Knights and Restoration Comedy," 1966.B1
Lacey, T. A., 1928.B4
La Fontaine. See Congreve, William.
Lamb, Charles, 1823.B1
"Lamb's Criticism of Restoration Comedy," 1943.B3
Langhans, Edward A., 1966.B16; 1973.B10
"Language and Action in The Way of the World, Love's Last Shift, and
    The Relapse," 1973.B15
"Language and Character in Congreve's The Way of the World," 1973.B8
"The Language of Eros in Restoration Comedy," 1974.B8
Lann, Eugene, 1941.B2
Lardner, Dionysius, 1838.B1
"Law and the Dramatic Rhetoric of The Way of the World," 1971.B9
Lawrence, W. J., 1925.B7; 1926.B2
The Learned Lady in England, 1650-1760, 1920.B2
Lectures on the English Comic Writers, 1819.B1
Leech, Clifford, 1951.B4; 1962.B6
"Leeds University and the Yorkshire Tradition: II. William Congreve,
    Local Worthy," 1949.B7
Legouis, P., 1966.B18
Le Public et les Hommes de Lettres en Angleterre au Dix-huitième
    Siècle 1660-1744, 1881.B1
"Les voies de la critique récente: Comment elle étudie la comédie
    de la restauration," 1966.B18
L'Etrange, A. G., 1878.B2
"Letter LXX. To Euphronius [etc.]," 1749.B1
Letters & Documents, 1964.A3
Letters Concerning the English Nation, 1733.B1
Lewis, Mineko S., 1973.B11
"Libertine and Précieux Elements in Restoration Comedy," 1959.B2
"The Libertine Gentleman in Restoration Comedy," 1965.B4
"'A Libertine Woman of Condition': Congreve's 'Doris,'" 1973.B9
"The Library of William Congreve," 1954.B4; 1955.B5
The Library of William Congreve, 1955.A7
Library of William Congreve, 1922.B4; 1939.B2; 1942.B4; 1949.B3, B4;
    1954.B4; 1955.A7, B5
Life of William Congreve, 1888.A3
Lightfoot, John Ewell, Jr., 1973.B12
Likenesses of Truth in Elizabethan and Restoration Drama, 1972.B11
"The Limits of Historical Veracity in Neoclassical Drama," 1972.B16
Lincoln, Stoddard, 1963.B5, B6
Link, Frederick M., 1976.B7
Literary Anecdotes of the Eighteenth Century, 1812.B2

"Literary Criticism from the Restoration Dramatists," 1934.B6
A Literary History of England, 1948.B5
Literary Landmarks of London, 1885.B1
Literary Meaning and Augustan Value, 1974.B4
Literary Relics, 1789.A1
Literary Studies, 1919.B1
"Literature No 'Document,'" 1924.B5
Lives of the Most Eminent English Poets, 1781.B1
The Lives of the Poets of Great Britain and Ireland, 1753.B1
Loftis, John, 1959.B6; 1966.B19; 1972.B16
"London Playhouses, 1700-1705," 1932.B4
The London Stage, 1660-1800, 1960.B1; 1961.B5; 1962.B11; 1965.B12;
    1968.B8
The London Stage, 1660-1800: A Critical Introduction, 1968.B1, B2,
    B9, B13
Lott, James David, 1967.B6
Love, H. H., 1964.B9; 1972.B17; 1973.B13; 1974.A7
"Love for Love," 1966.B13
"[Love for Love: A World of Opposing Values]," 1972.B30
Love for Love: Theatrical History, 1921.B5
Love Letters of the Past and Present Century, 1888.B2
"Love, Scandal, and the Moral Milieu of Congreve's Comedies," 1971.B13
"Lowndes' Editions of Congreve," 1974.B10
Lund, Serena M., 1933.B4
Lyles, Albert M., 1970.A6; 1974.B10
Lynch, Kathleen M., 1924.B4; 1926.B3; 1938.B2; 1951.A11; 1953.B2;
    1965.A2
Lyons, Charles R., 1964.B10; 1971.B10

M. M., 1942.B4
Macaulay, T. B., 1840.B2
Macaulay, T. C., 1935.B4
McCarthy, Mary, 1956.B5
McClelland, Charles Blake, 1970.A7
McCollom, William G., 1971.B11
McComb, John King, 1977.B5
McCulley, Cecil Michael, 1952.B4
McDonald, Charles O., 1964.B11
McDonald, Margaret Lamb, 1975.B8
McDowell, Margaret Blaine, 1954.B6
McKillop, Alan D., 1939.B4
McLaughlin, John Joseph, 1966.B20
McManaway, James G., 1964.B12
McNamee, Lawrence F., 1968.B10; 1969.B6; 1974.B11
Magill, Lewis Malcolm, Jr., 1949.B6
Mallet, David:
    --as author of "A Poem to the Memory of Mr. Congreve," 1930.B3;
    1939.B4; 1973.B1
    --text of "A Poem to the Memory of Mr. Congreve," 1729.B1
Malone, Edmond, 1800.B1

Mann, David Douglas, 1969.A8; 1973.A7; 1975.B9
"Manuscript Texts of Poems by the Earl of Dorset and William
    Congreve," 1964.B3
Marino, Mary Eleanor Gray, 1974.B12
"Marital Discord in English Comedy from Dryden to Fielding," 1977.B2
Marshall, Geoffrey, 1975.B10
"Masking and Disguise in the Plays of Etherege, Wycherley, and
    Congreve," 1970.B4
Masters of the Drama, 1940.B3
Mathewson, Louise, 1920.B1
Matrimonial Law and the Materials of Restoration Comedy, 1942.B2
Mau, Hedwig, 1936.B5
Maurocordato, Alexandre, 1967.B7
Memoirs of the Life, Writings, and Amours of William Congreve Esq.:
    --as subject, 1970.B19
    --text, 1730.A5
Meredith, George:
    --compared with William Congreve, 1971.B19
    --on William Congreve, 1897.B1
Merrin, James, 1948.B3
Merydew, J. T., 1888.B2
Mignon, Elisabeth Louise, 1943.B4; 1947.B4
Milburn, D. Judson, 1966.B21
Miles, Dudley H., 1910.B2; 1916.B2
"Military Influences on Theme, Plot, and Style in English Comic Drama
    from the Glorious Revolution to the Death of Queen Anne,"
    1973.B2
Miner, Earl, 1966.B22; 1974.B13
Minor, Charles Byron, 1957.B6
"Mirabell and Restoration Comedy," 1972.B25
Miscellanies, 1886.B2
"'The Mixed Way of Comedy': Congreve's The Double-Dealer," 1974.B3
"Modes of Satire," 1965.B8
Mohanty, Harendra Prasad, 1966.B23
Molière (Jean Baptiste Poquelin), influences on William Congreve,
    1890.A1, A2; 1907.B1; 1910.B2; 1931.B4; 1938.B4; 1965.B9
"Molière and English Restoration Comedy," 1965.B9
"Molière and the Restoration Comedy in England," 1907.B1
"Molières Einfluss auf Congreve," 1890.A1
Molloy, Joseph Fitzgerald, 1886.B1
The Moment and Other Essays, 1947.B6
"Money: God and King, Economic Aspects of Restoration Comedy,"
    1971.B4
Monk, Samuel H., 1960.B5
Montagu, Lady Mary Wortley, 1729.B2
Montgomery, Guy, 1929.B8
Moore, John Brooks, 1923.B4
"The Moral and Aesthetic Achievement of William Congreve," 1955.A6
"Moral Aspects of Restoration Comedy," 1954.B5
"Moral Purpose in Restoration Comedy," 1954.B6

"Morals of the Restoration," 1916.B2
Morris, Brian, 1972.A7
Morse, Charles, 1922.B2, B3
"Mr. Congreve Comes to Judgement," 1966.B10
Mudrick, Marvin, 1955.B6
Muecke, D. C., 1969.B7
Mueschke, Paul, 1929.B9
Mueschke, Paul and Miriam, 1958.A5
Muir, Kenneth, 1949.B7; 1965.B5; 1972.B18
Myers, Charles Robert, 1971.B12
Myers, William, 1972.B19
"The Myth of the Rake in 'Restoration' Comedy," 1977.B3

Napieralski, Edmund A., 1969.B14
Nathan, George Jean, 1948.B4
National Union Catalog:
    --Pre-1956 Imprints, 1970.B14
    --1956 to 1967, 1970.B15
    --1968 to 1972, 1973.B14
The Nature of Comedy, 1930.B2
"The Neo-classic lyric, 1660-1725," 1944.B2
Nettleton, George Henry, 1914.B2
A New View of Congreve's Way of the World, 1958.A5
The New Woman: Her Emergence in English Drama 1600-1730, 1954.B3
Nichols, John, 1812.B2
Nickles, Mary A., 1972.A8
Nickson, Richard, 1972.B20
Nicoll, Allardyce, 1923.B6, B7; 1925.B8
"No Cloistered Virtue: Or, Playwright versus Priest in 1698,"
    1975.B17
Nolan, Paul T., 1953.A5; 1957.B7; 1959.B7; 1962.B8
Norell, Lemuel N., 1962.B9
Norris, Edward T., 1934.B2
"A Note in Montague Summers's Edition of The Way of the World,
    Corrected," 1960.B5
"Note on Congreve," 1921.B2
"Notes toward a History of Restoration Comedy," 1966.B27
Novak, Maximillian E., 1969.B8, B9; 1970.B16; 1971.A7, A8, B13;
    1976.B8
"'A Novel,' 'Romance,' and Popular Fiction in the First Half of the
    Eighteenth Century," 1973.B16
Noyes, George Rapall, 1936.B6
Noyes, Robert Gale, 1960.B6

"Of 'One Faith': Authors and Auditors in the Restoration Theatre,"
    1977.B7
"Of the Character of Congreve as a Writer of Comedy," 1804.B1
Ohara, David M., 1957.B8
The Old Drama and the New: An Essay in Re-Valuation, 1923.B2
"Old Men and Women in the Restoration Comedy of Manners," 1943.B4

Olshen, Barry Neil, 1970.B17; 1972.B21; 1974.B14
"The Omitted Scene in Congreve's Love for Love," 1963.B4
"On the Artificial Comedy of the Last Century," 1823.B1
"On the Comic Writers of England. No. IX. Wycherley and Congreve,"
    1871.B1
"On the Date of Congreve's Birth," 1935.B2
"On the Relation of Congreve's Mourning Bride to Racine's Bajazet,"
    1904.B1
O'Regan, M. J., 1959.B8
Ovid. See Congreve, William.

Paine, Clarence S., 1940.B6; 1941.B3
Palmer, John, 1913.B4; 1914.B3
"The Paradox of Congreve's Mourning Bride," 1943.B5
Parfitt, George, 1972.B22
Parsons, Philip, 1972.B23
"Passion, 'Poetical Justice,' and Dramatic Law in The Double-Dealer
    and The Way of the World," 1972.B1
Payne, Rhoda, 1963.B7
Pearson, Ralph, 1926.B4
Peltz, Catherine Walsh, 1944.B2
"Perennial Favorites: Congreve, Vanbrugh, Cibber, Farquhar, and
    Steele," 1976.B6
"Period, Style and Scale," 1965.B1
Perry, Henry Ten Eyck, 1925.B9
Persius, influence on William Congreve, 1932.B3
"The Personal Element in Dryden's Poetry," 1974.B7
Persson, Agnes Valkay, 1970.B18; 1975.B11
"The Philosophical Assumptions of Congreve's Love for Love," 1972.B12
"A Play: Scenario or Poem," 1960.B7
"Players and Playhouses, 1695-1710 and Their Effect on English
    Comedy," 1973.B10
The Playgoer's Handbook to Restoration Drama, 1928.B2
The Play-Reader's Handbook, 1966.B31
"The Plays of William Congreve," 1922.B3
"Plot and Character in Congreve's Double-Dealer," 1968.B6
"Plot and Meaning in Congreve's Comedies," 1972.B19
"A Poem to the Memory of Mr. Congreve":
    --as subject, 1930.B3; 1939.B4; 1973.B1
    --text, 1729.B1
"Poetical Justice, the Contrivances of Providence, and the Works of
    William Congreve," 1968.B19
The Polished Surface: Essays in the Literature of Worldliness,
    1969.B5
"I. Political Themes in Restoration Tragedy. II. The Dramatic Use of
    Hobbes' Political Ideas. A Chapter from Political Themes in
    Restoration Tragedy," 1936.B7
Pool, E. Millicent, 1938.B3
Pope, Alexander, influenced by William Congreve, 1975.B6
Popson, Joseph John, III, 1974.B15

"The Structural Functions of Rake Characters in Restoration Comedy,"
    1973.B6
Stuart, Donald Clive, 1912.B1
Studies of a Litterateur, 1921.B7
"A Study of Dramatic Comedy," 1952.B4
"A Study of the Critical Theory of the Restoration Drama as Expressed
    in Dedications, Prefaces, Prologues, Epilogues, and Other Dramatic
    Criticism of the Period," 1953.B3
"A Study of the Development of the Theme of Love and Duty in English
    Comedy from Charles I to George I," 1970.B3
"The Style and the Wit of the Restoration Comedy of Manners," 1940.B1
"A Stylistic Analysis of the Comedies of William Congreve," 1969.A7
"A Stylistic Study of the Comedies of Etherege, Wycherley, and
    Congreve," 1974.B9
Suckling, Norman, 1965.B9
"Suicide in Eighteenth-Century England: The Myth of a Reputation,"
    1960.B3
Sullivan, William Arnett, Jr., 1971.B17
Summers, Montague, 1921.B4-B6; 1923.A1; 1934.B4, B5
"Sunlight of the Mind . . . ?" 1971.B19
Sutherland, James, 1969.B15
Swaen, A. E. H., 1935.B5
Swedenberg, H. T., 1971.A8
Swinburne, Algernon C., 1877.B1
Symons, Julian, 1945.B6

Tatum, Nancy R., 1961.B7
Tave, Stuart M., 1960.B8
Taylor, Charlene Mae, 1965.B10
Taylor, D. Crane, 1931.A4
Teeter, Louis B., 1936.B7
Temple, Richard, 1730.B2
"A Tentative Calendar of Daily Theatrical Performances, 1660-1700,"
    1945.B2
"The Text of Congreve's Love for Love," 1975.B5
Teyssandier, H., 1971.B18
Thackeray, W. M., 1853.B1, B2
"The Theatre: Ibsen and Congreve," 1925.B6
The Theatre Book of the Year 1947-1948: A Record and an Interpreta-
    tion, 1948.B4
Theatrical Criticism in London to 1795, 1931.B2
"Thematic Development in the Comedies of William Congreve: The
    Individual in Society," 1976.B9
Themes and Conventions in the Comedy of Manners, 1965.B7
"Theory of Comedy in the Restoration":
    --by Robert D. Hume, 1973.B7
    --by James Merrin, 1948.B3
"The Theory of Comedy in the Restoration and Early Eighteenth
    Century," 1957.B4
The Theory of Drama, 1931.B3